FIRST ASCENT

FIRST ASCENT

Stephen Venables

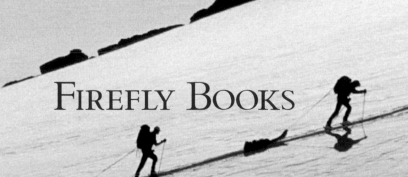

FIREFLY BOOKS

A FIREFLY BOOK

Published by Firefly Books Ltd. 2008

Text copyright © 2008 Stephen Venables
Design and layout © 2008 Octopus Publishing Group Ltd.

All rights reserved. No part of this publication may be reproduced, stored in a retrieval system, or transmitted in any form or by any means, electronic, mechanical, photocopying, recording or otherwise, without the prior written permission of the Publisher.

First printing

Publisher Cataloging-in-Publication Data (U.S.)
Venables, Stephen, 1954–
    First ascent : pioneering mountain climbs / Stephen Venables
[192] p. : col. ill., maps ; cm.
Includes index.
ISBN-13: 978-1-55407-403-7
ISBN-10: 1-55407-403-7
Summary: Accounts of the first to conquer the world's greatest mountains. Features first hand accounts from the world's most renowned climbers; includes supplemental information and photographs.
1. Mountaineering — History.   2.Mountaineers — Biography.
I. Title.
796.522092/2 dc22 GV199.89.V46 2008

Library and Archives Canada Cataloguing in Publication
Venables, Stephen, 1954–
    First ascent : pioneering mountain climbs / Stephen Venables
Includes index.
ISBN-13: 978-1-55407-403-7
ISBN 10: 1 55407 403 7
    1. Mountaineering — History.   2.Mountaineers — Biography.
3. Adventure and adventurers — Biography. I. Title.
GV199.89.V45 2008   796.522092'2   C2008-900248-2

Published in the United States by
Firefly Books (U.S.) Inc.
P.O. Box 1338, Ellicott Station
Buffalo, New York 14205

Published in Canada by
Firefly Books Ltd.
66 Leek Crescent
Richmond Hill, Ontario L4B 1H1

Developed by Cassell Illustrated:
Commissioning Editor: Laura Price
Editor: Jenny Doubt
Creative Director: Geoff Fennell
Layout: Ashley Western
Picture Research: Emma O'Neil
Production: Caroline Alberti

Cover photography: Front: Huntley Ingalls; Back: Alan Kearney
Printed in China

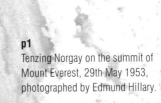

p1
Tenzing Norgay on the summit of Mount Everest, 29th May 1953, photographed by Edmund Hillary.

p2–3
Conrad Anker, John Krakauer, & Alex Lowe skiing amonst the fairytale summits of Antarctica's Queen Maud Land, en'route for making the first ascent of Rakekniven.
Inset: First ascent of Eiger North Face (left) and Annapurna (right).

p4–5
High on the West Face of Cerro Torre, photographed by Thomas Ulrich.

CONTENTS

6   INTRODUCTION

10   PILGRIMS, KINGS, & PROPHETS

16   MONT BLANC, 1786

22   THE GOLDEN AGE OF ALPINE CLIMBING

34   NEW HORIZONS

48   SMALL IS BEAUTIFUL

56   HIMALAYA – ABODE OF SNOW

66   THE BIG ALPINE WALLS

76   EIGHT THOUSAND METERS

88   BRAVE NEW WORLD

98   NEW WAVE OF ALPINE CLIMBING

110   HIMALAYAN RENAISSANCE

130   UNTOUCHED SUMMITS OF THE NEW WORLD

144   FREE ROCK

160   GAMES CLIMBERS PLAY

INTRODUCTION

We spent the night sitting upright, with our feet hanging over the edge and our backs pressed against a wall of smooth granite. Foam pads insulated us from the snow window ledge on which we sat. From the necks of our down sleeping bags, nylon slings protruded, clipped to a steel peg we had hammered into a crack above us, to make quite sure neither of us rolled over and fell a thousand meters back down the mountain face we had been climbing for the last three days. Above us, the wall curved out of sight, black against the starry sky, unknown, unexplored.

I won't say that it was the most comfortable night of my life, but I slept intermittently and, apart from a slight apprehension about the next day's climbing, I was reasonably content. The hard part was getting going in the morning, forcing stiff limbs and numb fingers to function efficiently in the biting cold of dawn. Packing away sleeping bags, lacing boots, lashing crampons to your boots and sorting out the ropes is a fiddly business, particularly when you are operating from a ledge no bigger than a narrow bench. But once we got going and the blood flowed I warmed to the task, thrilled to discover that the crack I had eyed up the previous afternoon was climbable, then overjoyed to discover huge handholds right on the lip of an overhang I had been worrying about all night.

Then my companion Dick took over, leading up an almost vertical square-cut corner filled with ice just solid enough to support the spiked tips of his crampons. Everything was working out nicely, I thought, as I paid out the ropes with one hand and took pictures with the other, then put down the camera to gaze out at all the other peaks crowding the horizon.

Above the corner I took over again, tiptoeing right, puzzling out the moves, linking tiny ice smears on the smooth rock to work sideways to another crack, where I could slot in a solid wedge for security. As I looked back a shaft of sunlight finally shone across our north face to illuminate Dick's red helmet and soon I was able to remove gloves and feel the rough crystalline granite warm under my fingers. This tactile movement over the vertical face of the mountain was intoxicating – pure physical pleasure, somewhere halfway between gymnastics and ballet. Intoxicating also was the linking of hidden clues, the revelation of secrets, the realization of the imaginary

Main picture
Conrad Anker and John Krakauer skiing on the Antarctic ice sheet, en route for the first ascent of the magnificent tower Rakekniven, in the background.

Inset
The author following Dick Renshaw across scary ice on summit day, first ascent of Kishtwar Shivling, Kashmir Himalaya.

line we had sketched up this blank canvas. It was hard work, of course, defying gravity, moving our bodies and our sacks full of gear through the thin Himalayan air, nearly 6,000 meters above sea level; but, late that evening, when we finally settled into our sleeping bags, thrilled tonight to be lying full stretch on bed-sized ledge, we enjoyed all the deep satisfaction of a hard day's task completed.

That day's climbing in Kashmir was one of the best of my life. What transformed pure physical delight into something deeper was the fact that no-one had been here before. Every twist and turn and surprise of this route was our own discovery; finding a way through this hardest section on the fourth day of the climb, we could dare to hope, for the first time, that we might actually reach the summit. The top wasn't everything: what counted more was the quality of the journey. Nevertheless the summit – that obscure object of our irrational desires – gave shape and focus to the journey: it was an endpoint, a goal, a reward which would afterwards add a retrospective glow to the whole experience. And this particular summit was doubly special, because no-one had ever reached it before.

The following day, after ten hours hard, hard work on frighteningly steep ice, we made it and two days after that we were safely down at our base camp, relaxing beside a stream in a glade of birch trees, enjoying the delicious sensation of completing the journey and returning to earth, hardly believing that just two days earlier we had been standing on that remote white point in the sky that I had been dreaming about for four years.

According to the local people the mountain was called Shivling – a common Hindu name which means lingam, or phallus, of Shiva. We distinguished this mountain by calling it Kishtwar Shivling, after the nearest market town. It is one of several peaks, mainly Himalayan, where I and my companions have been lucky enough to be first to the summit. None of those summits has been particularly high or outrageously difficult, but it was till immensely satisfying to be there first.

That sounds terribly egocentric and smacks a bit of neo-colonial aggrandizement. No-one could deny that mountaineering is quite an egocentric pursuit, or at least quite a selfish one. However, the being first has nothing to do with some kind of "conquest." No mountaineer ever uses the word "conquest," unless, as Edmund Hillary famously did, he is talking about conquering his or her own inner weaknesses. Mountains are never conquered. But occasionally we are lucky enough to find an interesting way up them – and, we hope, back down them – and if we happen to be first, the pleasure lies in the exploration, in the lure of the unknown.

For most people "first ascent" probably conjures up images of a high, pointed, inaccessible snowy peak – of a summit. That is a wonderfully graphic symbol of aspiration and of course it is hugely satisfying to be first to the top of an actual peak. But what really counts is how you reach that peak. So, although I was only the 204th person to reach the summit of Everest, I felt very happy to have got there by a new route, with a small four-man team stretched to its absolute limit. Many of the first ascents in this book are in that vein – first ascents of new routes up a mountain, or first ascents in a new, more sporting style.

Not all climbs even lead to a summit at all. For instance, the British mountaineer Joe Brown is not known best for making the first ascent of the world's third highest mountain, Kangchenjunga: most climbers know him as the legendary rock

climber who was first to climb Cenotaph Corner – a
35-meter-high lump of ryolite stuck half way up a
heather hillside in North Wales. Most Himalayan
climbers derive as much satisfaction (or probably
more satisfaction if they are honest) from a sunny
rock climb near sea level, as they do from reaching a
remote high altitude summit.

So, I have chosen in this book to try and cover the
whole game of mountaineering, from the smallest
boulders to the summit of Everest and I have attempted to make the coverage both global and historical,
starting with the earliest ascents recorded by Man.
That means that the scope is almost limitless. Within
that boundless field, I have tried to concentrate on
ascents that have in some way been groundbreaking.
I have included quite large number of mountains or
mountain faces, such as the Matterhorn and the
North Face of the Eiger, which have the kind of mythic status it is hard to ignore; but I have also tried to
include a few esoteric oddities to tempt the reader
down less well-trodden paths. There is probably an
unrealistically high proportion of first ascents by
British climbers. I fear there is an element of personal
bias here. However, part of the reason is that British
climbers offer a particularly rich wealth of written
records to dip into. It also happens that many of the
mountaineers who started on the small but geologi-
cally varied mountains and cliffs of these little islands
have, over the years, gone on to make their mark
amongst the biggest and most remote vertical land-
scapes in the world. They have also played quite a big
role in exploring new ground and experimenting
with new notions of what is possible. And that is what
this book is really all about.

Stephen Venables

THE FIRST MOUNTAINEERS:
PILGRIMS, KINGS, AND PROPHETS

Left
The harsh granite desert which the Israelites had to cross on their escape from Egypt, seen from the summit of Mount Sinai.

Below
Moses – proto-mountaineer – receiving the Ten Commandments on the summit of Mount Sinai, as imagined by a nineteenth-century Spanish engraver.

THE FIRST MOUNTAINEER WAS PROBABLY THE man – or woman – who climbed over the rim of Africa's Rift Valley to initiate homo sapiens' migration north to Eurasia. From the dawn of human existence, high country appealed to our innate sense of adventure. Even if mountains were not climbed for their own sakes, they had to be crossed, to see what lay beyond. Once human society moved beyond a simple hunter-gatherer existence and developed the art of trade, mountain ranges had to be braved to move essential goods between peoples. For instance, one of life's most basic essentials, salt, has been carried for centuries over the high Himalayan passes from Tibet to India, in return for fabrics and manufactured goods.

One of the wildest passes in Central Asia is the Karakoram Pass, five-and-a-half thousand meters above sea level. The first recorded crossing was in AD 399 by a Chinese Buddhist pilgrim, Fa Hian, who called the surrounding peaks Tsung Ling – Onion Mountains – because he found wild leeks which seemed to help alleviate his altitude sickness.

The most famous crossing of Europe's Alps was made not for trade, but war. In one of the most improbable outflanking manoeuvres in military history, Hannibal and his Carthagenian troops entered Rome through the back door, marching up through the Iberian Peninsula to what is now France, then crossing the Alps – with their secret weapon, elephants – to descend on Italy. Almost two thousand years later, Napoleon did the same thing (minus the elephants).

To this day a marble sculpture at the chapel on the St Bernard Pass immortalizes Napoleon's campaign, thanking him for liberating the local mountain people from the yoke of the Habsburg emperor. That hospice chapel has been the place of worship for generations of monks who live on the remote pass, cut off for months each year by the winter snow.

The poet Petrarch was one of the first people known to have climbed a mountain purely for his own amusement, when he and his younger brother ascended Mont Ventoux, in Provence, in 1336. But in his account, the ascent becomes a metaphor for something deeper, reinforcing that notion, deep in the human psyche, of the mountain as holy sanctuary. Recalling the famous Greek Orthodox monastic community – and the home of the earlier classical gods – he wrote, "I began to understand Athos and Olympus, since I found that what I heard and read of them was true of a mountain of far less celebrity." Even this modest Provençal hill inspired noble thoughts. "The life of the blest is indeed set on a high place, straight is the path which leads to it, many are the hills which intervene, and the pilgrims must advance with great strides from virtue to virtue. Lofty is the end of all things, the termination of life, to which our peregrination leads."

It was on a mountain top that the first great prophet, Moses, received the laws which form the entire basis of the Judaeo-Christian tradition. He had led his people out of Egypt and across the Red Sea, but the Promised Land was still a long way off and the people were getting dispirited, trudging through the desert. "They took their stand at the foot of the

Left
J.M.W.Turner's grandiose
interpretation of Hannibal's
army crossing the Alps.

Right, above
The mountain as holy sanctuary.
In this engraving by Louis Haghe,
Mount Sinai towers with
exaggerated steepness over
the Convent of St Catherine.

Right, below
Mont Aiguille near Grenoble was
first climbed in 1492, on the orders
of the French king, Charles VII. The
ascent was not repeated for another
342 years.

mountain. Now Mount Sinai was wrapped in smoke, because the Lord had descended upon it in fire; the smoke went up like the smoke of a kiln, while the whole mountain shook violently. ... Then the people stood at a distance, while Moses drew near to the thick darkness where God was." Like Jesus in the wilderness centuries later, Moses spent "forty days and forty nights" on the mountain and when he eventually came down, bearing the tablets of stone on which were inscribed all God's laws for his people, including the central Ten Commandments, "Moses did not know that the skin of his face shone because he had been talking with God."

For Hindus, Buddhists and followers of Shinto, the mountains are also imbued with divinity, to the point where the actual mountain itself becomes an object of reverence. In China thousands of pilgrims each year make the ascent of Omei Shan. Likewise for the Japanese pilgrims who climb the conical volcano of Fuji. Most famous of all is Mount Kailas in Tibet, close to the source of the great Himalayan rivers Indus, Ganges and Brahmaputra. Every year thousands of Hindu and Buddhists pilgrims make the *parikrama*, the clockwise journey around the mountain, to get closer to enlightenment. Some Western mountaineers have tried unsuccessfully to get permission to climb the mountain, but most climbers, I think, would prefer Kailas to remain unclimbed, inviolate, for ever.

HIGH ALTITUDE SACRIFICE

Many of the highest peaks of the Andes were climbed for the first time over 500 years ago, long before the development of "mountaineering" as a pastime. In a gruesome variation on the holy summit theme, the Inca high priests used mountain summits as altars for the sacrifice of young children. This practice of *capacocha* was described by the seventeenth-century Spanish chronicler, Father Coba. He recorded the pathetic story of Tanta Carhua, a ten year old girl who was taken to meet the emperor before being escorted to her high altitude death. According to Coba, she said, "You can finish with me now because I could not be more honoured than by the feasts which they celebrated for me in Cuzco."

It was only three centuries later, with the discovery of a boy's mummified body on the summit of El Ploma, that modern archaeologists began to find proof that these sacrifices really happened. The indigenous pack animals, llamas, were used to carry soil and stones to altitudes of nearly 6,000 meters, for the building of an elaborate tomb. The child would be given maize spirit to drink, perhaps to ease the fear and pain, then left to die of exposure, or killed outright.

One of the most remarkable modern discoveries was in 1995 by the mountaineer and anthropologist, Johann Reinhard, who was exploring the summit crater of a volcano called Mount Ampato, when he found a girl's body, wrapped in fine wool, lying amongst the rocks at about 6,100 meters. Sarita, was about twelve years old and had been killed by a blow to the skull. It seemed that her body had been preserved under ice for 500 years, but had recently slid down the crater slope during a volcanic eruption. Like other sacrificial victims, she had been entombed with gold and silver and ceremonial pots. Her body was so well preserved that it was possible to do DNA tests on her blood, showing that she was completely unrelated to the modern inhabitants of villages below Mount Ampato, confirming the stories of victims being escorted long distances to their sacrifice.

ROYAL CONQUEST

Like any other field of human endeavour, mountaineering has been subjected to its fair share of nationalist and militarist manipulation, not least in one of the very first recorded alpine ascents. Unlike Petrarch's private pilgrimage up the gentle slopes of Mont Ventoux, this was a full-scale siege, complete with ladders and iron spikes, carried out by one Captain Antoine de Ville and his regiment, on the express orders of the French king, Charles VII in 1492, the year Columbus discovered America. The peak in question was a spectacular monolith called Mont Aiguille, on the limestone plateau of the Vercors, near Grenoble and de Ville placed the cross and banner of his king on the summit. It was not reached again for another 342 years.

That kind of military assault seems anathema to the modern climber. Far more appealing are those scientists, artists, and poets who enjoyed the mountains in a spirit of curiosity and wonder: people like doctor of medicine Konrad Gesner, who wrote in 1542 that "the soul is strangely rapt with these astonishing heights," or the eighteenth-century Swiss painter, Kaspar Wolf of Argau who painted the high mountains for their own sake, or Albrecht von Haller, who published a poem extolling the beauty of the Alps. And there were the monks, who were often keen scientists and naturalists. It was four monks from the Swiss village of Engelberg who made the first ascent of the Titlis in 1744. In 1779 the Prior of the St Bernard hospice, a keen botanist called Abbé Laurent-Joseph Murith, made the first ascent, with two local hunters, of Mont Velan, which he called an "icy colossus."

Foreigners, too, became interested in these exotic mountains. English gentlemen became the first alpine tourists, and in 1741 William Windham joined three English students from Geneva, to visit the valley of Chamonix, climbing through the forest to Motenvers, and becoming the first visitors to set foot on the glacial ice of the Mer de Glace, one of the glaciers fed by the snows of the highest alpine peak of all, the moutain which was once called Mont Maudite (the accursed mountain) but later became known as Mont Blanc.

Mount Kailas, the mountain sacred to millions of Hindus and Buddhists, towers over the Tibetan plateau, close to the sources of four of the great Himalayan rivers – Tsangpo/Brahmaputra, Indus, Ganges, and Sutlej. Every year thousands of pilgrims make the journey around the mountain, many of them prostrating themselves full length on the ground, every stony step of the way. But the summit remains untouched by humans. Long may it remain that way.

Main picture and Far Right
Horace Benedict de Saussure (portrayed, far right, by Jean-Pierre Saint-Ours) was Professor of Natural Philosophy at the Geneva Academy. He was just twenty when he first saw Mont Blanc and offered a prize to the first men to reach its summit. Twenty-six years passed before that was finally achieved in 1786. The following year de Saussure repeated the ascent himself. In this aquatint by Grundmann, his party of 18 guides, laden with food, wine, camping equipment, and scientific instruments, is seen negotiating the chaotic jumble of crevasses known as "La Jonction."

THE ROOF OF WESTERN EUROPE:
MONT BLANC, 1786

MONT BLANC, THE WHITE MOUNTAIN, IS colossal. Even today, satiated with global superlatives, we can still feel awed by that gleaming dome, which seems so remote and ethereal, so impossibly high above the Chamonix valley. The vertical interval from valley floor to summit is nearly 4,000 meters – greater than the rise from base camp to summit on Mount Everest. On Everest that interval starts at much greater altitude, so the whole climb is on snow and ice, whereas the ascent of Mont Blanc from Chamonix starts through woods and meadows. Nevertheless, it is still a huge mountain, unrivalled king of the Alps, the roof of Western Europe.

CASH PRIZE FOR THE SUMMIT, 1760

The Genevan scientist Horace-Bénédict de Saussure was just twenty when he first visited Chamonix in 1760. He later wrote, "The majestic glaciers, separated by great forests and crowned by granite rocks which rise to incredible heights, offer one of the most magnificent and impressive sights imaginable." De Saussure came from a wealthy family and decided to offer a cash prize to the first team able to reach

the summit of Mont Blanc. To a village of impoverished farmers, hunters and traders, this was serious inducement and soon parties were attempting to find a way onto the huge glaciers cascading from the distant summit.

In 1760 the world's first balloon flight was still to come. Unlike the people of the high Andes or the Himalaya, Europeans had little experience of traveling above 3,000 meters. Virtually nothing was known about the effects of altitude. Nor had anyone seriously attempted to travel through heavily glaciated country – nothing as awesome as the immense ice cataracts which spill down Mont Blanc's northern slopes. This was dangerous terrain, riven by huge crevasses up to a hundred meters deep, often yawing many meters wide, or concealed by fragile snow bridges. Where the ice mass was stretched over bulges in the bedrock, it formed *séracs* – giant tottering towers of ice, threatening to collapse without warning. To explore this alien landscape, the pioneers brought cumbersome ladders to cross the biggest chasms. On steep ice slopes they had to chop steps with heavy wood axes. Unlike modern mountaineers, they had no crampons on their feet and had to try and maintain balance with the help of the hunter's alpenstock – a long wooden pole with a steel point at one end.

In 1775 a party managed to reach a subsidiary summit of Mont Blanc called the Dôme du Goûter. Later that summer another party got slightly higher, towards the Aiguille du Goûter. The team included a student home for the holidays from Turin University, called Michel-Gabriel Paccard. More attempts followed, all of them defeated by the sheer complexity of finding a way through the convoluted ice masses which spill from Mont Blanc's summit, and by the sheer scale of the enterprise.

The race came to a head in 1786 when a party managed to reach an isolated outcrop of rock below the final Bosses ridge leading to the summit. They baulked at this icy camel-back, and turned round, defeated. But one member of the team, a young crystal hunter from Chamonix called Jacques Balmat, hung around, exploring the rocks below the Bosses, searching for the amethysts and other semi-precious stones. By the time he set off down after the others darkness was falling. Disorientated amongst the maze of crevases on the glacier, he was forced to stop and scrape a hole in the snow with his alpenstock. He must have spent a miserable night, shivering in his frozen hollow, but he survived. Not only that, he was encouraged by his ability to cope in this alien high altitude world – so much so, that he determined that he – Jacques Balmat – would be the one to succeed finally in reaching the summit.

BALMAT, PACCARD, & THE SUMMIT: 1786

Paccard, the student who had tried the mountain eleven years earlier, had now finished his studies and was back in Chamonix. Balmat seemed to recognize a fellow adventurous spirit, and asked Paccard to team up with him. On 7 August, 1786, the two men made the long climb through the forest, then on above the tree line, to spend the night on a rocky shoulder still marked on the map as the Gîte Balmat, 2,589 meters above sea level. From here onwards almost the entire route would be on snow and ice.

They left the gîte at first light on 8 August, weaving their way around crevasses, passing the landmarks which had now become familiar to the Chamonix pioneers – La Jonction, Les Grands Mulets and, eventually, Le Grand Plateau. By the time they reached this great snow bowl, their eyes were smarting from the harsh glare of afternoon sunshine. And, at 4,000 meters above sea level, their breathing was becoming steadily more laboured, their muscles more weary. Yet they still had to climb another 800 meters to surmount the final dome.

To the right was the Bosses ridge which had defeated Balmat two months earlier. Nowadays, with steel crampons giving secure footholds, that knife-edge doesn't seem a big deal, but in 1786 they didn't have those aids. So Balmat and Paccard decided to head left instead, contouring up a slope which seemed less exposed. In fact, this ancient passage, as it became known, poised above giant ice cliffs, was no walk and it wasn't until 6:12 pm that the two men emerged onto the huge domed roof of the mountain, watched from nearly 4,000 meters below by one Baron von Gersdorf who clearly saw, through his binoculars, a red cloth fluttering from a wooden stick.

Balmat and Paccard measured a temperature of –7.5°C. Their barometer gave a reading of just over 5,000 meters. We know now that the actual height is 4,807 meters. We also know that – descending without crampons or ice axes, rushing back down steep ice slopes, then stumbling frantically though the jumbled chaos of yawing crevasses at La Jonction

Left
For the early pioneers the glaciated slopes of Mont Blanc presented an alien but fascinating new world to discover.

Below
Mont Blanc's domed summit rises 4,807 meters above sea level. This aerial view from the north shows the Bosses Ridge on the right and the precarious *ancien passage* above shadowy ice cliffs, climbed by Balmat and Paccard on the first ascent in 1786.

in the failing light – it was a brilliant achievement for these two proto-alpinists to get all the way back to their gîte by midnight, twenty hours after setting out on their historic climb.

The following day the two heroes were welcomed back to Chamonix. De Saussure, now Professor of Natural Science at the Geneva Academy – the man who had initiated the race to the summit 16 years earlier – rushed over to Chamonix immediately and attempted to repeat the ascent. He failed, but returned the following year and, accompanied by a huge team of local porters carrying ladders, blankets, food, wine, stoves, and scientific instruments, made the second ascent of Mont Blanc.

For Paccard, the triumph of the first ascent turned sour, when a fellow Chamonix resident spread malicious rumours that he had been dragged to the summit by Balmat. Although Paccard scotched the report, establishing that it was he, not Balmat, who had chosen the route, his reputation was damaged. In 1887 when the famous statue was erected in Chamonix, it showed Balmat, not Paccard, pointing the way to de Saussure. It was only on the bicentenary, in 1986, that a statue was finally erected to Paccard.

The former crystal hunter, Jacques Balmat profited from his success, repeating the climb many times and in 1808 guiding to the summit a Chamonix girl called Marie Paradis, who became the first woman to climb Mont Blanc.

SOUTH SIDE STORY

All the early attempts on Mont Blanc were made from the north side. However, a short distance south from the summit, there is a subsidiary point called Monte Bianco, from which much steeper precipices drop towards the Italian village of Courmayeur. In the twentieth century the gullies and buttresses on this wild Italian side would inspire some of the greatest advances in mountaineering, but already in 1865 an English party led by A.W.Moore, with Swiss guides Jakob and Melchior Anderegg, made the first big new route, way ahead of its time – a very steep ice ridge called the Brenva Spur.

The west-facing Brenva Face is one of the biggest snow and ice walls in the Alps, threatened by frequent avalanches. The South Face is steeper, with thin ribbons of ice separated by spectacular buttresses of red granite – scene of many difficult new routes in the late twentieth century.

There are now well over a hundred routes up Mont Blanc.

"The majestic glaciers, separated by great forests and crowned by granite rocks which rise to incredible heights, offer one of the most magnificent and impressive sights imaginable." This modern aerial photo captures all the majesty which so enraptured De Saussure. The Chamonix valley in the foreground and the Italian plains to the south are deep in shadow, while the last rays of the day illuminate the roof of the Alps.

THE GOLDEN AGE OF ALPINE CLIMBING

Above
Early British visitors were enthralled by the picturesque drama of the Alps. This watercolor by J.M.W.Turner depicts the Devil's Bridge on the Gotthard Pass.

Left
Not strictly "Golden Age," but this classic 1886 image by the Italian photographer Vittoria Sella, still captures the spirit of the mid-1800s. Alessandro and Gaudenzia Sella (the latter heavily protected against solar radiation) are climbing the Wetterhorn with the famous guide, Joseph Maquignaz. Behind them, in dark shadow, looms the North Face of the Eiger, which will become the notorious "last great problem of the Alps" in fifty years time.

BRITS INVENTED MOST THINGS, INCLUDING mountaineering. Or so we like to think. There is no doubt that British climbers did help to popularize the Alps. And they did, during the so-called "Golden Age" of alpinism in the mid- nineteenth century, snatch virtually all the highest summits on Europe's watershed. But, as they were the first to admit, those Victorian judges, dons and clergymen, with their prodigious beards and huge appetites for filling their long summer holidays with healthy adventure, relied heavily on the skills of local Swiss, French, and Italian hunters-turned-guides to reach their summits. And, before the British arrived on the scene to hog the lion's share, Swiss climbers had already nabbed a few of those summits.

1810
JUNGFRAU
VOLKER, BORTIS, MEYER

One of the greatest prizes after the Mont Blanc summit was the Jungfrau, the gorgeous culmination of the triptych – Ogre, Monk and Maiden – which dominates the skyline south of Switzerland's capital, Bern. In 1810 two chamois hunters, Alois Volker and Josef Bortis, reached the north summit with

Hieronymus and Johann-Rudolf Meyer. The following year Johann-Rudolf's nineteen-year-old son, Gottlieb, reached the higher south summit (4,185 meters).

The Meyers sponsored the first Swiss mountain maps; they were pioneer cartographers. Over in the Silvretta mountains, in eastern Switzerland, it was botanists who made the first ascent of Piz Linard, specifically to search for the upper limit of alpine plant species. The highest peak in the Berner Oberland, the Finsteraarhorn, was first attempted by a team led by the geologist Professor Hugi, after whom a saddle on the mountain – the Hugisattel – is named. The Agissizjoch nearby is named after a pioneering glaciologist, Louis Agassiz. Both Hugi and Agassiz influenced the British glaciologist James Forbes to visit the Alps and out of Forbes' fascination with the glaciers grew a passion for climbing to the summits.

MOUNTAIN TOURISTS: INTRODUCING THE FIRST BRITISH MOUNTAINEERS

Other British travelers were also drawn to the Alps. Britain's most celebrated painter, J.M.W. Turner, made several journeys to capture the grand romanticism of high mountain country, as did his champion, the painter and critic, John Ruskin. Jumping on the bandwagon of this new appreciation for mountain

THE ALPINE CLUB

During an ascent of the Finsteraarhorn in 1857, an English group including Edward Kennedy and William Mathews discussed the possibility of forming an association for experienced mountaineers to share information and ideas. That autumn Mathews hosted a dinner at his house where names were suggested and on 22 December 1857 the world's first mountaineering association, the Alpine Club, was founded with just twelve members. The first president was the Irishman John Ball. This slightly later group, 1865, includes, seated left, Leslie Stephen, who became president the following year. At the back, on the right, is Peter Taugwalder.

The mighty northern triptych of the Bernese Oberland, from left to right – Eiger, Mönch, and Jungfrau, seen across the deep gulf of the Lauterbrunnen valley. In the bottom left corner, unimagined by Victorian pioneers, is the Schilthorn cable car station which featured in the 007 movie, *On Her Majesty's Secret Service*.

scenery, Thomas Cook brought his first tourists to the range in 1863 to see the mountains which by now had become the regular summer haunt of those bearded British proto-mountaineers.

The beards came, by and large, from the wealthy upper middle class. Many of them were lawyers. Sir Alfred Wills, for instance, was the judge who sent Oscar Wilde to prison. John Ball was a rich Irish lawyer and Member of Parliament, with the private means to travel extensively through the eastern Alps, writing books about his journeys and, in 1857, making the first ascent of Monte Pelmo, in the Italian Dolomites.

However, they were not all born with silver spoons in their mouths. Two, in particular, came from humble backgrounds and perhaps it was because they had had to pull their way up the social ladder that they became such forceful alpinists.

John Tyndall, like Ball, was an Irishman. He started his working life as a surveyor for the Ordnance Survey, studying in his spare time. He moved to England, eventually procured a teaching post, continued studying, gained a PhD, and was then made a fellow of the Royal Society. In 1853 he was appointed Professor of Natural Philosophy at the Royal Institution. There he worked alongside scientific giants such as Michael Faraday, pioneering studies in physics, biology, and glaciology. Amongst his many scientific achievements was the identification of greenhouse gases, and today his name is commemorated in the John Tyndall Centre for climate change research.

The other forceful upstart was a young engraver's apprentice from London, called Edward Whymper. By all accounts he was rather an earnest, opinionated young man, but he had real artistic talent and was commissioned in 1860 to travel to the Alps and come back with a series of sketches for the London publisher William Longman. In Zermatt he found himself rubbing shoulders with the founding fathers of the new Alpine Club and staring up at the one mountain which, more than any other alpine peak, has an immediate, unmistakable personality – a uniquely shaped monolith with an aura of impregnability. Forbes had pronounced the peak "unscaled and unscaleable." Ball had declared that "alone among the great peaks of the Alps it will preserve the epithet 'inaccessible.'" Ruskin had called it "the most precipitous and the strongest mass in the Alps." Very soon the names of both Whymper and the older John Tyndall would be associated indelibly with this towering fortress. It was, of course, the Matterhorn.

Above
Gustave Doré's lurid reconstruction of the Matterhorn disaster, when the rope broke, sending Croz, Douglas, Hadow, and Hudson plunging 1,200 meters to their deaths. Edward Whymper was one of the three survivors. The portrait (left) shows him on his first visit to the Alps, a rather earnest, ambitious young engraver, for whom the Matterhorn would become an obsession.

EDWARD WHYMPER'S ALPINE FIRST ASCENTS

Between 1864 and 1866, climbing with a variety of partners, Whymper achieved a fine tally of first ascents, including:

Pointe des Ecrins
Aiguille d'Argentière
Aiguille de Trélatête
Aiguille Verte
Grandes Jorasses (Pointe Whymper)
Grand Cornier
Ruinette
Matterhorn
Tête de Valpelline

From a technical point of view, his most astounding achievement was the first crossing of the Col Dolent. On the descent, Michel Croz worked for seven continuous hours cutting steps in the 50 degrees ice, where a single slip by any member of the party would probably have spelt disaster.

Above
One of Whymper's engravings,
used to illustrate his classic
bestseller *Scrambles in the Alps*.

1865
THE MATTERHORN
EDWARD WHYMPER

One and a half centuries on, the Matterhorn still never disappoints and you can see how it has transformed Zermatt from a cluster of impoverished peasants' huts to a glitzy resort with new hotels going up every year. The mountain still seems impregnable, steeper than it actually is, towering in defiant isolation.

When Whymper first saw the Matterhorn in 1860 he was not actually very impressed with the mountain as an aesthetic object. But he was an ambitious man and he decided that mountaineering was for him. The following summer he cut his teeth with an ascent of Mont Pelvoux, in the Dauphiné Alps, then traveled over to Zermatt, hoping to try the first ascent of the Weisshorn, only to hear that John Tyndall had just beat him to it. Perhaps it was that rebuff which focussed his ambitions on the Matterhorn, for he almost immediately made enquiries about hiring a guide to attempt what was becoming known as the last great problem of the Alps.

Tyndall had already tried the Matterhorn. So had Jean-Anthoine Carrel, who lived in Breuil, on the Italian side of the peak. In fact, Carrel had become quite proprietorial over the mountain which his people called Cervino. Now, after much haggling over prices, he agreed to accompany Whymper up the Southwest Ridge from Italy – a route which appeared less formidable than the Northeast Ridge on the Swiss side.

Over the next three years, Whymper made no less than six attempts on the Italian Ridge. Sometimes Carrel agreed to accompany him; other times he used Swiss guides. Frequently the guides deserted him, terrified by electric storms or avalanches or falling rocks. On one occasion, in 1862, Whymper stayed alone in his little tent and pushed on to a new height record, before deciding to turn back. On the way down he slipped and fell, bouncing from rock to rock, suffering concussion and very nearly disappearing over a 300-meter drop.

"I was perfectly conscious of what was happening, and felt each blow; but, like a patient under chloroform, experienced no pain. Each blow was, naturally, more severe than that which preceded it, and I

Above
One of Zermatt's classic chocolate box views: on the right the Dent Blanche, first climbed in 1862 by Jean-Baptiste Croz, Edward Kennedy, Johann Kronig, and C.Wigram; on the left the seemingly impregnable Matterhorn, with Whymper's Hörnli ridge descending rightward, towards the camera.

remember thinking, 'Well, if the next is harder still, that will be the end.'"

After recovering at a local inn he tried again, but failed. A few days later Tyndall was seen close to the summit, having reached within about 300 meters of the top. In 1863 and 1864 Whymper was back to try again, and was again frustrated.

During 1864 Whymper climbed with the French guide Michel Croz and was impressed. So in 1865 he hired Croz again, later recalling that, "the programme which was drawn up for this journey was rather ambitious, since it included almost all the great peaks which had not then been ascended." It was a campaign which few modern mountaineers could match, not least the huge distances walked between each peak, traversing glaciers and crossing high passes day after day. But Whymper wasn't going to be satisfied without the crowning glory of the Matterhorn.

RACE TO THE TOP

Croz was now committed to joining another client, so Whymper made his own way to the Italian side of the mountain. There he met Carrel, who announced vaguely that he was working for an Italian gentleman. Carrel was secretive and evasive about his plans. Meanwhile his client, Felice Giordano, wrote to a friend in Turin, "I have tried to keep everything secret, but that fellow whose life seems to depend on the Matterhorn is here, suspiciously prying into everything. I have taken all the competent men away from him, and yet he is so enamoured of this mountain that he may go up with others and make a scene."

Which is precisely what Whymper did, the moment he heard that Carrel's team had set off for the Matterhorn. Supremely fit, he rushed over the Thedule Pass to Zermatt, bumping into Lord Francis Douglas, brother of the Marquis of Queensberry and a keen mountaineer. The two men agreed immediately to team up for a race against Carrel, hiring an old Swiss guide, Peter Taugwalder and his son to come as guides. At dinner that night in the Monte Rosa Hotel, they discovered that the Reverend Charles Hudson was also planning an attempt, with none other than Whymper's old guide Michel Croz. Thwarted yet again, and fearful of getting entangled in competitors' ropes, Whymper suggested

Right

Nowadays, in high summer, it is not unusual for 200 people or more to climb the Hörnli ridge in a single day. For all its mystique, the Matterhorn is probably an easier mountain than the one in the background – the Weisshorn, first climbed by John Tyndall's party in 1861.

reluctantly that they join forces. Reluctance turned to anxious regret when Hudson then insisted on bringing his young, comparatively inexperienced, friend Douglas Hadow.

So it was a cumbersome team of seven which set off the next morning to walk up through the woods and meadows to the rock prow which juts from the foot of the Matterhorn's Northeast Ridge, known as the Hörnli Ridge. After all the fruitless attempts from the south, Whymper had now decided to try the seemingly impossible Swiss ridge. Gloomy impatience gave way to new hope when the Taugwalders returned that afternoon to the bivouac spot where they were camping out, to report that they had made fast progress up the lower part of the ridge. Close-up, it was actually easy angled.

By dawn the next morning the whole party was on its way, zigzagging up a series of gullies and terraces, making fast progress on the east flank of the ridge. Higher up they took to the dizzy crest, climbing up onto the kinked "Shoulder" which is such a feature of the mountain. Then the ridge got much steeper – so steep that they were forced to traverse rightwards onto the shady slabs of the North Face.

Climbing techniques had not advanced a great deal since the first ascent of Mont Blanc 79 years earlier. However, the guides did now carry ice axes for cutting steps in hard ice, and everyone wore nailed boots, which provided some purchase both on rock and ice. But in comparison to modern climbers, they were woefully under-equipped. On passage like this, teetering over an 1,100-meter drop, if one man slipped, only the instant reaction of the others could save him: they had no slings or pegs to make anchors on the rock, no proper system for "belaying."

Instead, they relied on trust and high levels of skill. They were very fit, very nimble, and very fast. By one o'clock that afternoon they had traversed back onto the ridge, which now eased off a little, until at two o'clock they were rushing up a final snowslope and gathering on the jagged crest of the peak, staring straight down the south side, to see Carrel's party still 300 meters below the summit. The Swiss-French-English team had won the race and Whymper, after seven unsuccessful attempts, had finally achieved his dream.

Above
The other side of the Matterhorn. In Bradford Washburn's masterful aerial photo, the Italian Ridge rises from the south, on the right. Both Whymper and Tyndall attempted this route repeatedly and the highpoint on the horizontal shoulder is called Pic Tyndall. The route was completed to the summit by Anton Carrel's party, a few days after Whymper's successful ascent from the Swiss side. On the left is the more savage Zmutt Ridge, which was climbed 14 years later, in 1879, by Burgener and Mummery.

Below
The Walker family and friends, on their summer holidays. Lucy Walker, first woman to climb the Matterhorn, is in the back row, sitting to the right of her favorite guide, Melchior Anderegg. At the right end of the middle row is A.W.Moore, who made the first ascent of Mont Blanc's Brenva Spur in 1865. Horace Walker sports a white beard and prodigious ice axe.

In one of the less chivalrous episodes in mountaineering history, the triumphant party started shouting, then hurling rocks down at the Italians. Whymper then came over all sensitive and poetic, writing afterwards:

"The atmosphere was perfectly still, and free from all clouds or vapours. Mountains fifty – nay, a hundred – miles off, looked sharp and near ... There were the most rugged forms, and the most graceful outlines; bold perpendicular cliffs and gentle undulating slopes; rocky mountains and snowy mountains, sombre and solemn, or glittering and white, with walls-turrets-pinnacles-pyramids-domes-cones-spires! There was every combination that the world can give, and every contrast that the heart could desire."

TRIUMPH TO TRAGEDY

They spent a glorious hour on the summit. Then the main party started down, while Whymper lingered to write all of their names on a piece of paper, which he placed in a bottle left in the snow. Then he and Peter Taugwalder hurried down to catch up with the others.

Young Hadow was struggling and Lord Douglas was concerned. So he asked Whymper and old Peter to tie on to the main party, so that there would be more men above to hold the rope, should Hadow slip. Then they continued as a rope of seven.

FIRST WOMAN TO CLIMB THE MATTERHORN

Prominent amongst the British alpine pioneers was Horace Walker, after whom the Pointe Walker on the Grandes Jorasses is named. His sister Lucy, climbing in a print dress and living off sponge cake and champagne, made 98 climbing excursions, usually in the company of Melchior Anderegg, including the first female ascent of the Matterhorn in 1871. When asked why she never married, she replied, "I love mountains and Melchior, and Melchior already has a wife."

Hadow had just made the first ascent of the most coveted peak in the Alps. It was his first experience of this kind of steep terrain. On the way up he had coped well, but now he was looking straight down one of the most terrifying precipices in Europe. On this very steep terrain he was probably facing into the slope. Croz, the French guide, went first, waiting below each step to help Hadow, taking each boot in his hands and guiding it to the holds. The Matterhorn's rock is notoriously fickle, often loose and, on this northern slope, often coated with a slick of verglas. As Croz waited for Hadow, slack rope would have gathered between them. Above Hadow, Hudson and Douglas followed, balancing on small holds, trying to avoid getting too much slack in the rope.

Whymper watched anxiously from above. The lower two climbers were partially obscured by an outcrop and all he saw was a sudden flash of Hadow's shoulders before Croz let out a scream. Then he saw both men tumbling, whipping the rope tight and plucking first Hudson and then Douglas from the slope. The three higher men braced themselves, but a second later there was a loud snap as the rope between young Taugwalder and Douglas broke.

"For seconds we saw our unfortunate companions sliding downwards on their backs, and spreading out their hands, endeavouring to save themselves. They passed from our sight uninjured, disappeared one by one, and fell from precipice to precipice ..."

The three survivors spent a miserable night shivering on the mountain, before returning to Zermatt, victory soured by this terrible tragedy. The following day Whymper went up to the Matterhorn Glacier with some fellow English residents. There, on the great snow shelf at the foot of the 1,200-meters-high north face, they found the mangled remains of three of the victims. Douglas's body was never found. Croz's was horribly dismembered, but Whymper identified the beard stuck to a piece of his jawbone. In Hudson's jacket he found a letter to the dead man's wife; his watch had stopped at 3:45 pm.

The broken rope can still be seen in the Zermatt museum. It is pitifully thin: it doesn't look much more substantial than sash cord. Back in London, Queen Victoria was so shocked by the accident that she asked whether mountaineering couldn't be banned. Whymper himself was so shaken that he more or less gave up alpine climbing. However, he did travel to Ecuador to make the first ascent of Chimbarazo and he used his wonderfully dramatic etchings to illustrate his best-selling *Scrambles in the Alps*, which concludes, "Climb if you will, but remember that courage and strength are nought without prudence, and that a momentary negligence may destroy the happiness of a lifetime."

There is nothing like a gruesome accident to add lurid appeal to a climb, particularly when the mountain in question is so spectacular. The first ascent of the Matterhorn caught the public imagination like no other. However, as Whymper's party had proved, accident notwithstanding, the mountain was not actually as hard as everyone had assumed. The difficulty lay more in the imagination than in the actual terrain.

So let's not forget some of those other Victorian pioneers, including Whymper's rival, John Tyndall. He didn't quite make it on the Matterhorn, but he did pull off the first ascent of what many people nowadays would consider a harder – and more classically beautiful – mountain on the other side of the valley – the Weisshorn.

1861
THE WEISSHORN
BENNEN, TYNDALL, & WENGER

Tyndall made his ascent by the knife-edged East Ridge, with his guide Johann-Joseph Bennen leading the way. "The ridge became gradually narrower, and the precipices on each side more sheer ... Bennen .. tried the snow by squeezing it with his foot, and to my astonishment began to cross it. Even after the pressure of his feet, the space he had to stand on did not exceed a hand-breath." After six hours of continuous effort they stopped for food and drink, before continuing, until, finally, "clearly within reach, a silvery pyramid projected itself against the blue sky." On reaching the final point, Tyndall, the rational, analyti-

cal scientist, was quite overwhelmed. "I had never before witnessed a scene which affected me like this ... An influence seemed to proceed from it direct to the soul; the delight and exultation experienced were not those of Reason or Knowledge, but of Being: I was part of it, and it of me, and in the transcendent glory of Nature I entirely forgot myself as a man ..."

Any alpinist could agree with those noble sentiments, but most wouldn't dare express them so fulsomely.

OTHER GREAT PIONEERS OF THE GOLDEN AGE OF MOUNTAINEERING: LESLIE STEPHEN

Another of the great pioneers of the "Golden Age" was Leslie Stephen, who chose a deliberately flippant title for his classic mountaineering book – *The Playground of Europe*. His favourite stamping ground was the Berner Oberland, where his first ascents included the Bietschorn and the Schreckhorn, the latter by a dramatic rock ridge. Master of understatement, he described the final ridge as "significant enough for men of weak nerves."

Over in the Zermatt region, Stephen made the first ascent an elegant spire called the Zinalrothorn, only to discover that the summit was completely flat.

Left
John Tyndall, pioneering scientist
and mountaineer, commemorated
today in the John Tyndall Center
for Climate Change.

Below
A recent photo by mountain guide
Martin Moran, of the Weisshorn's
East Ridge.

Below, right
"This puzzle of stone" – the
Campanile Basso in the Brenta
Dolomites, one of the last great
alpine summits to be climbed,
by Otto Ampferer and Karl Berger,
in 1899.

"I had almost said the top, but the Rothorn has no top. It has a place where a top manifestly ought to have been ... It ended in a flat circular area a few feet broad, as though it had been a perfect cone, with the apex cleanly struck off. Melchior and Jacob [Anderegg] set to work at once to remedy this deficiency of nature by building a suitable cairn."

Like Whymper, Stephen was a prodigious walker. Back in Britain his "Sunday Tramps" covered huge distances on foot whilst discussing the great philosophical issues of the day, and he thought nothing of walking sixty miles from Cambridge to London, to attend a dinner. Another quality he shared with all his fellow pioneers was an aversion to undue risk. Matterhorn excepted, by and large the early alpinists avoided accidents and they tended to retire gracefully from extreme climbing, in Stephen's case to concentrate on huge literary projects such as founding the *Dictionary of National Biography*, and to fathering two famous daughters – Vanessa Bell and Virginia Woolf.

LAST UNTOUCHED SUMMITS

By the 1890s virtually all the alpine peaks had been climbed. But in the Brenta Dolomites near Trento there remained one soaring pinnacle called the Guglia di Brenta, later known as the Campanile Basso.

A famous writer on alpinism, Walter Pause, called the Campanile "this puzzle of stone." In 1897 one Nino Pooli led the first attempt to solve the puzzle. Although his team didn't reach the top, they managed to climb chimneys and ramps on the east side leading to a huge ledge, the "Stradone Provinciale" which led round to the northeast face. Here, protecting themselves with steel "pitons" hammered into cracks, they managed to continue to a high ledge. Ignorant of Pooli's attempt, two years later Otto Ampferer and Karl Berger were depressed, on reaching the ledge to find rusting pitons and empty wine bottles. But then their spirits lifted as they found a note from Pooli wishing future parties better luck.

Ampferer led on up the final wall, hands searching for holds in vertical cracks, boot toes balancing on tiny nubbins over the huge void. This was later given the second highest grade – Five. The Campanile was only eclipsed in 1911 when an outstanding rock climber, Paul Preuss, climbed a new direct route, straight up the east face, unroped, solo. On reaching the summit he then soloed back down the whole route. By now alpine climbing had entered a new era. The main summits had all been climbed and the fascination now lay in finding new, harder routes to those summits.

LESLIE STEPHEN'S ALPINE FIRST ASCENTS

Rimpfischorn
Alphubel
Blümlisalphorn
Oberaarhorn
Schreckhorn
Monte Disgrazia
Zinalrothorn
Lyskamm West
Cima di Fradusta
Cima di Ball
Mont Mallet
Bietschorn

Stephen also took part in first ascents of two famous passes. In the Berner Oberland, long before the railway was built, his party was first to cross the Jungfraujoch. On the Grandes Jorasses he was first to reach a saddle which he called Col des Hirondelles, because he found several swallows frozen in the snow during their attempt to fly over the Alps.

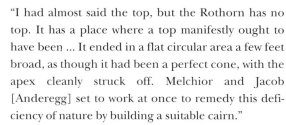

Denali, "The Great One," highest mountain on the North American continent, also known as Mount McKinley, with the North Summit on the left and the higher South Summit on the right.

FREDERICK COOK WAS A FIBBER, A TELLER OF porkies, a congenital liar. But you have to admire the Brooklyn doctor for the sheer effrontery of his hoaxes; and for the fact that his brazenly false claims to two of the world's greatest geographical prizes were at least founded on a life of adventurous exploration.

THE DOCTOR, THE WRITER, & HIS CHALLENGE

He had already made a name for himself exploring the Arctic and joining the first party ever to overwinter in Antarctica, when he found in 1902 an article in *National Geographic Magazine* which concluded, "The writer would strongly urge that if the expedition is undertaken that it be put under the direction of a man who is not only an experienced mountaineer but who has also had long training in frontier life and exploratory work, for the success of the expedition must depend in very large measure on its leadership."

FREDERICK COOK
MCKINLEY ATTEMPTS
1903 & 1906

The writer was Alfred Brooks. The expedition he proposed was to make the first ascent of North America's highest peak, Mount McKinley. Five years earlier, during the Klondike gold rush, a prospector called William Dickey had named the mountain after Senator William McKinley, a keen advocate of the gold standard, and had stated, correctly, that it was the highest mountain on the continent, rising to over 6,000 meters above sea level. Now Brooks had carried out a comprehensive survey of the peak, getting to within ten miles of its foot.

The pace of exploration was frenetic. Alaska, which had only recently been sold by Russia to the fledgling USA, was a vast wilderness promising adventure – and the possibility of profit – to ambitious prospectors, miners, hunters, and missionaries. As for McKinley – the crowning peak which the local Indians called simply Denali, "The Great One" – it was on a scale that made the European Alps look like effete hillocks. It was gigantic. But the biggest problem of all was just getting to the foot of the mountain.

Frederick Cook decided that he was the man to tackle the problem. He found money, put together a team and in the summer of 1903 landed on the southern coast of Alaska at Cook Inlet (named after the other, Captain, Cook). From here they had to travel nearly 400 miles through forest and swamp, to reach the northwest side of the mountain. Men and horses were plagued by clouds of mosquitoes and horseflies, their skin erupting in festering sores. For most of the 48 days of the approach the mountain was hidden by rain and mist. Yet, once they reached the mountain, they did manage to climb up its northern flank, following a steep snow ridge to an altitude of about 3,300 meters.

Back in Manhattan, Cook talked up the mountain at the Explorers Club, American's answer to the Royal Geographical Society. Spurred on by competition, he raised money for a second attempt in 1906. Some members of the first attempt were prepared to face again the swampy horrors of the Alaskan tundra in mid-summer. New to this torment were the mountaineers Herschel Parker and Belmore Browne. Also new on the team was a Montana blacksmith called "Big Ed" Barrill.

This time Cook decided to try the mountain from the south, even though it looked impossible to the experienced climbers on the team. Looking from a small peak near the Tokositna Glacier towards an even bigger glacier, the Ruth (named for Cook's daughter), they were confronted by a sprawling tangle of glaciers and ridges, with no obvious way through to the gigantic southern wall of McKinley itself, with the summit still 5,000 meters above them.

Cook announced that he would just do a recce with Barrill. So Browne was astounded three weeks later, back at the coast, to hear a rumour that Cook had reached the summit of McKinley. When Cook appeared he announced vaguely that he had found a surprisingly easy way up the mountain.

This time he was lionized in New York, lecturing to packed halls about his epic climb. Later he wrote up the story in *Harper's* magazine, publishing a photo of Barrill holding the Stars and Stripes on a surprisingly rocky summit. Browne was con-

had been whitened out in the *Harper's* version. Browne also noticed that the eminence Barrill was standing on looked remarkably similar to a peak in another photo of the Ruth Glacier – about 20 miles from the summit of McKinley.

Parker and Browne began to voice their disbelief. Even Cook's friends at the Explorers Club began to doubt him. But by now, 1907, the doctor was away again, "hunting walrus" in the Arctic, only to reappear in Denmark, hailed as a hero who had just become the very first person to reach the North Pole.

Robert Peary, who had devoted most of his life to polar travel, and was making the final preparations for his journey to the North Pole, was livid. The Danish government soon admitted that they had been duped. Meanwhile, Ed Barill signed an affidavit to say that the previous year's summit photo was a hoax. Browne and Parker even mounted an expedition to locate the rocky bump near the Ruth Glacier and recreate the photo, demonstrating that Cook had been nowhere near Mount McKinley. Yet still large sections of a gullible public supported the charismatic Cook, insisting that no-one had disproved his claims.

vinced that the photo was a fake and the following year that conviction was strengthened when Cook published his book *To the Top of the Continent*. Topographical detail about the actual route remained absent. As for the "summit photo," this time it included another background peak, which

Left
Modern expeditions fly in to Denali. A hundred years ago it was very different. On his first attempt Cook had to travel nearly 400 miles from the coast, traversing tundra and mosquito-ridden swamps. On the second attempt, defeated by the gigantic scale of the mountain, he faked a "summit photo" (above left) of Ed Barrill. The following year, 1907, his former colleagues Belmore and Brown identified the location of the photo; Cook's "summit" was nearly 20 miles from the actual top of Denali.

Above
A modern climber gazes south
from 4,900 meters on Denali. In
the background, on the right, is
Mt Foraker. According to Archdeacon
Stuck, the Tanana Indians used to call
Foraker "Menlale" – Denali's Wife.

MCKINLEY NORTH SUMMIT, 1910

In Alaska, at the mining town of Fairbanks, the locals were stirred by Cook's book to try McKinley themselves. Rising to a bar-room taunt that he was too fat to climb a mountain, the Welsh prospector Thomas Lloyd put together a team. Rather than face summer swamps and man-eating insects, they set off sensibly on 21 December 1909, using dog sledges to cross the frozen tundra from the north, heading for the Muldrow Glacier which gives access to McKinley's northwest flank.

By March 1910 the miners were on the mountain, cutting steps in the ice with coal shovels and wearing home-made irons strapped to their moccasins. Despite their complete lack of mountaineering experience, three of the team, Charley McGonagall, Pete Anderson, and E.C Davidson, reached the northern of McKinley's two summits, where, on 3 April 1910, they erected a fourteen foot spruce pole with a 12x6-foot American flag on top, which they reckoned would be visible from Fairbanks, 150 miles away. It was an astounding feat – carrying that huge pole to an altitude with less than half the oxygen pressure at sea level. On their 18-hour summit day the three men climbed up and down 2,500 meters. But then their

leader, Lloyd, blew it all by over-egging the cake, telling everyone in Fairbanks that he had lost enough weight to get to the summit himself, and that the team had also climbed McKinley's higher South Summit. No-one could see the flag, but the story was sold in all its hyperbolic glory to the *New York Times*, prompting people to wonder whether this wasn't just another hoax.

1913
HIGHEST SUMMIT
HARPER, KARSTENS, STUCK, & TATUM

In 1912 Parker and Browne returned yet again to McKinley and repeated the miners' route, almost to the South Summit. Looking across to the North Summit, they failed to spot any flagpole. But in Fairbanks there was an English clergyman, Archdeacon Stuck, who wanted to believe that the miners had made it, even though he had doubts over the full detail of Lloyd's boastful account. Right from the start he had been fascinated by the mountain. He had always been convinced that Cook was a liar, stating that Cook would only climb McKinley when a railway was built

to the summit. He was determined to solve the mystery, saying, "I would rather climb Mount McKinley than own the richest gold mine in Alaska." In 1913 he finally organized his own expedition.

Archdeacon Stuck was 49, so he took some younger companions. Billy Karstens, aged 34, was known as the Seventy-Mile Kid, from his gold-panning days on the river of that name. Robert Tatum was a twenty-one-year-old trainee priest. Walter Harper, also twenty-one, was Stuck's adopted son.

Like the miners, this team traveled in the winter, getting established on the mountain in the early summer. During the approach they shot four caribou, boiled down the meat and mixed it with butter to produce 200 highly nutritious meat balls for mountain rations. Laboriously they relayed loads up the mountain, stocking a whole series of camps, gasping in the thin air, wilting under the extremes of heat and cold.

On 6 April they were approaching their final camp when Walter Harper suddenly shouted, pointing up to the North Summit. There was the huge pole, planted three years' earlier by Lloyd's team: the Fairbanks climbers had climbed the North Summit.

But the true prize was still unclaimed. Clambering stiffly out of the his tent the next morning, Stuck had six pairs of socks stuffed inside his moccasins, and still his feet were cold; but he pushed on up the final snow slope.

Above
Modern climbers on what has become the "normal" route up Denali, the West Buttress.

Right
Hudson Stuck's companions on the first successful ascent of the mountain. Left to right: Robert Tatum, Esais, Harry Karstens, Johnny Fred, and Walter Harper.

"Walter, who had been in the lead all day, was the first to scrabble up; a native Alaskan, he is the first human being to set foot upon the top of Alaska's greatest mountain, and he had well earned the life-long distinction. Karstens and Tatum were hard upon his heels, but the last man on the rope, in his enthusiasm and excitement somewhat overpassing his narrow wind margin, had almost to be hauled up the last few feet, and fell unconscious for a moment upon the floor of the little snow basin that occupies the top of the mountain."

They made a cross out of tent poles, then stood around it to say the Te Deum. As Stuck put it, "there was no pride of conquest ... rather the feeling that a privileged communion with the high places of the earth had been granted." What a contrast to Frederick Cook's deluded egotism and Thomas Lloyd's garrulous stretching of the facts. And how fitting that Archdeacon Stuck should entitle his book *The Ascent of Denali*, using the local name which has now, finally, become the official name for the highest mountain in North America.

Walter Harper was killed in a steamboat accident in 1916. Stuck was heartbroken and died himself four years later. As for the great hoaxer, Cook, he never retracted his story and he was last heard of in 1915 announcing that he was going to make the first ascent of Everest. He was arrested and detained by the British authorities in Calcutta.

Even with twenty-first century equipment, Denali remains a formidable challenge, with ferocious blizzards and the altitude accentuated by the arctic latitude. In this picture the neighboring peak of Foraker appears through clouds of blasted spindrift.

The controversial race to the top of Denali could be seen as the patriotic struggle of a pioneer nation recently released from the shackles of British domination. But, despite losing America, the British Empire flourished and her mountaineers, reared on the European Alps, sought ever more exotic challenges. In 1892 a future President of the Alpine Club, Martin Conway, led the first modern mountaineering expedition to Central Asia, exploring the immense glacial highways of the Karakoram range in northern Kashmir. However, Conway's more immediate project was the Andes of South America.

"It was on the 13th of July 1898 that I sailed from Southampton by the Royal Mail Company's steamship *Don*, the same boat that nineteen years before carried Mr Whymper to his famous journey of exploration in the Great Andes of Ecuador. Like him, I was accompanied by two Alpine guides from the village of Val Tournanche, Antoine Maquiagnaz and Louis Pellissier by name. ... Maquiagnaz, in 1897, was HRH the Duke of the Abruzzi's leading guide in the journey which resulted in the first ascent of Mount St Elias in Alaska."

Conway and his alpine guides landed at Valparaiso, in Peru, and continued overland to the world's biggest high altitude lake, Titicaca, in Bolivia. In his subsequent account, Conway enthused about the famous reed boats and celebrated the bright clear light of the high plateau bordering the Andes –

the altiplano. "The freshness of all the sights and novelty of the scene even awoke the interest of Maquiagnaz, who seldom allowed the calm of his indifference to be disturbed by the strangeness of his surroundings."

They continued by horse-drawn coach over the border to Bolivia. On their left, as they journeyed south, the snow summits of the Cordillera Real (Royal Mountains) rose above the pink and tawny altiplano. In 1898 none of these mountains had been climbed and Conway was intent on trying the highest mountain of all – the great triple-peaked massif of Illimani, which dominates Bolivia's capital, La Paz.

From La Paz they followed the dusty road through a maze of eroded earthy gullies, then climbed up to a higher shelf of land beneath Illimani, basing themselves at Cotana finca. Describing the workforce at this estate, Conway displayed the full arrogance of the unreconstructed colonialist, writing, "a traveller can only regard with astonishment the manner in which the millions of Indians are actually kept in order by the small white population."

The ensuing narrative, as he journeys up the lower slopes of the mountain, is punctuated by tirades against the tiresome, idle Indian porters, who keep deserting the alpinists to get drunk at fiestas. Eventually they cut down the luggage, proceeding with just one Indian man and a boy, sharing out "two tents, warm fur sleeping bags of reindeer skin, cooking apparatus, provisions, and instruments." But, faced with a steep ice-choked chimney, the remaining two Indians desert: "Their cup of dread had been steadily filling; here it overflowed. They dropped their loads, cast off the rope and fled."

Above
Martin Conway, President of the Alpine Club and Liberal MP for the City of Bath.

Right
Bolivia's capital, La Paz, would have looked a bit different in 1898, but the view south to the triple summits of Illimani remains almost unchanged.

Below
Luigi Amedeo di Savoy, the Duke of Abruzzi (seated left) was nephew to the King of Italy and led the first attempt on the world's second highest mountain, K2.

FIRST ASCENT OF MOUNT ST ELIAS BY DUKE OF ABRUZZI.

The first great Alaskan peak to be climbed was Mount St Elias. Like so many mountains around the world it had its first European sighting by Captain Cook – on St Elias's Day. It was first climbed in 1897 by a huge team, sledging up the glaciers from the Pacific coast, led by the Italian Duke of Abruzzi, who would later establish a new record of closest to the North Pole. On returning to the Alaskan coast his aristocratic complexion was ravaged by insect bites and he commented, "I have conquered the Mount St Elias, but the mosquitoes, they have conquered me."

Undaunted, the Europeans continued, helped by the Spanish Señor Guillen from the finca, "who seemed absolutely to revel in the newly opened world of snow." They managed to drag their cumbersome luggage up to a final camp on the Cambaya Glacier, on the south side of the mountain. Here they slept briefly before setting off for the summit.

"Before two o'clock the next morning we had left camp and were winding our way up in the darkness among great yawning crevasses. A single candle in a pocket-lantern was our only light in the great solitude of the abode of snow. The snow was hard as rock and we made rapid progress ... Two and a half hours from camp we stood upon the very crest of the Cordillera Real, and we looked down an appalling precipice of at least 14,000 feet into the black depths ... the dim and vague horror of that almost fathomless plunge into the dark gulf at our feet was one of the experiences that it has been worth living to know."

They were looking down the east side of Illimani, where the great continental divide plunges into the vast steamy expanse of the Amazon basin. Up here they were now well over 6,000 meters above sea level. Curiosity satisfied, Guillen turned back, leaving Conway to continue with his two guides, cutting steps across a steep ice slope, past a subsidiary peak. The traverse led to a plateau below the final ridge, where the altitude really began to hit: "The remainder of the ascent was a featureless grind, and all suffered severely. The lifting of each foot in its turn was a tragic effort. Presently everything became unreal and dreamlike. I fell into a semi-comatose condition, but plodded on all the same."

Those words will resonate with anyone who has toiled in the thin air, dazzled by the blinding light reflecting off snow, determined grimly just to complete the self-imposed task. Conway eventually got his reward: "'Monsieur, à vous la gloire,' said Maquiagnaz, as he moved aside for me to stand first upon the highest point of snow." Illimani, Bolivia's highest mountain and one of the highest in the whole of the Andes, had been climbed.

Descending a couple of hours later, coming back past the subsidiary summit to the south, the party found a piece of woollen cord lying in the snow. Conway explained. "Tradition asserts that many years ago an Indian desperately dared to invade the secret places of the great god Illimani. He was last seen from below, seated on this point where we sat. He never came back to the abodes of men, for the god turned him into stone; so I named the peak Pico del Indio."

1894
AORAKI/MOUNT COOK
TOM FYFE & GEORGE GRAHAM

The Maoris called it Aoraki – the "Cloud Piercer."
The white settlers called it Mount Cook, after the
great sea captain; and they named the whole range
which dominates New Zealand's south, the Southern
Alps. The Southern Alps are reminiscent of Europe's
Alps, but here there is a wildness long since ban-
ished from Chamonix or Zermatt. Dense temperate
rain forest and dangerous rivers, fed by the melting
snows of huge glaciers, make any approach arduous.
Nowadays climbers tend to drop in by plane or
helicopter, as they do in Alaska. In the nineteenth
century they footslogged every inch of the way, once
Samuel Butler had thrown down the gauntlet,
writing, "There is a glorious field for the members
of the Alpine Club here. Mount Cook awaits them
and he who first scales it will be crowned with
undying laurels."

FREDA DU FAUR'S FIRST ASCENTS

The first woman to climb Aoraki Mount Cook was
the Australian, Freda du Faur. Provincial society
disapproved of her unchaperoned outings in the
wilderness with only men for company, but she was
determined, writing, "From the moment my eyes
rested on the snow-clad tops I worshipped their
beauty and was filled with a passionate longing to
touch those shining snows, to climb to their heights
of silence and solitude, and feel myself one with the
mighty forces around me."

In 1910 she became the first woman to reach
the summit. She subsequently became the first
woman to make the Grand Traverse linking all
three summits. Here she poses with her climbing
partners Alex and Peter Graham.

Above
Marmaduke Dixon and companion using skis improvised from reaper blades on the long glacier approach to Aoraki/Mount Cook.

Left
A modern climber on Aoraki/ Mount Cook.

It was an Irishman, the Rev William Green, who arrived first, in 1882, with two Swiss climbers, Emil Boss and Ulrich Kaufmann. They traveled by train and then horsecart to the Birch Hill sheep station, then set off on foot through the untracked scrub along the bank of the long Tasman Glacier, passing beneath the immense East Face of Aoraki, then turned left up the Hochstetter Glacier to the Grand Plateau to get onto the Linda Glacier and the north-west flank of Aoraki's highest summit. They did incredibly well, getting within about 50 meters of the summit before one of Aroaki's notorious storms swept in from the ocean, sending them scurrying back down.

SECOND ATTEMPT AT MOUNT COOK & THE ADVENT OF TOURISM IN NEW ZEALAND

Tourism arrived in New Zealand and The Hermitage was built alongside the other great glacier sweeping under Aroaki's West Face – the Hooker. In 1891 the first alpine hut was constructed beside the Tasman Glacier and provided a staging post for two locals, George Mannering and Marmaduke Dixon to attempt the peak. Then rumour spread that another Irishman, Edward Fitzgerald, was planning to sail to New Zealand with the great Swiss guide, Matthias Zurbriggen.

Local efforts to claim the prize redoubled. Dixon tried again, recycling a pair of agricultural reaper blades to make skis for the long snow approach Then on 20 December, midsummer 1894, another local team – Tom Fyfe and George Graham – found a route onto the Empress Glacier and the West Ridge. They reached the Middle Peak but were daunted by the one-kilometer long connecting ridge to the northern High Peak. Determined to beat Fitzgerald and Zur-briggen whose ship was about to land in New Zealand, they returned after just four days rest with Jack Clark. On 24 December they camped at the head of the Hooker valley and on Christmas Day continued up the Sheila Glacier to get onto the North Ridge of Aoraki. Climbing in nailed boots, they found a route over three big rock steps and continued up a final snow ridge to the highest peak of the Southern Alps, reaching the summit at 1 pm. Aoraki Mount Cook, as it is now officially known, was climbed.

Fitzgerald arrived in 1895 to discover that he was beaten. As consolation, he and Zurbriggen made the first ascent of New Zealand's second highest summit, Mount Tasman. Zurbriggen then made a solo ascent of Mount Cook's Northeast Ridge. The Zurbriggen Ridge remains a classic route up the mountain.

SLIDING SUMMIT

At about midnight on 14 December 1991 an estimated six million cubic meters of rock fell from the High Peak, crashing 2,700 meters down the east face and continuing 6 kilometers across the Tasman Valley. In an instant the summit was lowered by 12 meters to a new height of 3,754 meters above sea level.

1889
KILIMANJARO
MEYER, PURTSCHELLER, & LAUWO

At the Treaty of Berlin in 1885 the British and Germans divided up East Africa. Queen Victoria got Mount Kenya and the Rwenzori mountains, and would also have got Africa's highest mountain if the Kaiser had not insisted on drawing a bulge in the Tanganyika border, to put Kilimanjaro inside his territory.

So it was fitting that a German, Hans Meyer, should be the first to Kilimanjaro's summit with Ludwig Purtscheller and the Tanganyikan Yohanas Kinyala Lauwo, in 1889. The Rwenzori's highest peaks, on the borders of what are now Uganda and Congo, were first climbed twenty years later by the indefatigable Duke of Abruzzi. Mount Kenya fell to a British geographer called Halford Mackinder in 1899.

1899
MOUNT KENYA
BROCHEREL, MACKINDER, & OLLIE

Like Kilimanjaro, Mount Kenya is an extinct volcano, its lower slopes cloaked with different climatic zones of lush vegetation, ranging from tropical forest to dense bamboo to a unique heath land of giant heathers giving way to the bizarre shapes of giant lobelias and groundsels. Unlike Kili's rather boring dome, the Kenyan volcano has eroded to leave a ring

of jagged peaks surrounding a central precipitous tower of granite with two sharp summits. It is fashionable to pour scorn on the supposed insensitivity of imperial explorers, but it was actually Sir Halford Mackinder who suggested naming the two summits Nelion and Batian, after two famous Maasai chieftains. As for the name for the whole mountain, that came from the Wakamba tribe; *Kiinya* means cock ostrich and refers to the markings of white equatorial snow on dark rock; the name of the mountain was subsequently given to the whole nation state created by the British.

Mackinder trained as a lawyer, but he was more interested in geology, zoology, botany, and exploration. So he left the Law in 1887 to set up an embryonic Geography department at Oxford University. Ten years later he hatched his plan to climb Mount Kenya, spending two long summer vacations training in the Alps. On 8 June 1899 he left London for Africa, knowing that he had to be back in October for the start of his Geography department's first term as an official honours degree course. Like most of his contemporary mountain explorers, he took with him two alpine guides, César Ollier and Joseph Brocherel. He was also accompanied by two British naturalists.

From Marseilles they sailed through the Suez Canal to Mombasa. Undaunted by a smallpox epidemic, they continued up country, using the new railway to reach Nairobi. Then the adventure started in earnest.

"From the railhead we plunged into unmapped country in one day. On the Athi plains, a prairie of

Above, left
Snow on the Equator: the ancient volcano of Kilimanjaro towering just across the Kenya-Tanzania border, from the Amboseli national park.

Above, right
The author's companions tackling the first part of MacKinder's original route up Mount Kenya, in 1987.

Above, left
Looking across the Gate of the Mists from Nelion to Mount Kenya's higher twin, Batian.

Above, right
Mount Kenya from the south, with Batian on the left and Nelion on the right. Further right are the sunlit snowslopes of the Lewis Glacier.

sweet grass, thousands of head of game were grazing. Sometimes we saw herds of 1,500 zebra, Wildebeeste, and hartebeeste mingled. On more than one occasion the caravan was charged by a rhinoceros. We steered across the open by the prominent mountain Donyo Sabuk, with the white dome of Kilimanjaro visible at sunset and sunrise 100 miles to the south, and 100 miles to the north the striped peak of Kenya ... Through this land we marched, 170 strong, for everything had to be carried on men's heads. The food which would be required by the white men on the foodless mountain was packed in 25 lb tin-lined cases, each containing a day's complete rations for six men."

As well as rhinoceros, they had to contend with hostile slave traders and local tribes who fell out with Mackinder's bearers, murdering two of them while Mackinder was hacking a route through the bamboo that encircles the lower slopes of the mountain.

COFFEE PLANTERS' PARTNERSHIP

The ascent of Mount Kenya was not repeated until 1929, when a young coffee planter called Eric Shipton teamed up with District Commissioner Percy Wynn-Harris to make a variation on Mackinder's route, making the first ascent of Nelion, before crossing the Gate of the Mists to Batian. The following year, with another coffee planter called Bill Tilman, Shipton climbed the much harder West Ridge of Batian, continuing over Nelion, to make a complete traverse of the mountain, by a hard rock climb, in a single day. It was the beginning of a great partnership which, over the next six years, would achieve astonishing feats of exploration in the greatest range of all, the Himalaya.

By mid August Mackinder and the two alpine guides had passed the highest plant zone of giant groundsels, shaped like unearthly candelabra, to reach the Lewis Glacier. From here the real climbing started, up a rock wall which to this day boasts a "Mackinder's Chimney," leading to the South Ridge of the slighter lower summit, Nelion.

The ridge bristled with spiky towers and they ground to a halt, forced to spend a night in the open, shivering in the cold wind, beating their hands and feet to ward off numbness. In the morning a big chasm stopped them. They retreated. Mackinder descended to the valley to collect more supplies.

On 12 September they climbed back to the ridge, carrying a tent. They continued on the 13th, this time traversing off the ridge onto the tiny Darwin Glacier and then diagonally up to the Diamond Glacier which descends from the Gate of the Mists between the two summits. Here, ice climbing above 5,000 meters on the Equator, the going got tough. "It frequently took thirty blows to cut a single step." But eventually they reached rocks on the far side and climbed onto Batian's summit at midday. Fearful of the approaching afternoon storm, they soon hurried down, "descending cautiously through a mist of ice crystals" and getting back to their camp by the Lewis Glacier at 10 pm. Mackinder hurried back to Nairobi, and "thence ... returned with all speed to the coast and to England, arriving on October 30, only a week late for the recommencement of my work at Oxford."

This page
Mass assault on Haskett-Smith's original route up Napes Needle. The lower pair are in the Wasdale Crack, with a third climber belaying on the Shoulder. The summit climber is belaying his companion up the awkward crux move which Haskett-Smith climbed solo, on sight. And then had to reverse!

Right
Typical nineteenth-century gear including nailed boots copied from the farmers and shepherds who first tramped the high fells.

SMALL IS BEAUTIFUL

ROMANTIC POET SAMUEL TAYLOR COLERIDGE famously experimented with mind-altering drugs. He was also one of the first people to describe the cathartic thrill of rock-climbing. Descending from the summit of Scafell Pike, one of the highest peaks in the English Lake District, in 1802, he got lost in the mist and found himself veering towards the brink of a rocky precipice. " ... I was beginning according to my custom to laugh at myself for a madman, when the sight of the crags above me, and the impetuous clouds just over them, posting so luridly and so rapidly northward, overawed me..." ; But the madman managed to get a grip, and escape the impasse. "O God, I exclaimed aloud, how calm, how blessed am I now." With canny prescience, he had found the one weakness in the cliffs, known to modern climbers as Broad Stand.

Coleridge was ahead of his time, as was the local shepherd, John Atkinson, who made the first recorded ascent of Pillar Rock in 1826. It was only in the latter part of the century that Pillar and the other Lakeland crags became the Mecca for rock pilgrims spending their robust, hearty holidays at the hotels beside England's deepest lake, Wastwater.

The summits of Great Gable, Scafell, and Pillar which overlook the lake might have seemed puny in comparison to the great alpine peaks, but their cliffs and gullies were a chance to perform miniature masterpieces of technical virtuosity. One outstanding virtuoso was Walter Parry Haskett-Smith, who first visited the Lake District in 1881, as a twenty-year-old Classics student from Oxford. That year he contented himself with long walks over the hills, but the following summer he began to grapple with the cliffs. At this stage climbers in Britain didn't bother much with ropes. Instead they relied on buckets full of nerve – none more so than Haskett-Smith who pulled off the most daring ascent of all.

1886
NAPES NEEDLE
HASKETT-SMITH

On the flank of Great Gable, invisible from the valley, there is a slender obelisk, an English version of Chamonix's famous "Aiguilles," called Napes Needle. From the valley you can hardly see it, but scramble up close and you see it reveals itself, detached dramatically from the surrounding cliffs. On the last day of his summer holiday in 1886, Haskett-Smith decided to attempt the Needle. Alone. The only obvious weakness was a wide crack splitting the base of the obelisk. Nowadays its edges have been worn smooth and bald by countless boots. In 1886 the crack was choked with turf and stones. Haskett-Smith scrambled his way up the crack, then teetered to a standing position on the "shoulder" – a ledge beneath the obelisk's final point.

He was now faced with an almost vertical rock wall, about three meters high cut by a horizontal crack at chest level. He hoped that the top of the wall – the Needle's summit – was flat, but he couldn't see. So he tossed up several stones. Just one stone lodged securely on the summit, but it was enough to give him confidence to commit to the blind moves. First he shuffled left and up, nailed boots teetering onto the horizontal crack. Next, as he described it afterwards:

"gently and cautiously transferring my weight, I reached up with my right hand and at last was able to feel the edge and prove it to be, not smooth and rounded as if might have been, but a flat and satisfactory grip. My first thought on reaching the top was one of regret that my friends should have missed by a few hours such a day's climbing ... my next was one of wonder whether getting down would not prove far more awkward than getting up."

As all the thousands of climbers who have since repeated the ascent can testify, reversing that "mantelshelf" move off the summit – even with the protection of a rope looped over the top – is indeed an awkward nervy business. Solo, with a fatal fall the likely result of failure, it was a brave tour-de-force.

1914
SCAFELL – CENTRAL BUTTRESS
HERFORD & SAMSON

Eight years later Haskett-Smith published the first climbing guidebook, grading the pioneer rock climbs of the Lake District. In 1903 Fred Botterill made history with the first "Very Severe" climb on Scafell Crag. Then in 1913 a brilliant young climber called Siegfried Herford made the first tentative moves to inspect the "Central Buttress" of the same cliff, decid-

ing that a huge detached slice of rock called the Great Flake, could be the key.

Herford returned in 1914 with two companions who, as befitted English gentlemen, named the grassy ledge below the main difficulties "The Oval" after the famous London cricket ground. By now rock climbing was roped, and Charles Holland "belayed" from a secure stance on The Oval, while Herford and George Samson fought their way up the deep chimney behind the Great Flake. There was a huge "chockstone" jammed halfway up the chimney. Hanging on with one arm, Herford managed with his other arm to tie a rope sling around this boulder. Then he untied from the main climbing rope and threaded it through the sling, before retying it. Now he had some protection from the rope, but he was too exhausted to go any further.

Herford and Samson lowered themselves back down. They returned in the morning, climbed back up the chimney and rethreaded the rope. Wedged precariously in the chimney, hanging on to the sling, Samson braced himself while Herford stood in his nailed boots on Samson's shoulder. Leaning out over the void, Herford reached blindly over the top of the chockstone, grappling for handholds while his left boot searched the overhanging edge of the Great Flake for footholds. The foot skidded and his weight began to lurch backwards, but Samson grabbed the boot and shoved back onto the hold, allowing Herford to make one more lunge upwards, over the

Left
One of the boldest early climbs on Scafell was Owen Glynne Jones' Direct Route of 1898. In this later picture by Walter Brunskill, Siegfried Herford is seen on the precarious "mantelshelf" move, belayed by George Samson.

Below
It was the same pair who achieved Britain's hardest rock climb before the First World War – Central Buttress. In Samson's photograph, Herford is preparing to leave the top of the Great Flake, the main difficulties now over.

Right
This is – or was – the crux of the route. In this modern photo by John Cleare, Ian Howell is tackling the Great Flake, which has subsequently fallen off, making the route even harder.

chockstone and up to the top of the Great Flake, where at last he could wrap his hands round a sharp edge – a positive handrail. Once there, the climb was as good as over.

Down at the hotel, another climber wrote in the log book, "the extraordinary nature of the difficulty of this climb can hardly be over emphasised." Central Buttress was harder than anything climbed to that date in Britain. Like so many talented young men of that generation, Siegfried Herford only lived a short while longer, dying on the Western Front in 1916. His contemporary, George Mallory, survived the trenches and, through his attempt and eventual death on Mount Everest, achieved global fame. Like Herford, Mallory was a talented rock climbing pioneer and before immersing himself in the great Everest adventure he made many first ascents in Britain. However, his favourite stamping ground was not the English Lake District but the slightly bigger, more austere, cliffs of Snowdonia. And it was here, in North Wales, that another leap forward was made in the 1930s.

1928
SNOWDON – LONGLAND'S CLIMB
JACK LONGLAND ET AL

If you're not Welsh, pronouncing Clogwyn Du'r Arddu can be a bit of a mouthful, so most visiting climbers call it simply, with a mixture of awe and affection, Cloggy. As a piece of rock architecture this cliff on the flank of Wales's highest mountain, Snowdon, is unique. It broods over a tiny lake, black rock stained green with the fecund moss and slime which flourish in Snowdonia's damp climate. But on a fine summer day, when the rain from the Atlantic finally dies away, Cloggy doesn't brood at all. The high "Pinnacle" gleams as the morning sun slants over the shoulder of Snowdon then slides swiftly across the smooth walls and vertical cracks of the East Buttress, then illuminates the West Buttress. By evening the whole cirque glows warm russet. Light reveals the unique structure of the cliff, in particular the great stack of left-slanting overlapping slabs which make the West Buttress so instantly recognizable and such a tantalizing challenge to climbers.

It was Fred Pigott, star of one of the oldest mountaineering associations, the Rucksack Club, who was first up the East Buttress, climbing the strenuous cracks and chimneys of Pigott's Climb in 1927. The following year he turned to the West Buttress, but others had already staked a claim. That Easter, the

THE BOLD POLE VAULTER

Two years after the Cloggy triumph, Jack Longland's hardest Welsh rock climb was actually a mistake. In 1930 he was climbing a well-known route on a cliff called Holly Tree Wall, when he took a wrong turn and found himself heading up a huge smooth rock spike, with absolutely nothing to clip the rope into. Describing it decades later, after a successful career in public education, he said, "I was a pole vaulter, which I think gives you very strong fingers, and I remember that the pull-out onto the actual blade of the javelin was very strenuous, though not dangerous – I had a belay about forty feet below me."

In other words, if he had slipped, he would have fallen at least eighty feet before – with any luck – his second had held him on the rope around his waist. Nowadays Javelin Blade is graded E1 (the first Extreme grade) and is reckoned to be the first route climbed at that standard in Britain.

moustachioed elder of British mountaineering, Geoffrey Winthrop Young, wounded during the Great War and now hobbling on a wooden leg, had watched from the lake shore as his protégés made the first tentative probe onto the West Buttress. Both men would later become famous for getting very close to the summit of Mount Everest. One was called Frank Smythe; the other was a student from Cambridge called Jack Longland. Rain drove them back, but two days later they returned and managed to start work on the route.

Peeling off great wadges of green turf, they were overjoyed to find underneath tiny but perfect holds – sharp, incut knobs and wrinkles in the ancient volcanic rock. Then rain halted play.

Spring came and Longland drove up to Wales for the Whit bank holiday weekend with a team of Oxford and Cambridge climbers. On the Monday they raced up to Cloggy, only to find a rope hanging from the West Buttress: the Rucksack Club had been there on the Saturday and Fred Pigott had managed to get beyond Longland's Easter highpoint. Now both teams met beneath the cliff and agreed to join forces. Piggott led back up to his highpoint, then, with chivalrous generosity, handed the lead over to Jack Longland, who he felt had prior claim.

The route followed a strip of rock, the furthest left of the stacked slabs, hanging out over the dank chimney called the Black Cleft. About sixty meters above the start, Longland had to step around to the right, onto another slab. As he later recalled in the *Cambridge University Mountaineering Journal*, Longland had to change from nailed boots to rubber-soled plimsolls for some very delicate climbing. And, like Herford on Scafell 14 years earlier, he protected himself by threading the rope through a sling attached to a chockstone; except this was not a natural chockstone, but a stone he placed himself – Britain's answer to the steel pitons which continental climbers were hammering into the cracks of alpine crags.

"My longest hesitation, on a little ledge below the rather unpleasant overhang which obviously had to be surmounted to secure a position on the next leaf of slab, was overcome by a triumph of organization. To me, protesting, were first sent up on the rope a pair of rubbers ... [then] I felt inside [the rucksack] and found two chockstones ... The first was a beauty and fitted like a City man into his bowler hat. ... Even so the next pitch was sufficiently emotive, the crisis being a turn on small straddling footholds into an outward facing position, and then a very awkward pull over the little wall on the right to a minute ledge on the next slab."

Pirouette complete, the Cambridge athlete continued up the "Faith and Friction Slab" until he reached a ledge, where, succumbing finally to continental temptation, he took out of his tweed jacket pocket a steel peg which he had picked up in the Alps

Right
The unmistakable cliffs of Clogwyn d'yr Arddu, known to climbers as "Cloggy." Evening sunlight highlights the East Buttress and Pinnacle, on the left, and the tilted overlapping slabs of the West Buttress, on the right.

Below
Easter 1928 beneath Cloggy. Left to right: Thomas Graham Brown, Mont Blanc pioneer; AB Hargreaves, rock pioneer; Frank Smythe of Everest fame; Jack Longland, first to broach Cloggy's West Buttress.

Right, below
Clogwyn d'yr Arddu, better known as "Cloggy." The left-slanting overlapping slabs of the West Buttress are on the right. Longland's Climb takes the thinnest, most left-hand, sliver of slab.

and, using a large stone for hammer, bashed it into a crack. Anchored securely, he brought Piggott up to join him. Higher up, it began to rain, so they stopped in a hollow to smoke their pipes. Then, undaunted by wettened rock, Longland flung himself at the final overhang, grappling gymnastically above nearly 200 meters of space, and swinging out onto the top of the cliff. He had succeeded in climbing the very first line up the West Buttress and to this day it is known as Longland's Climb.

SCOTLAND'S HIGHEST PEAK

The great forcing grounds for British rock climbing before the Second World War were the mountain crags of Snowdonia and the Lake District, and the smaller gritstone outcrops of the Peak District. But we shouldn't forget the bigger, almost alpine, cliffs of the Scottish Highlands, in particular the magnificent north face of Britain's highest mountain, Ben Nevis.

The rock here – a pink rhyolite – is beautiful and during the long days of the northern summer it offers wonderful entertainment. But it is winter, plastered with an ephemeral coating of snow, rime, and blue ice, that the buttresses and gullies of Ben Nevis really come into their own. One of the most spectacular routes – popular to this day – is the turreted crest of the 650-meter-high Tower Ridge, which was first climbed in 1894 by an English team led by Norman Collie.

1906
BEN NEVIS — GREEN GULLY
PHILDIUS & RAEBURN

The most prominent local, Scottish, pioneer was Harold Raeburn, son of an Edinburgh brewer. As a middle-aged man he would travel 5,000 miles to Tibet, to take part in the very first Everest expedition with George Mallory. That was in 1921. As a younger man, in 1906, he pulled off with a Swiss climber, Eberhard Phildius, what may have been at that time the hardest ice climb in the world – the narrow, near vertical sluice of ice on Ben Nevis called Green Gully. With no crampons – just tiny nails in the soles of their boots – they cut steps for their feet, and holds for their hands. As Raeburn put it, "to hang on with one hand, while that long two-handed weapon, the modern ice axe, is wielded in the other, is calculated to produce severe cramps in course of time, and did so now."

Green Gully was only repeated twenty years later, by another great Scottish pioneer, Jim Bell, who

This page
Ben Nevis in winter. Tower Ridge was first climbed in winter in 1894, by Norman Collie (second from left in the picnic below). Above him is Cecil Slingsby, pioneer of many first ascents in Norway, handing a dram to Haskett-Smith of Napes Needle fame.

Opposite
Sandstone towers of Lower Saxony. Hauptdrilling (left) was climbed in 1920 and is given a modern grading of VIIIa . Schrammtorwächter (right) is even harder, and was first climbed in 1936.

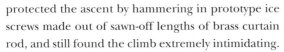

protected the ascent by hammering in prototype ice screws made out of sawn-off lengths of brass curtain rod, and still found the climb extremely intimidating.

1920s
LITTLE SWITZERLAND
FIRST GRADE VII CLIMBS

From the earliest days of British rock climbing, the aim was always, apart from the occasional shoulder of "combined tactics," to climb "free," without resort to artificial aids. Getting to the top wasn't the point: what mattered was how you got to the top. Contempt for steel ran so deep that pitons were rarely used, even for safety, so that technical skill had to be matched by uncommon boldness.

In the Alps, tackling bigger, smoother walls, climbers began to rely more on pitons to protect themselves. However, Britain did not have a monopoly on the pure ethic, because on the German-Czech border, in the valley of the Elbe, there was a region of sandstone towers, like fantasy castles, where Saxon climbers developed one of the most uncompromising ethics anywhere in the world.

The climbs they put up in the 1920s were technically harder than anything else at that time and, in order to preserve the beautiful towers in this region called Little Switzerland, in 1913 the Saxon climbers drew up a code. Climbs could only be attempted from below, avoiding the damage of "top ropes" sawing into the soft sandstone. Likewise, no pitons could be hammered into the delicate cracks; instead the leader had to protect himself by clipping his rope into a sling with its knot jammed into the crack. The art of knot-jamming became a Saxon speciality. If there were no cracks at all, then fixed steel ring bolts could be used, but they were widely spaced, so if you did fall off, you could expect to go a long way before the rope held you.

Under the modern grading system, several of the earliest Elbesandstein routes were Grade VII – amongst them the Wilder Kopf-Westkante, climbed by Emanuel Strubich in 1918 and the Hauptwiesenstein Rostkante, climbed in 1922 by Hans Rost, H. Wugk, and H. Arnold. Even harder were the routes pictured above – the first Grade VIIs in the world.

HIMALAYA — ABODE OF SNOW

Above
A member of Paul Bauer's 1933 Himalayan expedition examining giant rhubarb – Rheum nobile – on the approach to Kangchenjunga's Northeast Ridge, where Hans Hartmann tends the primus stove in a cave excavated from the ice.

Left
The Munich climbers failed on Kangchenjunga, but in 1936 they made the first ascent of neighbouring Siniolchu, "the most beautiful mountain in the world," seen here in the classic study by an earlier visitor to Sikkim, Vittoria Sella.

THE HIMALAYA IS GIGANTIC. IT STRETCHES over a thousand miles from Kashmir to eastern Tibet. Throw in the mighty Karakoram and Hindu Kush in the northwest, plus the eastern outliers stretching into Burma, and this greatest range on earth stretches closer to 2,000 miles.

VETS, BOTANISTS, & PUNDITS

Before anyone attempted to climb any of its summits, explorers led the way. There was the British vetinerary surgeon, William Moorcroft, who spent five years working his way through the mountains en route for the horse markets of Central Asia, only to end up murdered in Khotan; Geoffrey Vigne, the first westerner to explore the great passes of the Karakoram; and the three Schlaginweit brothers, one of whom, Adolf, suffered Moorcroft's fate and was murdered in Kashgar in 1857. Most adventurous of all were the native Indian "pundits," trained by the British to cross the Himalaya from India disguised as Buddhist pilgrims, to secretly survey the forbidden land of Tibet.

Many of the pundits started out through the tiny state of Sikkim, which is dominated by the world's third highest mountain, Kangchenjunga. Western interest in this beautiful mountain kingdom was first aroused by a botanist –the Director of Kew Gardens, Joseph Hooker, whose *Himalayan Journals* recorded his wanderings here in 1848 and 1849. It may have been the massed crates of rhododendrons and other exotic species packed up for shipment to England which aroused suspicion; whatever the reason, he was arrested and imprisoned under the orders of Sikkim's chief minister. He was later released, but the British East India Company in Darjeeling was so outraged that it promptly annexed a large part of southern Sikkim, whose terraced foothills provided a perfect environment for propagating the tea plants they had stolen from China.

The first climbers arrived in 1883 and over the next few decades a regular procession of European mountaineers made their way up through Sikkim's steamy tropical forest to the cooler rhododendron zone, and on to the high glaciers. The greatest prize was Kangchenjunga. Failed contenders included the psychopathic Satanist Aleister Crowley, "Beast 666"; the first serious campaign was made in 1931 by a big German expedition led by Paul Bauer.

THWARTED ON KANGCHENJUNGA

Kangchenjunga was eventually climbed from the southwest in 1955, but that face lies in Nepal, which was forbidden to foreigners in the 1930s. So in 1931 they had to make do with the Northeast Ridge – a Baroque concoction of crystal towers, cupolas and gargoyles, perched above huge precipices. Up this dizzy roof the Munich men hacked their way, sometimes tunnelling right through the ice towers which they could go neither over nor round. This was siege warfare, with teams of men ferrying supplies up a chain of seven camps, taking turns to go up to the front. They got to 7,400 meters before a ferocious storm forced them into a desperate retreat. It took days to fight their way down to the monsoon-soaked jungle, where one of them described the catharsis of reaching the first human habitation: "dishevelled, dead-beat, our nerves worn out with the wild struggle against nature."

They returned in 1933, but were stopped again, this time by a final slope of snow windslab poised to avalanche, which they dared not cross. Kangchenjunga's five summits remained untrodden, but Bauer did return again to Sikkim in 1936 with three companions, as training for a planned attempt on another Himalayan giant a thousand miles from Sikkim – Nanga Parbat.

1936
SINIOLCHU
GÖTNER, HEPP, & WIEN

For their 1936 training, the Germans attempted several of Kangchenjunga's satellite peaks, including one which had often been described as "the most beautiful mountain in the world" – Siniolchu. A team of Darjeeling porters helped the climbers carry loads to an advance camp at about 5,700 meters. From here the Germans continued alone to spend the next night at 6,100 meters. For this bivouac on an exposed

Right
One of several paintings by Edward Lear of the world's third highest mountain, Kangchenjunga, floating over 7,000 meters above the lush forests of Sikkim.

Below
A member of Paul Bauer's 1933 expedition walks the tightrope of the Northeast Ridge of Kangchenjunga, looking across to Siniolchu, which was climbed successfully three years later.

ALEXANDER KELLAS – SIKKIM PIONEER

One of the first and most successful mountaineers to visit Sikkim was the Scottish doctor, Alexander Kellas. Between 1907 and 1921 he took part in six Himalayan expeditions, nearly always traveling alone, apart from a few loyal helpers. He was one of the first people to employ Sherpas – members of a Tibetan tribe who settled in Nepal, immediately to the south of Everest, about 400 years ago. To boost limited earnings from trade and subsistence agriculture, many Sherpas traveled to Darjeeling to seek work with foreign expeditions; and Kellas was the first person to champion their toughness at altitude. In 1910 he made first ascents of two of Sikkim's highest peaks – Chomiomo (6,829 meters) and Pauhunri (7,125 meters). Despite this fitness, he died of a heart attack in Tibet, during the approach march of the 1921 Everest Reconnaissance Expedition.

FROM THE HIMALAYA TO THE ARCTIC

One of the pioneering climbing expeditions to Sikkim was made in 1907 by the Norwegian team of Monrad Aas and C.W.Rübenson. Climbing as a twosome, carrying their own supplies, they achieved what was probably an altitude record for the time when they reached an estimated height of 7,285 meters above sea level. They would have continued to the slightly higher summit of Kabru, if they hadn't been turned back by vicious cold winds. On the descent Rübenson slipped on steep ice and shot past Aas, who with great skill managed to hold his fall; but it was a narrow escape, as six strands of the hemp rope broke.

Rübenson is best known, though, for the climb he did three years later, in 1910, in the Arctic north of his native Norway. Here, above the sea inlet of Tysfjord, with A.B.Bryn and F.Schjelderup, he made the first ascent of Norway's most famous mountain, Stetind. The summit is only 1,381 meters above sea level, but it is a spectacular granite pinnacle, separated from the foresummit by a delicate knife-edge ridge. The key to this ridge – where you have to traverse above a huge drop hanging from your hands – was discovered in 1904 by a Yorkshireman called Cecil Slingsby; but the final honour of reaching Stetind's summit went to Rübenson's Norwegian team.

Right

The Rishi Gorge, sole approach to the Nanda Devi Sanctuary, first penetrated in 1934 by Eric Shipton and Bill Tilman, with the famous Nepalese Sherpa, Angtharkay. For much of the way, the route traversed precariously above drops of over a thousand meters.

ridge they had no tent and just huddled in the snow with their feet in their rucksacks. Bauer waited here the next day with E.Hepp, while A.Götner and Karl Wien continued up the gleaming Northwest Ridge to the 6,888-meter summit of Siniolchu.

The four men spent another shivering night on the ridge before descending. The following year on the massive snow-laden slopes of Nanga Parbat, both Wien and Heep were asleep in their tents at Camp Four, with twelve other men, when a massive avalanche struck the camp. When Bauer sent up a search party there was no sign of a single tent and it took six days, digging a trench ten feet deep, to dig out twelve of the buried bodies. Two were never found.

1936
NANDA DEVI
TILMAN & ODELL

Bill Tilman loved solving geographical puzzles, finding a way to the world's highest summits. But the biggest obstacles in the Himalaya have never been purely physical: jungles, river rapids, landslides and icefalls are nothing compared to the obduracy of civil servants. Arriving in Calcutta in 1936 as the advance scout for an attempt on Kangchenjunga, Tilman was told that his Anglo-American expedition could not have a permit.

Ever phlegmatic, Tilman accepted the alternative peak on offer – the twin-summited holy goddess peak of Nanda Devi, six hundred miles to the northwest, in the Indian state of Garhwal. In fact, the bureaucrats' obstruction was a godsend: at 7,816 meters above sea level, Nanda Devi's main summit was nearly 800 meters lower than Kangchenjunga, so the team stood a much better chance of actually getting up the mountain. More to the point, it was Tilman, with his friend Eric Shipton, who had two years earlier found the elusive route through the ring of peaks protecting Nanda Devi's "Sanctuary".

That route involved some serious bushwhacking up a deep river gorge, with some dangerously exposed traversing across smooth slabs hundreds of meters above the river. Getting a team of eight climbers, high altitude porters and several weeks' supplies up the gorge was a logistical nightmare.

Minor food gripes notwithstanding, they were a harmonious bunch, these Anglo-American pioneers. The American team had been selected by Charles Houston, a luminary of the legendary Harvard Mountaineering Club, who would later lead two

attempts on the world's second highest peak, K2. The British contingent included Noel Odell, a geologist who in 1924 had spent the best part of a fortnight living and climbing above 8,000 meters on Mount Everest.

Once they had reached their base camp in the Sanctuary, the eight climbers started work on Nanda Devi's South Ridge, which Tilman and Shipton had identified as a possible route to the summit. With help from Nepalese Sherpas, they took turns breaking trail and carrying loads, making a series of camps. The top camp was at 7,300 meters. Modest by nature, Tilman proposed Odell to represent the British on the final push to the summit. Charles Houston was selected to represent the Americans, but he suddenly came down with violent stomach cramps, so Tilman took his place. They set off at first light on 29 August 1936.

Afterwards, sitting in his study in North Wales, writing up the expedition, Tilman captured beautifully the tragic-comic purgatory of life at extreme altitude. "It was bitterly cold, for the sun had not yet risen over the shoulder of East Nanda Devi and there was a thin wind from the west. What mugs we were to be fooling about on this infernal ridge at that hour of the morning! And what was the use of this ridiculous coil of rope, as stiff as a wire hawser, tying me for better or for worse to that dirty-looking ruffian in front! Such, in truth, were the reflections of at least one of us as we topped a snow boss behind the tent, and the tenuous nature of the ridge in front became glaringly obvious in the chill light of dawn. It was

Left
The first glimpse of Nanda Devi's highest summit as the Rishi Gorge enters the Sanctuary. The final section of Tilman's South Ridge is profiled on the right.

Right
On summit day, 1936, the powder snow was "like trying to climb cotton wool" and every slip "cost six to eight deep breaths." Here Gilbert Harder repeats the climb in 1977. Behind him mist swirls round Nanda Devi's lower East Summit, first climbed by M. Karpinski's Polish expedition in 1939. The mountains of neighbouring Nepal stretch into the distance.

comforting to reflect that my companion in misery had already passed this way, and presently as the demands of the climbing became more insistent, grievances seemed less real, and that life was still worth living was a proposition that might conceivably be entertained."

They continued slowly, at first on pleasantly sound rock, but then on deep snow, "like trying to climb cotton wool," where every step "cost six to eight deep breaths" and "on top of the hard work and the effect of altitude was the languor induced by a sun which beat down relentlessly on the dazzling snow, searing our lips and sapping the energy of mind and body."

They were rewarded at 2 pm, when they climbed out onto a long, broad ridge of snow, with nothing more above it. "... After three-quarters of an hour on that superb summit, a brief forty-five minutes into which was crowded the worth of many hours of glorious life, we dragged ourselves reluctantly away, taking with us a memory that can never fade and leaving behind 'thoughts beyond the reaches of our souls.'"

FIRST ATTEMPTS ON EVEREST

Nanda Devi was in 1936 the highest summit yet reached by man. For Tilman it was a well-earned triumph, but perhaps he spared a thought for his regular exploring partner, Eric Shipton, who had been lured that year to join an unsuccessful attempt on Mount Everest. Both Tilman and Shipton were deeply involved in the pre-war attempts on the world's highest mountain; Shipton taking part in four expeditions to the mountain.

Although they failed to reach the summit during seven attempts between 1921 and 1938, the British Everest expeditions achieved a huge amount. They explored and mapped large tracts of Tibet. During Shipton's 1935 expedition they made first ascents of 22 peaks over 6,000 meters. On Everest itself, even though the southern flank in Nepal was forbidden to them, they unlocked the secrets of Everest's north and east faces in Tibet; and they established a series of new altitude records. In 1922, using a primitive oxygen set, George Finch and Geoffrey Bruce reached a new altitude of 8,320 m. Two years later, a medical missionary called Howard Somervell got

Above, left
The ebullient General Bruce sits at the center of his 1922 Everest Expedition. At the far left is George Mallory, who established a new altitude record, only to have it beaten a few days later by George Finch (to his left with fur collar) and the leader's nephew, Geoffrey Bruce (dark ear flaps).

Above, right
Two years later, the British got even higher on Everest. Here Howard Somervell photographs Edward Norton continuing alone towards the summit. Climbing without oxygen, Norton got within less than 300 meters of the summit. Three days later, somewhere near here, Sandy Irvine and George Mallory fell to their deaths.climb the conical volcano of Fui.

even higher, but then had breathing difficulty, and sat down to wait while his companion Edward Norton climbed on alone, only turning back at about 8,570 m, less than 300 meters from the top of the world.

It is possible that George Mallory, the official climbing leader of that 1924 expedition, got even higher three days later, with Sandy Irvine. It is even conceivable that they reached the summit, but we will probably never know. At some point, probably descending, they fell and the rope connecting them broke. Mallory's injured body was found, lying on a gravel terrace at 8,160 meters, seventy-five years later, in 1999.

In 1933 Lawrence Wager, Percy Wyn-Harris and Frank Smythe all got to a similar point to that reached by Norton. But that highpoint was not passed again until 1952, by which time a whole new route had opened on Everest, approached from the previously forbidden kingdom to the south – Nepal.

THE OXYGEN QUESTION

The British pre-war Everest expeditions were the first to experiment with using supplementary oxygen for mountaineering. Finch demonstrated its potential in 1922 and both Mallory and Irvine were using it on their fateful 1924 attempt. Before joining the 1921 reconnaissance on which he died, Alexander Kellas had given the matter thought. Working from personal experience in the field and from empirical calculations in the laboratory, he calculated the maximal rate of oxygen consumption of an unaided climber near the summit of Everest. He postulated that if the terrain were not too steep or difficult, it should be possible for very fit climbers to reach the summit of Everest without any artificial support, managing a maximum ascent rate, on the final section, of about 100 meters ascent per hour. This is exactly what Peter Habeler and Reinhold Messner were to achieve, 57 years later, when they made the first oxygenless ascent in 1978.

THE BIG ALPINE WALLS

Left
The dark side of the Matterhorn towering over the Tiefmatten Glacier. On the left skyline is Whymper's Hörnli Ridge; the South Ridge is profiled on the right. Descending towards the camera is the harder Zmutt Ridge, with the North Face deep in shadow to its left. Immediately right of the Zmutt Ridge is the West Face, climbed in an extraordinary bold solo by William Penhall in 1879 – the same day Mummery's team climbed the Zmutt.

Right
The only known photo of Mummery in action, climbing his eponymous Mummery Crack on the Aiguille Grepon.

ALBERT FREDERICK MUMMERY LOOKED A BIT nerdish. Pale, tall, and thin, with spectacles, he was an unlikely mountaineer. Yet, as he wrote of his first trip to the Alps, "At the age of fifteen the crags of the Via Mala and the snows of the Théodule roused a passion within me that has grown with the years, and has to no small extent moulded my life and thought."

When he applied to join the Alpine Club in 1880, aged twenty-five, he was turned down. Perhaps the Club elders disliked the fact that Mummery was in trade – he inherited a profitable tanning business from his father – but their real objection seems to have been the style of his actual climbing: he was that most despicable person – an innovator! Not content simply to repeat others' routes, he set out deliberately to find new, harder ways to great alpine summits, or to reach summits so inaccessible that no-one had managed yet to get to them. He sought climbing difficulty for its own sake.

BURGERNER & MUMMERY

Albert Mummery's most celebrated climb was the first ascent of the Northwest Ridge of the Matterhorn – the Zmutt Ridge. Back in 1865, during their simultaneous climbs of the Southwest and Northeast ridges, Carrel and Whymper had tackled the easiest lines up the great pyramid; with the Zmutt, in 1879, Mummery notched up the difficulty. He also, like Whymper fourteen years earlier, found himself racing for the prize.

His rival, William Penhall, was first on the ridge, getting to the top of a prominent row of pinnacles called "The Teeth" before retreating. A day later, Mummery arrived with his guide Alexander Burgener, to bivouac at the foot of the ridge. With their two assistant guides, they made a jolly party, enjoying "a heterogeneous mixture of red wine and marsala, bottled beer and cognac." They set off long before dawn, climbing quickly to the Zmutt's prominent snow ridge and over the jagged Teeth. Then they saw what had defeated Penhall – steep, smooth, slabs, veneered with verglas. Later Mummery described Burgener in action on this section: "It was obviously practicable but it was equally obvious that the slip of one meant the destruction of all who were roped to him."

No-one slipped and the four men eventually completed the first ascent of the Zmutt Ridge. Looking across to their right, they saw Penhall in hot pursuit, climbing alone up the Matterhorn's West Face – a truly futuristic route up a notoriously dangerous wall which has rarely been repeated.

Mummery also tried the Matterhorn's remaining unclimbed ridge, the Fürggen. In Chamonix he was drawn to the russet spikes of the Aiguilles. He was first to the north summit of the Aiguille Grand Charmoz and first, with Benedikt Venetz, to climb the neighbouring Aiguille Grépon, where the awkward, cussed *Fissure Mummery* still flummoxes experienced rock climbers.

The Alpine Club eventually allowed him to enter their portals, but eyebrows were still raised, particularly at his increasing tendency to climb hard routes without guides. Many of his alpine climbs were made with his wife Mary Petherick and, after one of his later ascents of the Grépon with women climbers, he commented on how quickly the aiguille had gone from being an impossible climb to "an easy day for a lady."

After Mummery, British pioneering rather petered out in the Alps. However, we should not forget Geoffrey Winthrop Young who, with trusty guides such as Josef Knubel, continued the search for difficult new routes during the years immediately before the First World War. Nor should we forget a rather cantankerous Fellow of the Royal Society, Professor Thomas Graham Brown, who developed an almost obsessive love affair with the Brenva Face of Mont Blanc.

1927, 1928, 1929
MONT BLANC – BRENVA TRIPTYCH
THOMAS GRAHAM BROWN ET AL

This eastern aspect of Mont Blanc is more Himalayan than Alpine – an immense wall, with three huge buttresses protected by massed tiers of hanging ice cliffs, and separated by deep gullies where avalanches crash down with terrifying frequency. But there was nothing rash about Graham Brown's infatuation. He watched and studied and calculated, timing his climbs minutely. Here is how his companion Frank Smythe described the approach to the first of Graham Brown's big three climbs on the Brenva Face in 1927:

"At 2 pm ... we saw ... that the traverse, which lies over ground of unrelenting steepness, involves the passage of no less than four couloirs. Of these, three were constantly swept by falling stones, and one formed the chute for the enormous ice avalanches that fall from a mass of tottering ice-pinnacles, hundreds of fee-high, at the edge of a small hanging glacier perched up on the side of the mountain. To attempt a crossing while the hot sun was shining on the face would be suicidal; we must wait for it to pass, and for frost to curb the activities of the stone and avalanche fiends."

So they waited, "sometimes chatting, more often in silent contemplation of our surroundings, whilst the smoke from our pipes stole up the red granite crags in peace offering to the Mountain King whose inmost sanctuary we were about to invade. ... The sun left us at 3:52 pm, but we waited for the snow to harden properly. At 4:50 pm we knocked out our pipes, strapped on our heavy rucksacks, and set off for the *Red Sentinel*."

Later that evening they chopped a narrow ledge out of the ice beneath the protecting granite tower which Graham Brown had called the *Red Sentinel* and crawled into their tent sack. By dawn the next day they were on their way up the main buttress and that afternoon they emerged on the summit of Mont Blanc. The following year they climbed the central buttress, which they called *Route Major*; and in 1929 with Alexander Graven and Alfred Aufdenblatten Graham Brown completed his triptych by climbing the prominent fruit-shaped buttress of *The Pear*.

MUMMERY'S ALPINE-STYLE EXIT

Energetic and restless, Mummery retired from business to concentrate on the study of Economics, co-authoring *The Physiology of Industry*. And he sought bigger, more futuristic mountain challenges. In 1888, with Heinrich Zurfluh, he made the first ascent of Dych Tau (5198 m) in the Caucasus, in just eight-and-a-half hours. Nowadays Russian climbers rate it grade 5a and usually stop to camp half way up the route. However, his most audacious climb – and his last one – was in 1895, when, with just one Gurkha porter for companion, he reached an altitude of nearly 7,000 meters on the gigantic Diamir Face of the world's ninth highest mountain, Nanga Parbat.

What Mummery was attempting – an "alpine style" ascent, in a single push, up an unknown face of an 8,000 meter peak – was only pulled off successfully eighty years later, in 1975, by Peter Habeler and Reinhold Messner. Mummery himself disappeared shortly after his Diamir Face attempt, whilst trying to cross a high pass on Nanga Parbat. His companions assumed that he had been buried by an avalanche. He was only thirty-nine.

Above

The huge Brenva Face of Mont Blanc is threatened by batteries of immense ice cliffs – source of regular lethal avalanches. Studying the face obsessively, planning his tactics meticulously, Graham Brown giant eroded tooth succeeded in finding three separate routes up the face.

GHOST CLIMBER

Relaxing after the first ascent of the *Red Senitel*, Graham Brown commented, "You know, Smythe, throughout the climb I always had the most curious feeling that there was a third man on the rope, and I couldn't rid myself of it all the way up." Smythe also had this feeling, at one point seeing someone emerge from a difficult rock chimney to join him, when Graham Brown was in fact still twenty meters below him, out of sight. Four years later, alone on Everest, he experienced a similar hallucination, famously turning to hand a piece of chocolate to an imaginary companion.

Inter-War
EASTERN-ALP CLIMBERS
CONTINENTAL ICE WALLS

The British, having virtually invented alpine climbing, rather ran out of steam during the inter-war years. Apart from the great Brenva routes, there was little British innovation. More impressive were Frenchmen such as Lagarde and Segogne, tackling the tumbling ice mass of the Aiguille du Plan's North Face, or the Swiss, Robert Gréloz and André Roch, cutting their interminable staircase up the North Face of the Triolet – 900 meters of ice, never less than 50-degree angle, frequently steeper. But the really exciting innovation was going on in the Eastern Alps, on the vertical limestone walls being tackled for the first time by mainly Italian, German and Austrian climbers.

1925
FLEISCHBANK SOUTH-EAST FACE
ROSSI & WIESSNER

In Austria, close to the urban centres of Innsbruck and Munich, there is a cluster of limestone peaks called the Kaisergebirge (Emperor Mountains) – an arena for supremely skilful performances by bold young men. It was here, in 1913, that Hans Dülfer soloed a chimney-crack several hundred meters high, which is Grade VI. Twelve years later, on the adjoining Southeast Face of the Fleischbank, Fritz Wiessner and Roland Rossi made a route whose "Rossi overhang" is still a tough challenge today. Wiessner, a short, barrel-chested, hugely energetic man, later emigrated to North America, where he made the coveted first ascent of Mount Waddington, as well as the first pure rock-climbing ascent of Wyoming's Devil's Tower. He also, in 1938, almost reached the summit of the world's second highest mountain, K2.

These Grade VI rock climbs in the Eastern Alps were on a whole new scale of steepness and difficulty. Unlike British climbers on their dark mossy little cliffs, relying on the odd sling draped over a spike, the Teutons and Italians thought nothing of using the piton – a steel peg with an eye, hammered into a crack in the rock, then connected to the rope by a snaplink called a karabiner. It was often the only way of protecting themselves on soaring walls up to 900 meters high. When the holds ran out – or got too small – they would resort to "artificial" climbing, standing in stirrups suspended from the pitons.

1933
CIMA GRANDE NORTH FACE
EMILIE COMICI

The most spectacular limestone walls were in the Dolomites of the South Tirol. Germans set the bar, but by the Thirties Italian climbers, sometimes sponsored by Benito Mussolini, began to compete with the Germans on walls such as the South Face of the Marmolada, the Northwest Face of the Civetta, and the immense Brenta Alta. The names of those Italian pioneers are the stuff of legend: Detassis, Vinatzer, Micheluzzi, Rattim Cassin ... but perhaps the most famous was Emilio Comici, who said that his perfect route would follow the line of a drop of water falling from the summit.

Like giant eroded tooth stumps of limestone, the Tre Cime de Lavaredo, tower a thousand meters above the screes. The North Face of the Cima Grande (center) was the most celebrated route climbed by Emile Comici (seen posing in easier terrain in the photo left). The west tower – Cima Ovest – (on the right) fell to another great Italian pioneer, Riccardo Cassin.

Comici's water drop ideal was realized – almost – in his most famous creation, the North Face of the Cima Grande. The triple formation of the Tre Cima di Lavaredo is the most famous landmark in the Dolomites and the towers' north faces are uncompromisingly vertical, often overhanging. Comici's 1933 route up the central Grande follows an almost direct line up an unrelenting series of cracks and chimneys – a masterpiece which still remains high on the wish list of climbers visiting the Dolomites, seventy years on.

THE THREE GREAT NORTH FACES

The Eastern Alps, with their predominantly rocky peaks and small glaciers, were the perfect place to push standards; but the really exciting advances came when the Teutons and Italians exported their bold pizzazz to the glaciated giants above Chamonix, Zermatt and Grindelwald. French climbers were left straggling, as daring Germans arrived to attempt the ice-smeared buttresses of the Grandes Jorasses' North Face. The Swiss spluttered with astonishment in 1931 when the two young Schmid brothers from Munich raced up the 1,200 meters high North Face of the Matterhorn. And then, in 1935, another pair of brave Bavarians made the first attempt on the most notorious – and previously inconceivable – wall of all, the North Face of the Eiger.

What is it about the Eiger that so captures the public imagination? Most obvious is the sheer scale of its great northwest wall, the "Eigerwand." It is over a mile high; it is simply the biggest precipice in Europe. There is also the monumental simplicity of the thing – the geometry of the flat-topped triangle. But then, look closer, let your eye wander over its huge tilted, scooped plain, and your become mesmerized by the detail: the steely glint of tilted icefields, the yellow pallor of overhanging limestone – whole walls within walls – the spidery veins of snow and ice, weaving through overhangs. Then, on a summer's day, walk up beneath the wall, and you find the ground thick with the rubble of aeons – the shattered debris of

Right
The North Face of the Eiger (far right) is the biggest sheer face in Europe, over a mile high. A key to the first ascent was the delicate traverse discovered by Andreas Hinterstoisser in 1936 (near right) and repeated by Luke Hughes, during an ascent of the face fifty years later. Ironically, it was just by this spot that Hinterstoisser and his three companions died, during a desperate attempt to retreat off the face.

falling rock; hang around a short while and you will probably hear the boom and thud of more stones falling from the sombre amphitheatre above.

The Eigerwand is a big, moody, dangerous brute; but it has a kind of savage beauty which counterpoises the silvery elegance of its famous neighbour, the Jungfrau. It is also, uniquely amongst the great alpine north faces, incredibly public. It hangs immediately above the village of Grindelwald and can be seen even more clearly from the mountain railway station at Kleine Scheidegg.

1935, 1936, 1937
ILL-FATED EIGER ATTEMPTS
TONI KURTZ

It was here, clustered round the telescopes in August 1935, that the crowds watched while Max Sedlmayer and Karl Mehringer raced with flamboyant assurance up the first two thirds of the wall, only to be stopped in their tracks at a small ledge, right in the heart of the wall, unable to go up or down, as storm after storm swept in from the northwest, smothering the Eigerwand in fresh snow and ice, sending avalanches sweeping down the wall. It was only weeks later that a specially chartered plane, flying close to the wall, spotted one of the men standing upright in the snow, frozen to death; the other had disappeared.

In 1936 the public were treated to an even more gruesome accident. This time it was four climbers who teamed up, discovering what would become the classic line onto the face, sidling in from the right across a smooth slab still named after its author, Andreas Hinterstoisser. He used tension from the rope to lean leftwards across the slab, hammering in pitons where he could, to stop himself from swinging back in a huge arc. Once all his three companions were safely across, they pulled the rope through and continued up the wall. The next day they reached somewhere near the previous year's Death Bivouac. But one man had been injured by a falling rock and they decided to turn back.

As they retreated the weather broke. Rain and hail hammered them. An artillery barrage of loose stones whistled down from above. Then the temperature plummeted and snow fell. Coated in thick verglas, with no rope left in place, the Hinterstoisser Traverse was irreversible. So they tried abseiling directly down towards menacing overhangs.

It was then that something terrible went wrong. The details are blurred, but someone fell, plucking the others from their holds. For some reason Hinterstoisser became untied and fell 800 meters to the foot of the wall. Rainer was strangled on the rope. Angerer was yanked hard against a piton, where he soon froze to death. Only Toni Kurz remained alive, hanging in space beneath an overhang.

One of the many quirks of the Eigerwand is the railway which tunnels up inside the mountain, with a little window, the Stollenjoch, opening onto the wall, very close to the Hinterstoisser Traverse. The railway guard on duty that afternoon heard screams for help and climbed out onto a ledge, 800 meters up the face, to hear Toni Kurz crying for help, shouting that he was the only one left alive.

Later that evening a rescue team climbed out of the window. They could do nothing that night but promised to return the next day. Kurz survived the night, but when they came back in the morning there were icicles hanging from his boots. Instructed by rescuers, Kurz managed to climb down and cut down Angerer's body, releasing more frozen hemp rope, which he then had to unsplice into three strands to make a long enough length to lower down the overhangs to his rescuers. He then pulled up fresh strong rope. All this, he had to do with one hand and his teeth, because the other hand was a blackening frostbitten claw.

Eventually Kurz began abseiling down the new ropes, using a karabiner as a friction brake. But when he reached the knots joining the two ropes, he

Left
Another of Bradford Washburn's peerless aerial photographs – of the mighty North Face of the Grandes Jorasses. This was one of the great challenges for the finest alpinists of the Thirties. In 1935 Martin Meier and Rudolf Peters succeeded in climbing it by the Croz Spur, which rises directly towards the moon. But the higher Walker Spur, profiled on the left, remained an outstanding challenge for another three years.

couldn't feed them through the karabiner at his waist. The rescuers shouted to him to make one last effort – somehow to lower himself those last few meters – but the young man's extraordinary will to live finally ran out. He slumped over and hung dead on the rope.

By 1938 ten climbers had attempted the Eigerwand and only two had returned alive. One of those two was Wiggerl Vörg. Having proved that an attempt was not an automatic death sentence, he now returned with another extremely talented climber called Anderl Heckmair.

EIGERWAND CLIMBED
HARRER, HECKMAIR, KASPAREK, VÖRG

Shortly before he died in 2005, Anderl Heckmair published a final autobiography, beautifully illustrated with the photos of his youth – sepia images of a vigorous young man with a thick sweep of dark hair, large nose, and bright confident eyes, posing in lederhosen, or breeches, skiing, climbing, tramping through alpine woods with young friends, carrying equipment on an improvised go-kart ... To understand the climbing fervour of those young men risking their lives on the "last great problem" of the Alps, you have to imagine what it was like to grow up very poor, during the Depression. Most of them eked

out a living as manual labourers, spending every spare moment in the mountains. In those days there were no ski lifts, no helicopters. They walked everywhere, earning spare cash by carrying supplies to the mountain huts. Often they were unemployed – they were prototype climbing bums, revelling in freedom and the thrill of exploration. They were bold and ambitious and the lure of the most famous unclimbed wall in the world was irresistible.

Heckmair and Vörg prepared carefully, bringing the best equipment available from the sports shop in Munich, traveling to Switzerland and pitching their little tent in the meadow beneath the Eiger. Heckmair even landscaped the site, making a little paved entrance to the tent. They did several training climbs, including the ridges flanking the great scooped amphitheatre of the Eigerwand. They even did reconnaissance onto the wall itself, leaving a rucksack full of heavy gear just below the first big obstacle, the Difficult Crack. They were annoyed to bump into two Austrians also intent on the climb, but determined not to be put off.

The next day they came back up, before dawn, climbing very fast, then continuing with all their gear, up the Difficult Crack, over the Hinterstoisser Traverse and on towards Death Bivouac. Again they bumped into the two Austrians, Heinrich Harrer and Fritz Kasparek. Harrer was climbing without crampons, relying just on nailed boots, and the pair was moving very slowly. Reluctantly, Heckmair

Left
During the final stages of the Eiger
ascent, the four climbers had to
contend with ferocious avalanches
and sit out a miserable bivouac
(far left) in the Exit Cracks. They
were literally fighting for their lives.
Hence the jubilation when they
returned safely from the summit
on 24 July 1938, to be met by the
massed press of Europe. Left to right:
the two Austrians, Harrer and
Kasparek; and the two Germans,
Heckmair and Vörg.

offered to join forces and from then onward he led the whole way.

They continued higher than anyone had been before, following the line of least resistance up a gash called the Ramp, which slants left between bulging walls of smooth limestone. Here they bivouacked, sitting on two awkward ledges. The following morning Heckmair showed his real genius on the Waterfall Pitch, frozen overnight to bubbles of blue ice. Above that came the Ice Bulge. Then the vital traverse back right along the shattered rubble of the Brittle Ledges. Then another hard crack. And then the stupendous Götterquergang – the Traverse of the Gods – where a press aeroplane photographed the four men strung out above a drop of 1,500 meters.

By now the weather had broken. As they reached the icefield known as the Spider, avalanches were pouring down from the walls above, funnelled onto the men's heads. Several times they were swept off their feet and left hanging from ice pitons. Fighting now for the team's lives, Heckmair led on into the Exit Cracks, where they had to stop again to bivouac. Heckmair managed to sleep that night, leaning against the broad back of Vörg, who braced himself, staying awake to give his leader some rest.

Morning brought more snowfall. More avalanches. On one pitch Heckmair fell off and landed on Vörg, a crampon spike stabbing his companion's hand. He simply bandaged the bleeding hand and returned to the fray, fighting the avalanches, sweeping snow from what holds he could find, peering through the murk to find the correct way through a maze of gullies and chimneys. Following in Heckmair's steps, climbers still struggle on the famous Quartz Crack, and marvel at the genius of the man who then found the critical traverse left to a final insecure chimney, where there are virtually no cracks to hammer in secure pitons.

It was late afternoon on 24 July 1938 when Heckmair emerged onto the final icefield and then, in the cloud, almost climbed over its rim to fall down the South Face of the Eiger. Determined not to spend another night in the open, the four men rushed straight down the West Flank, arriving before dark at Kleine Scheidegg, where they were greeted by a crowd of admirers and journalists, who treated them to a night at the hotel and the hottest bath of their lives.

POLITICAL AFTERMATH

The moment they descended safely from the North Face of the Eiger, Heckmair, Vörg, Harrer, and Kasparek were summoned to meet the Führer. For Hitler, this Austro-German triumph on the most notorious alpine wall was perfect propaganda material, coming just after Germany's takeover of Austria in the Anschluss. For foreign critics, the political triumphalism was simply confirmation that the Eigerwand was an arena for fascist fanatics.

Heckmair was not a party member; in fact he had once voted Communist simply to poke fun at Hitler. But, as he said years later, what anonymous young climber wouldn't be flattered suddenly to be lionized by his head of state? That seems to have been the extent of his brush with Nazism.

Not so the Austrian, Heinrich Harrer, who was a member of the SA and then the SS. Success on the Eiger won him a place on the 1939 Nanga Parbat expedition, which was under the direct control of the Nazi party. Ever since the twenties there had been an undercurrent of anti-semitism and fascist enthusiasm in the Eastern Alps, particularly in the Austrian Alpine Club, but there were many who abhorred this subordination of mountaineering to racist ideology.

WALKER SPUR, GRANDES JORASSES

Heckmair's plan, after climbing the Eigerwand, was to rush straight over to Chamonix and bag the other great outstanding "problem" – the Walker Spur on the North Face of the Grandes Jorasses. But, while he and his Eiger companions were being treated to a luxury cruise courtesy of Adolf Hitler, their Italian rivals stole a march. Armed simply with a postcard picture of the Grandes Jorasses, Riccardo Cassin and his companions Esposita and Tizzoni rushed over the border from Courmayeur, found their way to the foot of the face and proceeded, at the very first attempt, to find a route up the 1,200 meters high granite spur. Heckmair had to content himself with the second ascent.

EIGHT THOUSAND METERS

Left and Below

Annapurna, the first 8,000-meter peak to be climbed. After many weeks' reconnaissance, the French team had just three weeks to find a way though the sprawling, avalanche-threatened glaciers of the North Face. On the final day, slanting rightward up the huge windblasted snowfield, Herzog and Lachenal were both badly frostbitten. Without the help of Rebuffat and Terray (seen snowblinded below) and the Sherpas waiting below, they would probably never have got back down alive.

IT ALL STARTED WITH NAPOLEON. IT WAS HIS government, revolutionary yet filled with traditional gallic zeal for all things rational, that instituted a new set of standard metric measures, including the meter – one ten-millionth of the length of the quadrant from the equator to the north pole which passed through Dunkirk. Later in the nineteenth century, when British and Indian surveyors began to measure the world's highest peaks, they stuck with Imperial feet. Thus Everest came out at 29,002 feet (later re-calibrated at 29,029 feet). But once German, French, Swiss, Austrian, and Italian climbers got in on the act, they preferred to measure Himalayan peaks in meters. Because only fourteen of the world's highest summits came out over 8,000 meters above sea level – and because climbing at that altitude happens to be close to the limit of human physiology – the number 8,000 acquired mythic resonance.

During the Twenties and Thirties several people managed to climb above 8,000 meters. Edward Nor-ton reached 8,570 meters on Everest in 1924; in 1938 Fritz Wiessner and Pasang Dawa Lama reached a similar height on K2; but no-one succeeded in getting to the *top* of an "eight-thousander." That became the all-consuming holy grail for Himalayan climbers when business resumed after the War, aided by the good news that Nepal, whose northern frontier is marked by eight of the giant peaks, was allowing foreign climbers to enter its borders for the first time.

1950
ANNAPURNA
HERZOG & LACHENAL

In Paris, the French Himalayan Committee jumped at the opportunity of Nepal's open border, racing to organize a crack team in time for the spring season of 1950. The leader was Maurice Herzog; his climbers included two hugely energetic, highly experienced alpinists who had just made the second ascent of the infamous North Face of the Eiger – Louis Lachenal and Lionel Terray. With Dr Oudot and film-maker Ichac, the team totalled eight. They were the first westerners ever allowed to travel north from the Nepalese town of Pokhara and search for a route up either Dhaulagiri or Annapurna.

The approach was an enchanted journey. With the help of Sherpas from the Everest region, they marched along forest trails, passing through beautifully paved villages reachable only on foot, where the people had never before seen Europeans. They climbed up and down over the tangled ridges of Nepal, at one point descending into one of the deepest gorges on earth – the Kala Gandaki. The only existing map was wildly inaccurate and their reconnaissance was largely inspired guesswork.

Weeks sped by and the monsoon clouds were already on their way when Herzog decided that their best chance lay up Annapurna. There was an ill-advised attempt on the fiendish Northwest Ridge before he agreed that the easier-angled North Face offered the only chance of success. The race was on – to climb one of the world's highest peaks, on sight, in the remaining fortnight before the monsoon arrived.

Everyone worked to the point of exhaustion, taking turns to break trail up the sprawling ice mass of the North Face, threatened for much of the way by snow avalanches and ice breaking from the great cliffs they called the Sickle. In just ten days Frenchmen and Sherpas established five camps, the last perched at the base of the Sickle. From here Herzog and Lachenal set off for the summit at dawn on 2 June.

Herzog's account, which in book form became an international bestseller, reveals a man riding a wave of euphoria, in a state of ecstasy, enhanced perhaps by the fatigue-suppressing drug Maxiton supplied by Dr Oudot. "This was a different universe – withered, desert, lifeless; a fantastic universe where the presence of man was not foreseen, perhaps not desired. We were braving an interdict, overstepping a boundary, and yet we had no fear as we continued upwards. I thought of the famous ladder of St Theresa of Avila. Something clutched at my heart."

Lachenal's diaries, however, tell a rather different story of a reluctant hero terrified of losing feet and hands to frostbite, continuing only because he knew that if he turned back his leader would carry on alone and probably never return. So they ploughed on together, through biting wind, until they stood on a sharp snow crest and looked down the awesome precipice of the South Face on the far side. They had climbed Annapurna – the first eight-thousander, the highest summit reached by man since Odell and Tilman had stood on Nanda Devi fourteen years earlier.

For Herzog, posing with the French tricolour, it was a transcendent moment. "How wonderful life would now become. What an inconceivable experience it is to attain one's ideal and, at the very same moment, to fulfil oneself. I was stirred to the depths of my being. Never had I felt happiness like this – so intense and yet so pure."

But Lachenal was desperate to escape this alien world and save his hands and feet. In the interests of lightness, the expedition had been equipped with insufficiently warm boots and his feet were like blocks of wood. As they hurried down through scudding spindrift, Herzog dropped his gloves. Delirious from a heady cocktail of Maxiton, anoxia, and success, he failed to take out spare socks in his rucksack as substitutes.

It was now late afternoon and thick cloud had enveloped the mountain. Herzog lost sight of Lachenal in the mist. At dusk he stumbled on the two little tents at Camp V where Lionel Terray and anther

crack climber, Gaston Rébuffat were waiting. They bundled Herzog into the tent then stared horrified at his hands which were white and wooden. Then, using Lachenal's nickname they asked, "But where's Bisquante?"

FROSTBITTEN RETREAT

Herzog didn't know where Bisquante was, so Terray rushed out into the mist shouting his name. He eventually found him lying in the snow. He had slipped on some ice, losing ice axe, gloves, and one crampon in a long fall. "My feet are frostbitten. Take me down! Take me down!" he pleaded. Terray explained that it would soon be dark, so Lachenal tore Terray's ice axe from him and tried to escape, before realizing he would have to wait for the morning.

Little was known about frostbite in 1950 and the recommended treatment was to try and whip the frozen flesh back to life with a knotted rope! All that achieved was to damage the frozen tissue irreversibly.

June 4 brought an intensification of the storm, with cloud and snow merging into a lethal blur. All day they struggled down, failing to find Camp IV, then at dusk falling into a concealed crevasse where they lay, shivering deliriously through a hellish night. Removing goggles to peer through the white-out, Rébuffat and Terray had become snowblind. To add insult to injury an avalanche swept into the crevasse, burying men and equipment in icy smothering powder. They awoke to a hideous dawn, scrabbling with frozen hands in the snow – two of them blind – desperate to retrieve buried boots.

They were very lucky: they found their boots. And they were blessed with fine weather for 5 June, allowing a rescue party to reach them from Camp IV. Now everyone worked to get the frostbitten summit pair and their snowblind rescuers off the mountain, which was horribly loaded with fresh snow. At one point on the lower face Herzog and two Sherpas were swept 150 meters in an avalanche before the rope snagged, saving them miraculously.

At base camp their suffering was not over. In those days there were no roads in Nepal, nor helicopters. So they had to trudge for days through forest and paddy field to the Indian border, slithering in the mud. Each night Dr Oudot inflicted agonizing injections in the groin, intended to limit the frostbite damage. But Lachenal and Herzog's digits were getting dangerously gangrenous and when they finally reached the railway, their train journey was punctuated by pauses to sweep pieces of amputated necrotic flesh from the carriage. When the team eventually

Right and Below
Mallory called it the Western Cwm. The Swiss expedition which first trod this hanging valley in 1952 called it The Valley of Silence. The lower picture, taken from Pumori, shows the infamous Khumbu Icefall tumbling out of the Cwm. The huge pyramid in the distance is Makalu, with Lhotse in front and Everest's summit on the extreme left. The top picture captures the extraordinary atmosphere of the cwm, as a team of porters heads towards the distant Lhotse Face, with Everest, again, on the left.

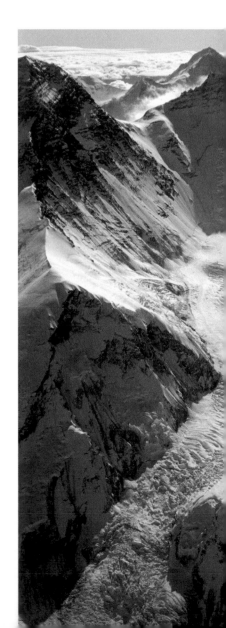

flew home to a heroes' welcome in Paris, and Herzog's bandages were removed, even the medics gagged at the writhing tangle of maggots feeding on his truncated finger stumps.

THE RACE FOR EVEREST

While Maurice Herzog's team were searching for a route up Annapurna, an American team led by Oscar Houston was in Sola Khumbu – the Sherpas' homeland just to the south of Everest. The team included the British veteran of pre-war attempts from Tibet, Bill Tilman. Looking up the fracture chaos of the Khumbu Icefall – the only way onto the mountain from the south – Tilman was gloomy about the chances of anyone climbing Everest from Nepal (the Chinese invasion of Tibet had ruled out any attempts from that side for the time being). But in London a young surgeon called Michael Ward was studying some recent aerial photos of the mountain which belied Tilman's gloomy prognosis. So Ward organized a small recon-naissance team for 1951 and asked Tilman's old exploring partner, Eric Shipton, to be leader. They were already on the march, in Nepal, when they were joined by two New Zealanders, one of whom was a young beekeeper called Edmund Hillary.

Ward's adventurous hunch proved correct: there was a way, albeit a dangerous way, up the Khumbu Ice-fall. The stage was now set for a full scale attempt on this new southern route up Everest, but Switzerland

got in first, securing a permit for both the spring and autumn of 1952.

The Swiss got within a whisker of climbing Everest in the spring of 1952. They pioneered the route up the Icefall to the extraordinary hanging valley of the Western Cwm, which they called the Valley of Silence; on up the huge ice slopes of the Lhotse Face; then the godforsaken, windblasted camp on the huge flat South Col; and finally the Southeast Ridge, where Raymond Lambert and Tenzing Norgay suffered a horrendous night at about 8,300 meters, shivering in their tent with neither sleeping bags nor stoves to melt snow for water.

They were breaking every rule in the book, yet still Lambert and Tenzing continued the next day, battling not just the wind and cold, but also their own malfunctioning oxygen sets. They reached an altitude of about 8,600 meters – higher than Norton's 1924 record – but to continue would have been suicidal.

The Swiss returned in the autumn, but discovered that trying to climb above 8,000 meters in October is almost impossible. By a strange irony, the prospective British Everest expedition for 1953 was testing equipment in Switzerland, at the Jungfraujoch, when news arrived that the Swiss had failed a second time on Everest. As the British leader, John Hunt, said later, "I can't deny that we were not extremely relieved to hear that the Swiss had failed."

1953
EVEREST
HILLARY & TENZING

Four months later, in the early spring of 1953, the British team set off from Kathmandu for the 170-mile march to base camp, accompanied by porters carrying thirteen tons of equipment. This was one of the best equipped, most thoroughly prepared expeditions ever to come to the Himalaya. It was also one of the most selfless, united teams. Yet, everything hung in the balance, rightup to the last moment. At one point it looked as though the great machine was going to grindto a halt. Even when the stores, including all the heavy oxygen cylinders, were lifted to the South Col, everything depended on luck with the weather.

On 26 May Tom Bourdillon and Charles Evans climbed higher than any human had been before, reaching Everest's South Summit, just 100 meters below the top. But experimental oxygen system was causing problems and, they had to turn back.

Three days later, greatly helped by starting from a much higher camp – a single tent perched precari-

Left
Efficient use of supplementary oxygen was deemed critical to success in 1953. Here Hillary checks Tenzing's set, before setting off from Advance Base on the final journey to the summit.

Below
Tenzing (right) photographed with the flags of Nepal, Britain and the United Nations, on the summit of Everest, 11 am, 29 May 1953. Two days later his companion Hillary luxuriates in success (left) with Band, dark-haired Ward and pipe-smoking Evans.

Right
The final obstacle below the summit, the Hillary Step, photographed by the author 35 years after it was first climbed.

ously on a narrow ledge at about 8,500 meters – Edmund Hillary and Tenzing Norgay set off at 6 am for the second summit attempt. By 9 am they were on the South Summit. After checking oxygen flow rates, Hillary continued, leading across a narrow ridge to an abrupt cliff about 18 meters high.

On the left, rocks sloped steeply down onto the 2,500 meters high Southwest Face. On the right, plastered precariously to the rock step, a large blob of snow overhung the 3,000 meters precipice of the East Face. Hillary squirmed up between snow and rock, then brought Tenzing up to join him. Beyond the cliff, the ridge eased off, but there were still several tantalizing snowy hummocks before they arrived on the highest mound of all.

Tenzing, the Tibetan who was born just a few miles from the summit, posed with the flags of Britain, Nepal and the United Nations. Back in Kathmandu there was an ugly row about who actually stood first on top (it was Hillary), as Tenzing was claimed as a hero by zealous Indian and Nepalese nationalists. In contrast to that political bickering, when the team stopped at Zurich airport on the way home to Britain, they were amazed to find the entire 1952 Swiss team waiting for them in the VIP lounge with champagne – a truly generous gesture from the men who so nearly climbed Everest first.

The Everest team were flabbergasted by the huge enthusiasm for their achievement – not just in Britain, but all over the world. Hillary, Tenzing, and Hunt became global celebrities overnight and their achievement inevitably overshadowed the other outstanding climb of 1953 – the first ascent of Nanga Parbat in the newly independent state of Pakistan.

1953
NANGA PARBAT
HERMANN BUHL

This was the mountain of destiny which had decimated the ranks of German and Austrian climbers during the 1930s. It was high up on the mountain's Silver Saddle that the German sahibs and their loyal Sherpas had frozen to death in the ferocious storm of 1934. The dead had included the leader, Willi Merkl. Now, nineteen years on, his nephew Karl Herrligkoffer was determined to complete his uncle's route to the summit of Nanga Parbat.

So, yet anther Austro-German team arrived in the Fairy Meadow beneath the gigantic, sprawling ice mass of the Rakhiot Face. Yet again they toiled under the fierce Asian sun, blazing a winding trail up the flank of the mountain to the rock tower called the Moor's Head and onto a sharp snow ridge leading to the Silver Saddle. Herrligkoffer, a mere figurehead, directed operations from below. The actual climbing team was highly competent, led by Peter Aschenbrenner. But the star with the greatest reputation was Hermann Buhl.

Buhl's CV of hard alpine climbs was almost unequalled in 1953. He was notoriously tough and famous for his many solo climbs. As an example of his ascetic drive, training for Nanga Parbat he climbed the 1,800-meter-high East Face of the Watzmann, a huge rock climb near Munich. He did it alone. In the night. In the middle of winter.

On the night of 2 July, Buhl and Otto Kempter slept at Camp V, just beyond the Moor's Head, ready for the two of them to attempt the summit the next day. The main summit of Nanga Parbat was over 1,200 meters higher. If you add to that the unavoidable descent into a dip called the Bazhin Gap, then the height rise is more in the region of 1,400 meters. And there is a horizontal distance of 4 kilometers! At that altitude it was a truly Herculean prospect.

Tense, impatient and unable to sleep, Buhl set off at 1:30 am on July 3, breaking trail for Kempter, who followed half an hour later. Like the French on Annapurna, they were climbing without oxygen. By 7 am Buhl was on the Silver Saddle. He continued across the huge plateau beyond, where he left his rucksack, carrying just what he could fit in his pockets. Continuing around the subsidiary summit of Nanga Parbat, he looked back to see that Kempter had turned around. One senses that Buhl was happy to continue utterly alone on this greatest journey of his life.

It was only at 2 pm that he reached the Bazhin Gap at 7,812 meters, where he took some Pervitin, a stimulant developed during the War to help f pilots stay awake. Then he looked at the ridge ahead. "300 meters still separate me from the main summit [and] these 300 meters contain the most difficult section of the whole ascent. A steep rock ridge covered with towers; vertical, sharp-edged upthrusts of granite with sharp cornices and covered in snow." He continues, admitting, "it is an extremely reckless undertaking ... I can often see right through the gap that has formed between the snow and the rock the climbing is grade IV and V standard". On his left the Rupal Face drops 5,000 meters – the biggest mountain face on earth.

A vertical tower blocks his way, so he has to find a devious traverse around it. "The rock is very brittle and demands extreme caution." Then an overhang blocks his way, "and thus I am forced to traverse a small

Below
A succession of German expeditions laid siege to the gigantic Rakhiot Face of Nanga Parbat during the 1930s. To reach the upper ridge on the left, they had to weave a labyrinthine route through spectacular crevasses. In 1937 sixteen men died in their sleep when a camp was stuck by a huge avalanche – one of the worst disasters in climbing history.

Below

During an earlier disaster in 1934, several Germans and their Sherpas died of hypothermia, marooned in a vicious storm at Camp 8. The same fateful route was followed in 1953, but with fewer camps. On the final push to the summit, the Austrian Hermann Buhl climbed alone over a height rise of 1,400 meters and a horizontal distance of 4 kilometers. By the time he returned to the top camp, 40 hours after setting out, his 29-year-old face seemed to have aged twenty years.

slope and later to climb a vertical-to-overhanging crack, and only by using my last reserves of energy am I able to work my way up the last few meters to the ridge."

And still there is a final snow ridge leading to a shoulder at 8,050 meters. Now it is 6 pm. The summit is only 75 meters higher but he has reached the end of his tether. So he drinks the last dregs of coca tea in his flask. It gives him a slight boost and, crawling on all fours, he drags himself to the summit of Nanga Parbat.

The long shadows in Buhl's summit photo show that the sun is about to set. Beyond the Tyrolean pennant fluttering from his ice axe, the Silver Saddle looks impossibly remote, far, far below. There is absolutely no chance of his getting back before nightfall.

Buhl spent the night about 100 meters below the summit, standing on a boulder, leaning against a sloping wall of rock, as there was nowhere to lie down. All he had to protect his torso was a vest, shirt and thin pullover – his thick warm one he had left in the rucksack. The temperature was probably –20º C or lower. Yet he survived and subsequently only lost the tips of two or three toes from frostbite. The real purgatorial trial came the next day, as the sun blazed down on the lone figure, struggling all the way back along that ridge. "I can no longer swallow or talk, even less shout,. Only blood and spittle come from

my mouth.." At last he reached his rucksack, but couldn't manage to swallow the food inside. Then, "out on the Silver Saddle I see two dots; I could shout with joy, now someone is coming up. I can hear their voices too, calling 'Hermann.' But then I realize they are rocks."

He limped on, hallucinating repeatedly, desperate for help. Only at 6:30 pm did he reach the Silver Saddle and look down the ridge beyond to the tents of Camp V where he saw two climbers. This time they were real and, 40.5 hours after setting out, he returned to the world of men. Photographed as he arrived at the camp, his emaciated, desiccated face had aged twenty years in two days.

1957
BROAD PEAK
BUHL, DIEMBERGER, SCHMUCK, & WINTERSTELLER

Nanga Parbat sealed Hermann Buhl's fame. Back at home in the Alps, undeterred by missing toes, he continued to excel on the hardest climbs and led an international team through foul weather to make the fifth ascent of the Eigerwand. But he wanted to climb another eight-thousander, on his own terms.

After his first choice of partners dropped out, he teamed up with Electrical Supply Manager Marcus Schmuck to attempt Broad Peak in the Karakoram range north of Nanga Parbat. This 1957 enterprise was to be quite different from Nanga Parbat, with just four climbers, and no high altitude porters carrying loads to the high camps. The other two climbers were Fritz Wintersteller, an electrician, and Kurt Diemberger, a reluctant student in Business Studies.

Diemberger and Wintersteller traveled by boat. Because of the Suez Crisis they took the long route round Africa, keeping fit by jogging round the deck, Wintersteller even doing 200 deep knee bends a day. A stocky, bullish man with a prodigious appetite, he had organized most of the expedition food. In Pakistan, when they all finally reached their base camp a hundred miles from the roadhead, it was he, according to his diary, who proved the tireless trail-breaker.

They laboured for a month, ferrying supplies up and down the long West Spur, making three camps and getting fit and acclimatized on the job. From Camp 3, on May 29, they climbed to a saddle at c.7,900 meters between two of Broad Peak's three summits. The higher lay up a steep ridge to the right. Buhl, the legendary survivor of Nanga Parbat, was struggling; "I drag myself along behind Markus. I don't

know what's wrong with me, just don't seem to have the right stuff today." So Wintersteller pushed ahead with Diemberger, taking six breaths to every step, ploughing a furrow to what seemed to be the summit. It was now 6 pm. It was also cloudy and difficult to tell whether the further summit they could glimpse was actually higher or not. All they could do was turn round, not getting back to Camp 3 until 10 pm.

The four men retreated all the way to base camp to rest and nurse niggling doubts about whether they really had climbed Broad Peak. Then on 7 June, three months after leaving Austria, they set off to climb all the way back up again. On 9 June they left Camp 3 again. It was 4 am and bitterly cold, as Schmuck wrote: "Soon, despite horsehair socks, wool socks, felt liners, boots and overboots, we can feel the cold in out toes."

All four men had to stop frequently to stamp and swing their legs, to warm numb toes. At 7,800 meters the had to sit down and massage their feet, especially Buhl, with his old frostbite injuries. Schmuck and Wintersteller then forged ahead and at 4 pm reached the point where Wintersteller and Diemberger had turned back on 29 May. "This time the view is clear – 400 meters away there is another, higher, peak which easily be reached by walking along a partly snow covered ridge."

It may have been "easy" but at 8,000 meters just walking is exhausting. A whole hour passed before Wintersteller was snapping stunning summit photos of Schmuck. Just as they turned round, Diemberger

Left and Above
The first ascent of an 8,000-meter peak by just four climbers, with no oxygen equipment or high altitude porters, was a revolutionary concept. In the team photo (bottom) the fresh-faced quartet of Schmuck, Diemberger, Wintersteller, and Buhl (left to right) pose at Salzburg Station. Many weeks later, in the far north of Pakistan, Buhl is photographed at Camp 2 on Broad Peak (above). From Camp 3 the team eventually reached the 7,800 meters saddle below the main summit. Buhl (left) contemplates the huge distance still remaining to the summit on 9 June 1957.

Above
Kurt Diemberger's famous photo captures the moment when Herman Buhl, having struggled all day with his old Nanga Parbat frostbite injuries, finally reaches the summit of Broad Peak, fifteen hours after setting out from Camp 3. Only the highest Karakoram summits remain illuminated by the setting sun.

arrived on the summit. Then, descending back over the forepeak, they passed Buhl, still forcing himself upward, still dredging up the old willpower.

It is now nearly dark, but, as Buhl writes in his diary, "I notice how quickly Kurt manages the last stretch to the forepeak. This inspires me and I say to myself, didn't we all, the whole team, want to get to the top?" Then Diemberger comes back from the summit, turns round, and accompanies his mentor up the final stretch, so that the two of them reach the top of Broad Peak at 7 pm when only the highest summits of the Karakoram are still glowing orange above the darkening depths.

Buhl and Diemberger didn't get back to camp until after midnight. Later, back in base camp, they reflected on their fantastic achievement: the first ascent of an eight-thousand-meter peak by just fours climbers, without any help from high altitude porters, nor oxygen. Emboldened by their achievement, a few days later Schmuck and Wintersteller made the first ascent of a 7,360-meter peak later named Skilbrum. Not to be outdone, Buhl and Diemberger set off to try another high peak called Chogolisa. But the weather turned and they had to retreat short of the summit. Descending through the cloud, following some way behind Diemberger, unroped, Buhl strayed from the tracks and walked out onto the edge of an over-hanging snow cornice, to plunge probably five hundred meters into a remote glacier basin. He was never seen again.

8,000-METER PEAKS

EVEREST 8,850 m
29.5.53 – Edmund Hillary (NZ), Tenzing Norgay (Tibet/India) (British expedition)

K2 8,611 m
31.7.54 – Achille Compagnoni, Lino Lacedelli (Italy)

KANGCHENJUNGA 8,586 m
25.5.55 – George Band, Joe Brown (UK)

LHOTSE 8,516 m
18.5.56 – Fritz Luschinger, Ernst Reiss (Switzerland)

MAKALU 8,463 m
15.5.55 – Jean Couzy, Lionel Terray (France)

CHO OYU 8,201 m
19.10.54 – Herbert Tichy, Sepp Jöchler (Austria), Pasang Dawa Lama (India)

DHAULAGIRI 8,167 m
13.5.60 – Kurt Diemberger (Austria), Peter Diener (Germany). Ernst Forrer (Switzerland), Albin Schelbert (Switzerland), Nawang Dorje Sherpa (Nepal), Nima Dorje Sherpa (Nepal).

MANASLU 8,163 m
9.5.56 – Toshio Imanishi (Japan), Gyalzen Norbu Sherpa (Nepal)

NANGA PARBAT 8,125 m
3.7.53 – Hermann Buhl (Austria)

GASHERBRUM I (Hidden Peak) 8,068 m
5.7.58 – Nicholas Clinch, Peter Schoening (USA)

ANNAPURNA I 8,091 m
3.6.50 – Maurice Herzog, Louis Lachenal (France)

BROAD PEAK 8,047 m
9.6.57 – Hermann Buhl, Kurt Diemberger, Marcus Schmuck, Fritz Wintersteller (Austria)

GASHERBRUM II 8,035 m
7.7.56 – Josef Larch, Fritz Moravec, Hans Willenpart (Austria)

SHISHAPANGMA 8,046 m
2.5.64 – Chen San (China), Doje (Tibet), Mima Zaxi (Tibet), Sodnam Doje (Tibet), Wang Fuzhou (China), Wu Zongyue (China), Xu Jing (China), Yungden (Tibet), Zhang Junyan (China)

Alan Hinkes took this photo from high on K2 in 1995. Broad Peak dominates the picture, with its highest summit on the right. To its left are the Gasherbrum peaks, number 1 to 4, from left to right. Floating above the clouds on the right, is the distinctive trapeze form of Chogolisa, where Herman Buhl died, a few days after his success on Broad Peak – the first person to make first ascents of two 8,000-meter peaks.

BRAVE NEW WORLD

AMERICA EMERGED TRIUMPHANT FROM THE Second World War as the richest, most powerful nation on earth. Yet her mountaineers still retained a touch of that naïve New World deference to Europe which Henry James's novels had chronicled so acutely. However, any lingering diffidence was about to melt away under the blazing California sun, where American rock climbers were about to redefine the sport of climbing on the giant granite walls of Yosemite Valley.

In his seminal history of North American climbing, Chris Jones tells the story of a Swiss émigré called John Salathé climbing a smooth granite wall, hammering pitons into a thin crack, until it petered out. But then, "closely examining the wall, he noticed a blade of grass growing out of a minute crack. 'By God,' he thought, 'if a piece of grass can come out, a piton can go in. So I takes a piton and drives and drives, but the piton chust bends.'"

Left, Above, and Right
Three views of the 900-meter high precipice, El Capitan – the "Captain" of the Yosemite Valley. In the winter scene, afternoon sunlight catches the crest of The Nose, dividing line between the North-West Face on the right and South-East Face on the left. The summer picture (above) shows the huge Heart formation halfway up the South-East Face – a prominent feature crossed by the Salathé Wall route. The photo below depicts is of the Northeast Face, "North America Wall," with The Nose soaring up the left skyline.

JOHN SALATHÉ & THE HARD STEEL PITON

Pitons of that era were made from malleable soft steel. So Salathé, a blacksmith by trade, took an old Ford Model A rear axle of hard steel and forged a piece of it into a piton. Returning to the unyielding crack, "I took my piton and I pound and pound, and it goes into ze rock."

Salathé was soon forging a whole range of hard steel pitons for his fellow Yosemite pioneers. He also invented the "skyhook" which could be hooked over tiny nubbins of rock to aid progress up a blank wall. With these new tools he climbed a giant detached granite spire which the indigenous Indians called the Lost Arrow. Then, in 1950, aged fifty-one, he teamed up with a student called Al Steck to make the first ascent of the 450 meter-high North Face of Sentinel Rock. The climb took five days.

Sentinel Rock was Salathé's last major climb. He had long since dropped out of the rat race, living as a proto-hippie, out of the back of a van, surviving off a diet of fruit and wild herbs. The stage was set for a brash new generation to move in and tackle Yosemite's bigger challenges, in particular the vast inviolate cliff called The Captain – El Capitan.

Yosemite climbing had been dominated so far by San Francisco climbers. In 1953 they weren't impressed when a cocky teenager arrived from the smog of Los Angeles and reputedly asked, "What have you guys got around here worth climbing?" But, in comparison to the other leading young upstart, Warren Harding, the teenaged Royal Robbins was positively effete. The two men were to become the biggest names – and determined competitors – in a generation of bold, colourful characters who really invented the modern phenomenon of "big wall climbing."

1957
HALF DOME
ROYAL ROBBINS

Salathé had shown how modern hard steel pitons could be hammered into the most incipient cracks – and removed repeatedly for use on successive pitches

Yvon Chouinard was one of the brightest new stars in the Californian climbing firmament. With Tom Frost, he invented the Rurp – the Realized Ultimate Reality Piton – a hatchet-shaped sliver of steel, not much bigger than a thumbnail, with a point no thicker than a knifeblade, enabling climbers to use minute cracks where before they would have had to drill holes and place bolts. At his Great Pacific Ironworks, Chouinard started manufacturing a complete range of pitons, then designed innovative ice climbing gear. The Chouinard/Frost team also invented aluminium alloy hexagonal and wedge-shaped "nuts" which gradually made hammering pitons almost obsolete. In the Eighties, fearful of an increasingly pernicious litigation culture, Chouinard sold his business to his employees (it became Black Diamond) and moved into "software," founding the phenomenally successful clothing company Patagonia. Here Chouinard is seen preparing his gear.

– to protect previously unimaginable climbs. They could also be used to aid progress – artificial climbing – where there were no hand or foot holds for free climbing.

In 1957 Royal Robbins grabbed the first big prize with Jerry Gallwas and Mike Sherrick – the Northwest Face of Half Dome. No-one had ever committed to such an immense wall. Rescue was simply not an option, so they took 300 meters of rope, in case they needed to retreat. Early in the climb Robbins performed a massive pendulum, swinging on the rope across blank rock to gain another crack system. They hauled gear up behind them in special sacks and spent four nights sleeping on ledges, all the time wondering how they were going to get through the huge summit overhangs. And then, on the fifth day, they discovered an escape – a foot wide gangway leading left beneath the overhangs, like the window ledge on a skyscraper, hanging over a stomach-churning void. From there, the summit was a mere formality. The great vertical slice of Half Dome Northwest Face was climbed.

Above
The wild-living, boozing, iconoclastic Warren Harding, who burnt out a series of partners during his protracted first ascent of The Nose, totalling 45 days of climbing. After completing the final 12 days push, he commented, "As I staggered over the rim, it was not at all clear to me who was conqueror and who was conquered. I do recall that El Cap seemed to be in much better condition than I was."

Right
Second man "cleaning" a pitch, removing the pitons and slings which will need to be used over and over again on subsequent pitches.

1958
EL CAPITAN – THE NOSE
WARREN HARDING

Warren Harding arrived in Yosemite that July to discover that he'd been beaten to the great prize. Determined to up the ante, he eyed up the even bigger cliff on the other side of the valley – 900 meters of

granite soaring in a single sweep to the flat top of El Capitan. No-one had previously dared before to consider it, but, entranced by the majestic prow where the Northwest met the Southwest Face, Harding stated uncompromisingly, "I'm gonna climb that goddamn line."

"The Nose" as the South Buttress became known, was a huge step into the unknown – as daunting, in its way, as the first Apollo mission to the Moon. The Nose of El Capitan is as tall as the biggest Dolomite walls in Europe, but steeper and much smoother. Apart from the psychological barrier of climbing above so much air, there was the deep fear of climbing into a deadend – of getting trapped high on the wall in a storm. And there was the questions of survival – how to haul enough water to spend an expected month on the wall, whilst being frazzled by the dessicating Californian sun.

Faced with these daunting logistics, Harding approached The Nose like a Himalayan expedition. He even named the bivouacs, Camp 1, Camp 2 etc. And he anchored a continuous line of ropes, enabling him and his various partners to travel up and down the route with supplies. That summer of 1957 they climbed the lower section, including a 130-meter-high wide crack where they had repeatedly to use their four wide pitons, made from the legs of an old stove they had found in a Berkeley rubbish tip. The fissure is known to this day as the Stoveleg Crack.

Winter arrived and they all went home. Harding returned in the summer of 1958, hammering his way

Left

The master at work: Royal Robbins on the first ascent of Salathé Wall, gaining maximum height before making a huge pendulum rightward across blank rock, to gain Sous le Toit (Under the Roof) Ledge.

Far Left

Tom Frost climbing through the big roof to gain the final headwall of Salathé Wall.

Right

More scenes from the golden age of El Capitan climbing. Clockwise from top left: Robbins contemplating his gear selection for the second ascent of The Nose; Frost, Robbins, and Chouinard settling in for the night at the Black Cave, first ascent of North America Wall; Tom Frost's view down the free-hanging rope to Robbins relaxing on El Cap Spire, during first ascent of Salathé Wall, pitch 21; the giddy view which deterred early generations: Frost looks down pitch 29 of The Nose to Pratt and Robbins relaxing at Camp VI.

This Page
Doug Scott photographs a climber working his way up The Nose, placing pitons for aid.

Right
Another Doug Scott photo, this one of the Austrian climber Peter Habeler belaying him across the roof traverse leading to the headwall of Salathé Wall, on an early ascent in 1972. (See Tom Frost on same pitch on page.92). Six years later Habeler became the first person, with Reinhold Messner, to climb Everest without supplementary oxygen.

up under the relentless sun. Despite the advances in piton manufacture, there were still sections where the cracks were too thin or simply non-existent. Here Harding resorted to bolts, using a hammer-driven bit to drill holes in the iron hard granite.

One of the strange ironies of the Land of the Free is its frequent authoritarianism. Yosemite, one of the world's first national parks, is run by officious park rangers, and in 1958 they ordered Harding to stop climbing during the high tourist season. But that autumn, refreshed with a new team, he climbed all the way back up the ropes, determined to complete the route. From Camp 4, with Wayne Merry, Harding finally tackled the prominent black triangle two-thirds of the way up the route – the Great Roof. They had been dreading this pitch, but an amenable crack in the back of the roof enabled them to work out to the lip at its right hand end, to belay in the most awesome position, hanging 600 meters above the pine trees on the valley floor.

They continued, day after unrelenting day, up a series of vertical and overhanging corners, to Camp 5, then Camp 6. On the eleventh day the weather seemed to be breaking, so Harding laboured all day and through the night, drilling holes by the light of his headtorch, up the final blank overhanging wall. Soon after sunrise he pulled over onto the top of El Capitan. The unthinkable wall had finally been climbed.

1961

Royal Robbins disappeared on army service. When he returned to "The Valley" in 1960 a new generation of Young Turks was flexing its prodigious biceps in the climbers' summer home amongst Yosemite's stately pines. Tom Frost had already repeated the first four pitches of Warren Harding's legendary route up El Capitan. Now Robbins enlisted Frost, along with Joe Fitchen and Chuck Pratt, for an audacious plan to show how a big wall might be climbed in the finest possible style.

This time there would be no fixed ropes: the team would just cut loose, commit themselves to the big pendulums on the route – knowing that retreat, thereafter, would be difficult, if not impossible – and go all out for the top. Working in two pairs, alternating leading and gear hauling, they climbed The Nose in just seven days. It had taken Harding and his friends a total of 45 days! Harding had also been forced to drill 125 holes for bolts, in addition to placing over 600 pitons. Casting his eye over the immense acreage of virgin rock to the left of The Nose, Robbins wondered whether there might be an alternative line up El Capitan – less direct, but following a more natural crack system.

The result, climbed later that summer by Tom Frost, Chuck Pratt, and Royal Robbins, was Salathé Wall. The climb took just six days and only thirteen bolts were drilled on the entire route. Ethically and stylistically, it was a big advance on The Nose. It finished up the most stupendous "headwall" overhanging at an angle of 95 degrees, with a single crack splitting the wall. Coming last up this section, Robbins had to follow by "prussiking" (climbing with special slip knot loops) up the free hanging rope. Even he, apparently, let out a shriek of terror as he cast loose from the anchor and found himself spinning on a single nylon rope over 800 meters of thin air.

Size talks in America, and on El Capitan and Half Dome the Californians had the biggest, steepest, most photogenic wall on the continent. But, a thousand miles to the east, the mountain state of Colorado had

its own unique attractions. Close to the university town of Boulder, where the Rockies rear up out of the immense American plain, climbers could grapple with the gorgeous red sandstone of the Flatirons and Eldorado Canyon. Deeper into the range, was their own vertical granite wall – the Diamond on the East Face of Longs Peak. Further west there was the savage gash called the Black Canyon of the Gunnison, with its extraordinary "Painted Wall." But perhaps the most unique climbing ground – the most quintessentially Wild West adventure – was the desert country surrounding Moab, Utah. It was on these monolithic red sandstone desert pinnacles that a lanky, laconic bricklayer by the name of Layton Kor made his mark.

1962

The names of the sandstone towers of Colorado, Utah and Arizona speak for themselves – Spider Rock, Totem Pole, Standing Rock. They represent the ideal inaccessible summit. They also owe their spectacular eroded shapes to the softness of the rock: they seem terrifyingly ephemeral. As Layton Kor put it, in a variation of Mallory's famous quotation, they had to be climbed, "not so much because they're there, but rather because they may not be there much longer."

Just getting to the foot of the towers was an adventure. Here is one of Kor's regular partners, Steve Komito, recalling a typical desert outing: "Even now I can still hear it, however muffled by the mists of time. That pitiless grinding of sandstone on steel causes an involuntary contraction of my abdomen. It's the underside of my recently purchased station wagon

dragging itself across a rut of slick rock on a meaningless joke of a road far from the comfortable haunts of men who know better than to drive a car like mine out into this unplayful sand pile high on the Colorado River Plateau."

At last they reach their objective. "Layton is bubbling with joy at having beaten Harvey Carter to this hidden treasure house. Huntley Ingalls is raving about the 'significant summit unique on the planet' and I'm wishing that it would maybe fall over now, so that we wouldn't have to climb it tomorrow."

"It" is an unclimbed monolith called Standing Rock, composed, as Komito put it, "of layers of Rye Krisp held in place by bands of moistened kitty litter." Casting himself as the reluctant hero, Komito describes his companions: "Huntley, scholarly and withdrawn, provides a sharp contrast to the roguish bricklayer with whom he has shared a number of desert derring-dos. They are both single-minded about knocking off these towers."

Over the next two days, climbing almost entirely on "aid" – knocking pitons into the crumbling layers, hauling themselves from one tenuous anchor to the next, they succeeded in making the first ascent of Standing Rock. On Everest, it would be a mere incident, lost in the bulk of the mountain; here, in the Colorado desert, it was a glorious summit in its own right. But Kor's restless energy was already looking overseas for new challenges and soon he would be traveling to Europe, to take part in a new wave of exploration sweeping across the biggest faces of the Alps.

Above, left
Peter Habeler working his way up the Headwall on Salathé Wall, 900 meters above the valley floor. The free-hanging ropes give an idea of the actual angle of the rock – about 95°.

Above, right
Colorado's "roguish bricklayer" and climbing genius, Layton Kor, with primitive gear on the first ascent Standing Rock.

Right
Kor and Komito at work, half way up Standing Rock – "layers of Rye Krisp held in place by bands of moistened kitty litter."

THE NEW WAVE OF ALPINE CLIMBING

Left
The soaring West Face of the Petit
Dru, with the reddish Bonatti Pillar
facing directly towards the camera.

Below
A different view, showing the
twin summits of Les Drus just left
of center, with the North Face in
shadow on the left. The sunlit West
Face in this 2005 picture is scarred
by the pale grey of huge rockfalls.
Later that year there was another
massive fall, when millions of tons
of granite broke loose. Walter
Bonatti's most famous climb, the
Bonatti Pillar, exists no more.

"I DON'T WANT TO DIE. I MUST NOT DIE, LINO,
Achille, can't you hear us? For God's sake help us!"

The light was fading and in a few moments it
would be dark. Walter Bonatti and the Hunza porter,
Mahdi, had laboured all day to carry vital oxygen
cylinders for the summit bid on the world's second
highest mountain, K2. But they couldn't find the tent
where Lino Lacedelli and Achille Compagnoni were
waiting for the oxygen cylinders. It was hidden, off to
the left, behind some rocks.

In the end, Bonatti and Mahdi had simply to cut a
ledge and sit in the snow, shivering through the bitter
long night, 8,100 meters above sea level. Mahdi
howled in terror and at first light fled back down the
mountain. Bonatti followed, leaving the oxygen
cylinders standing in the snow. About an hour later,
Compagnoni and Lacedelli traversed across the slope
from their tent, collected the oxygen and continued
to the summit of K2, winning fame and glory both for
themselves and for Italy.

For Bonatti, youngest member of the 1954 expedition, K2 was a bitter betrayal. Not only had he, the
most brilliant climber on the team, been passed over
for the summit; he had also nearly died supporting
the summit pair and received scant recognition for

his sacrifice: he was virtually written out of the plot in
the official accounts. He returned to Italy profoundly
depressed, hoping to find solace in the Alps. He
sought a kind of catharsis in the most beautiful, difficult, ambitious climb he had ever attempted.

1955
PETIT DRU – SOUTHWEST PILLAR
WALTER BONATTI

Aiguille des Drus is the name given to a twin-peaked
tower that rises above the snout of Mont Blanc's
longest glacier, the Mer de Glace. Even by its easiest
route up the back, first climbed in 1878, it is quite a
hard climb. But the real drama is on the front side,
facing the popular tourist viewpoint of Montenvers.
The North Face was a big breakthrough in 1934; the
first ascent of the smooth granite sheet of the West
Face of the Petit Dru was another step forward in
1952. Now Bonatti set his heart on the soaring pillar
to the right – the Southwest Pillar.

He had already attempted the pillar with Carlo
Mauri in 1953, before the K2 expedition. They
returned in 1955 but were again defeated by bad
weather – another disappointment to rub salt in the
wounds of K2. Rather than let the pillar go, Bonatti
became obsessive about it, determined to return. Not
only that, he decided on an audacious plan to
attempt the route completely alone.

He confided in a friend called Professor Ceresa,
who saw him off from Montenvers at 2 am on
15 August 1955. Several hours later he was toiling up
the couloir leading to the base of the pillar, struggling
to drag his 36-kilo rucksack behind him. But
this approach was horribly dangerous, bombarded by
falling rocks, so Bonatti retreated and decided on
a novel solution: he would descend from above,
abseiling into the couloir from the other side of
the mountain.

The following day with Ceresa, he climbed up to
the Charpoua Hut on the southeast side of the Dru.
Near the hut he found a dead butterfly. Tense with
anxiety over the terrifying task he had set himself, he
was overcome by empathy. "Poor living creature con-

demned to die in a cruel world whose existence you had not even suspected. In this last flutter I saw a drama of almost human dimensions. Who knows, I thought, with what horror you felt the first bite of cold, the dread certainty of death and the myriad regrets which I share with you? Poor little insect, my brother in misfortune in this place of death, how similar my fate is to yours. ... If tomorrow I do not succeed in getting up, my end will be the same as yours."

At dawn the next day, he suffered further agonies of dread as he reached the shoulder on the Dru and prepared to abseil into the horrible couloir. "The void there was absolutely terrifying, broken only by icy shadows and the sharp, vertiginous outline of the Southwest Pillar. In the half hour of rest which I allowed before the descent I lived through perhaps the most important moment of the whole climb. Till then every foot I advanced up the mountain had still allowed me the possibility of return, but beyond the gap that was no longer possible."

Then he set off down, abseiling ropelength by ropelength into the depths, manhandling the unwieldy burden of his huge sack laden with food, bivouac gear, rope, pitons and wooden wedges. Half way down, hammering in a piton anchor, he struck his left hand, slicing off the end of his ring finger. Almost fainting with pain and blood loss, he had somehow to bandage it, then sort out a bivouac at the foot of the pillar. Then he discovered that his fuel can had spilt. Most of his food was spoilt. Far more serious, he couldn't use his stove to melt snow for water. And he still hadn't started the actual climb!

Most people would have packed it in. But Bonatti had phenomenal drive. Over the next six days he survived off 2 packets of biscuits, a tube of condensed milk, four little cheeses, a tin of tuna, a tin of pate, a small flask of cognac, and cans of beer. The climbing was incredibly sustained – pitch after pitch of near vertical granite, much of it requiring artificial aid from pitons. Bonatti had a system of self-belaying, using his monstrous rucksack as a second man. After completing each pitch he had to abseil down, then climb back up the rope, removing the pitons, then hauling up the sack. In other words he actually climbed the whole of the Southwest Pillar twice and descended it once.

THE GREAT ROOF

By the fifth day his hands were so swollen and lacerated that he had to use his teeth to open his clawed fingers. And now he had to find his way around a monstrous granite roof. Up to the right he spotted a jumble of stacked blocks above the roof. Tying a bun-

dle of pitons and wedges to one end of a rope, he made a kind of bolas, then swung and threw it up into the air to catch on the rock jumble. Then he prepared to swing across in a giddy pendulum, dangling a thousand meters over the base of the Dru.

"A last unnerving moment of hesitation, a last inward prayer for safety, and when uncontrollable tremors ran over me and my strength seemed about to go, I shut my eyes for an instant, held my breath and let myself slip into space, held only by my hands around the rope. For a moment I had the sensation of falling with the rope, then my forward flight slowed down, and almost with a jerk I felt myself swinging backwards. The anchorage had held!"

But he still had to climb up the rope, trying not to jerk it, terrified that the dodgy anchor might collapse and send him plummeting to his death. "When I had to leave the rope in order to grasp the rock flakes, I found myself hesitating another moment. I feared,

WALTER BONATTI'S LEGACY

Walter Bonatti's legacy of first ascents, including the Karakoram summit of Gasherbrum IV (7,925 meters) is phenomenal. For fifteen years he was probably the most outstanding mountaineer in the world. Then in 1965 he made the brave decision to give it all up. For his swansong, to mark the hundredth anniversary of the first ascent of the Matterhorn, he climbed a new direct route up the North Face. Because he was Bonatti, he did it alone. In winter. Then, liberated from the prison of ambition, he embarked on a new life as a roving photo journalist, making long but reasonably safe journeys through some of the world's finest wildernesses. In 2007 when the Alpine Club was looking for one outstanding mountaineer to invite to its 150th anniversary celebrations in Zermatt, the choice was obvious – they invited Walter Bonatti.

THE FALL OF THE BONATTI PILLAR

After his extraordinary solo ascent, the Bonatti Pillar became one of the most coveted hard rock climbs in the Alps. The first person to repeat a solo ascent was the Welshman Eric Jones; and the route was later soloed by the photogenic darling of the French media, Catherine Destivelle. Now Bonatti's most famous route no longer exists. The recent warming of the Alps has caused several huge rockfalls on the Petit Dru, as the subterranean ice gluing together huge plaques of granite, melts. After the biggest rock fall, in 2005, the whole of the Bonatti Pillar fell into the valley. Where there was once a soaring pillar of golden weathered rock, there is now an immense grey scar.

indeed expected that the whole thing would collapse on top of me." But it didn't. Above the flakes the climbing remained phenomenally hard and it was only on the sixth day that it finally eased off. Using forearms and elbows whenever possible, sparing his horribly painful hands, he swarmed up the final easy ridge and stood alone on the summit of the Petit Dru. He had done it utterly alone. He had climbed the Southwest Pillar. And after that day it was no longer called the Southwest Pillar: it became known as the Bonatti Pillar.

ANGLO-SAXON ALPINE RENAISSANCE

Walter Bonatti set the pace in postwar alpine climbing, but there were soon keen competitors snapping at his heels. After going through a rather moribund period in the Thirties and Forties, British alpinists were now enjoying something of a renaissance. Names such as Brown, Whillans, Patey, and Bonington were being inscribed on new alpine masterpieces. In 1961 Chris Bonington, Don Whillans, Ian Clough, and Djuglosz succeeded on a route from which Bonatti had led an epic retreat, losing four of his six companions in the storm, just a month earlier. The route, up Mont Blanc's Central Pillar of Frêney, was the highest, remotest technical rock climb in Europe.

Americans too were making their mark. On the Petit Dru, to the left of the Bonatti Pillar, the Californians, Royal Robbins and John Harlin used their extreme big wall techniques, honed on the cliffs of Yosemite, to force a new ultra-direct line up the West Face.

Like Bonatti, John Harlin was a driven man with a huge ego, hungry for extreme experiences. He was also, like Bonatti, inventive, creative; and he had a sensitive side: realizing that his job as a U.S. Airforce bomber pilot, in the event of a Third World War, was to obliterate the beautiful city of Prague, he asked to be transferred to ground duties. He spent every weekend and holiday driving hundreds of miles from his German base to the Alps until he retired from the Airforce, to set up a climbing school in Switzerland. It was from this base in Leysin, where he lived with his wife and two children, that he planned what was to be the ultimate alpine climb – a direct line straight up the middle of the biggest, most famous wall of all – the North Face of the Eiger.

1966
EIGER DIRECT
HASTON, HUPFAUER, LEHNE, STROBEL, & VOTTELER

Harlin had already climbed the original 1938 route – the first American to do so – and knew just how dangerous the Eigerwand could be. His proposed Direct ran straight into the main line of fire from avalanches and falling rocks, funnelled down from the Spider. After a couple of abortive forays he realized that the only safe way to attempt the line was in winter, when all the loose rubble would be frozen in place.

He planned for the early winter of 1966, inviting the Colorado aid-climbing specialist Layton Kor and a notoriously tough, ambitious Scotsman called Dougal Haston. He also invited the English climber Chris Bonington, who had doubts about the project but couldn't bear not to be involved: he got round the problem by coming as photographer for the *Daily Telegraph* and ended up, despite all his former doubts, leading one of the hardest pitches on the route.

Right from the start, the team seemed plagued by bad luck. When they assembled on 6 February the weather was bad. Then Harlin dislocated his shoulder skiing. Undeterred by the injury, he returned on 19 February, to discover that a rival German team had already climbed 500 meters up the Direct line. So the next day Harlin's team used the German ropes to reach the First Band. Here, determined to move independently, they were forced to climb horribly smooth overhanging rock to just the left of the Germans' more natural line. It took Layton Kor four hours to gain just 30 meters, before placing a bolt to abseil off.

Left

Transferring skills from the desert towers of the Wild West, Layton Kor demonstrates his artistry on the crucial traverse round the Central Pillar, Eiger Direct, in the dead of winter.

Below

John Harlin, instigator of the Eiger Direct, sits our a six day storm with Dougal Haston at the Death Bivouac snowcave, during the worst alpine winter for many years..

That night a storm arrived, with winds of 75 miles-an-hour down at Kleine Scheidegg. Up on the face, Kor and Dougal Haston cowered under a bivouac sack, almost drowning in torrents of freezing spindrift.

COMPETITIVE EDGE

And so it went on, day after day, week after week, as the rival parties pushed out their parallel lines of ropes up the centre of the Eigerwand. To combat the worst winter alpine winter in years, the Harlin team ended up digging a snowcave at Death Bivouac.

From here Heckmair's 1938 route slants off to the left, up the Ramp. The Harlin route went straight up, with Kor leading one sensationally hard pitch to get round the base of the Central Pillar. A true craftsman, tapping tiny knifeblade pegs into incipient cracks, the 6' 4" Coloradoan engineered his way up almost blank rock, refusing to deface the Eiger by drilling any unnecessary bolts.

Then yet more storms blew in. Kor retreated to Kleine Scheidegg, while Haston and Harlin sat it out for six days in the tiny snowcave, occasionally poking an ice axe through the outer floor and looking straight down to Grindelwald, some one thousand five hundred meters below. Harlin then became ill with bronchitis and they had eventually to retreat.

Two days later, on 19 March, Harlin left hospital with bronchitis medication, determined to complete his great project, now that the weather was improving again. His wife wrote from Leysin, "Don't play with the gods up there ... we give all our support thru this last stretch." His seven-year-old daughter, Andréa, wrote, "Dear Daddy, I hope you come back home pretty soon. I love you very much." Nine-year-old John wrote, "I passed the exams for the college secondaire. I wish you good luck! Try to make it to the top!"

Those letters were the last contact he ever had with his family.

Two days later, back at the snowcave, he received a radio message from the *Daily Telegraph* reporter, Peter Gillman, that a German climber had been spotted in the Fly – the little icefield above and right of the Spider, immediately beneath the final headwall. The race was on.

LAST NIGHT AT DEATH BIVOUAC

Kor set off immediately from Kleine Scheidegg, hoping to catch up with Haston and Harlin, who now started up the ropes from the snowcave in the middle of the wall. Haston went first, with Harlin following about quarter of an hour behind. They were using jumars – camming ascenders used to climb fixed ropes. On this section around the Central Pillar most of the ropes were free hanging. To save weight, they had used thin 7-mm-diameter ropes – under ideal conditions quite adequate to hold a man's weight, but here, stretched taut over rough edges, horribly susceptible to wear and tear.

At the end of one particularly giddy section, as Haston heaved up over an edge, he noticed that the rope's sheath was slightly frayed. But he shouted no message of warning to Harlin. It was Peter Gillman, the *Telegraph* reporter watching 1,500 meters below, who witnessed what happened next.

"What I saw when I trained the Kleine Scheidegg telescope on the face at 3:15 pm on 22 March will stay with me for ever. ... As I peered through the telescope, following the line of fixed ropes up the face, I knew at once, beyond any conceivable doubt, that I had seen a man falling to his death. I saw a figure dressed in red, limbs outstretched, turning over slowly, finally, in the air clear of the face. I tried to follow the figure but it disappeared behind a buttress and all I saw were chunks of snow tumbling out of a couloir by the Death Bivouac and another climber standing nearby, presumably transfixed by what he too had seen. I gave an involuntary shout and the others who crowded round the telescope tried to suggest that I had seen a rucksack or an anorak. I wanted so much to agree but I knew it was not so, ... Chris and Layton set off on skis towards a patch of debris which we had located below the face, while I guided them with the telescope and a radio. At 4:35 pm Chris radioed: 'It's John. He's dead.'"

Don Whillans, working at the American School in Leysin, had the grim task of going round to the Harlins' house to deliver the terrible news. As Harlin's son recalled forty years later, "I was playing in bed with my sister and friends next door. One look at Mom, coming through the door, told us something was terribly wrong."

Up in the Fly, high on the Eiger, Sigi Hupfauer, Jörg Lehne, Günther Strobel and Roland Votteler were stupefied to hear of Harlin's death. Haston joined them and they agreed to team up and complete the route together, as a memorial to the man whose huge energy and ambition had initiated the project. The weather broke yet again and they endured three nights of miserable shivering on tiny ledges and days of extreme climbing, before emerging on the summit icefield in a blizzard on 25 March, the day John Harlin was buried in the Leysin graveyard.

FAST AND LIGHT

Eleven years later, on the way home from an expedition to Afghanistan, a young British law student called Alex MacIntyre stopped off in Switzerland to climb what was still regarded as one of the hardest routes in the Alps – the Harlin Route on the Eigerwand. With American climber Tobin Sorenson, MacIntyre took just four days to complete what in 1966 had required a full scale Himalayan siege lasting six weeks.

MacIntyre and Sorenson weren't necessarily better climbers than Harlin, Kor, and Haston. They were just moving with – or slightly ahead of – the times. Alpine climbing had taken off again in the Seventies, particularly on the steep ice and "mixed" faces of ice, snow and rock. Better ice gear helped: crampons, ice axes, and ice screws engineered to give greater precision and confidence. But attitude was probably the main factor – man's desire to experiment and explore.

Left

The lost generation. Alex MacIntyre was one of the most eloquent and innovative stars of a new generation of alpinists to hit the Alps in the mid seventies. Here he is seen in Tibet in 1982, with another exceptional climber of the time, Roger Baxter-Jones, in the balaclava. MacIntyre died a few months later, on Annapurna. Baxter-Jones, a popular alpine guide, died three months later, when he and his client were killed by a collapsing ice tower on the Aiguille du Triolet.

WALTER CECCHINEL & JAGER

The twin-summit Drus has always been a forcing ground, particularly the showy south and west faces of the Petit Dru. But there is also a secret, hidden corner, facing northeast, where a sliver of ice runs straight up to the notch between Grand and Petit. This "Drus Couloir," unthinkable to earlier generations, became one of the most coveted first ascents in the early Seventies.

The most prominent contender was Walter Cecchinel. He got part way up the Couloir in 1970. Two years later competitors got higher before being defeated by blank rock. Cecchinel returned in January 1973 with a medical student called Claude Jager and succeeded in making the first ascent of what was probably the hardest ice and mixed climb to have been made in the Alps.

It had always been assumed that winter was the only season safe for the Drus Couloir, but in fact it was repeated the following July by a team including Adoubert, a pastor whose religious vocation was matched by an equal vocation for extreme climbing. He was also delightfully hedonistic. Describing his team's bivouac half way up the vertical rock barrier in the middle of the Drus Couloir, he recorded the following:

"In the middle of the couloir that evening, we had a luxurious meal again: pernod, salted tit bits as an aperitif, paté of goose, slices of pineapple, cakes, and a flask of Burgundy. We were looking after our morale. The cuisine may not have been grande but it was certainly haute."

The following day they completed the upper half of the Drus Couloir. In his personal account, Adoubert analysed eloquently the thrill of steep ice climbing:

"Now began that very special dance, a rhythmic ballet in four movements, a mixture of barbaric and primitive gestures, and classical movement. ... The best dance, like the best toreador, strikes only once. ... One doesn't murder the beast or the wall – it's a question of style, or ecology, or spirit, of going to the limit of risks ..."

GABARROU & BOIVIN

A few miles from the Drus, clearly visible to all the skiers who whoosh down the Vallée Blanche each winter, there is another blue ribbon of ice, set deep between russet pillars of granite – the Super Couloir of Mont Blanc du Tacul. Two British climbers, Mo Anthoine and Bill Barker, spent several winter days attempting it before being defeated by its glassy iron hard surface.

Then a young Frenchman called Patrick Gabarrou snatched the prize with Jean Marc Boivin, in May 1975. Climbing in the early summer, they had the advantage of longer days and, perhaps, softer ice, while still avoiding the stonefall danger of high summer. Moving with rapid Gallic élan, they dispatched the Super Couloir in two days of climbing. Gabarrou went on to pioneer a wealth of new routes probably unequalled in the history of alpinism and is still find-

ing new corners to explore, over thirty years later. Boivin made many more first ascents. In 1988 he made the first parapente jump from the summit of Mount Everest but two years later he was killed base-jumping off the Angel Falls in Venezuala.

1976
GRANDES JORASSES CENTRAL COULOIR
COLTON & MACINTYRE

The new ice climbs by French stars such as Cecchinel, Gabarrou and Boivin were quickly repeated by young British and American alpinists thirsty for adventure, who then started finding their own new routes. Prominent amongst this talented generation were John Bouchard, John Porter, Gordon Smith and

Above and Right
The Super Couloir of Mont Blanc du Tacul: John Harlin III, whose father died on the Eiger when he was a child, photographed here in 2005, thirty years after the first ascent of the couloir. The equipment has become more sophisticated – and the climbing, by modern standards, less extreme – but the sunless cleft has lost none of its compelling atmosphere.

Terry King. But the one with the wildest gleam in his eye was the law student who pulled off the first "alpine-style" ascent of the Eiger Direct – Alex MacIntyre. And it was he who plucked perhaps the finest alpine plum of the mid Seventies – the Central Couloir of the Grandes Jorasses.

MacIntyre was bright and well versed in alpine history. The very names of the three main rocky spurs on the Grandes Jorasses – Walker, Whymper and Croz – honour Victorian pioneers. And, as Mac-Intyre pointed out in an excellent article for *Mountain* magazine, the first brave Germans to attempt the North Face in the early Thirties had tried the big icy depression between the spurs, two of them, Brehm and Rittler, being killed in 1931 by falling stones.

Attempting the Central Couloir 45 years later with Gordon Smith, MacIntyre was also threatened by stonefall from the Whymper Spur: "then with an ear-splitting bang, night turned to day, and the whole spur was raked, strafed and peppered from end to end – flashing, sparking, reeking of the devil, granite on granite at terminal velocity ... so we aborted the mission."

Sensible chap. But he was highly ambitious and covetous of this line up one of the most famous faces in the Alps. He also wanted to cock a snook at two of the world's most famous climbers, Chris Bonington and Dougal Haston, who had spent twelve days during the winter of 1972 failing to get up the route. Bonington had called his article "Too Cold For Comfort." Four years on, attempting the route in summer, MacIntyre entitled his version, "Cold Enough For Comfort."

He returned a month after the first attempt, during a night of hard frost, climbing this time with a Yorkshireman called Nick Colton. To avoid the immense gaping *bergschrund* – the terminal crevasse at

Below
The hardest section of the Central Couloir soars directly above the Scottish climber Dougal Haston, during an abortive winter attempt with Chris Bonington and Mick Burke in 1972. They found it "too cold for comfort." Fourteen years later, climbing in summer – but starting at night when loose rocks were well frozen in place – Alex MacIntyre found it just "cold *enough* for comfort."

Above
Dave Hesleden during a recent
ascent of the Colton-MacIntyre route,
photographed by Simon Richardson.

the bottom of the Couloir – they sneaked in from the left, starting up the lowest rocks of the classic Walker Spur. They set off at 10:30 pm, climbing fast and unroped, and by 2:30 the next morning they were at the top of the first big icefield, at the start of a much steeper, narrower gullet, "sorting the gear roping up, peering and wondering, because it looked steep up there. At least, it looked steep as far as you can throw a head-torch. There was no moon and it was dark in the couloir."

They continued by the light of their headtorches, the gullet "steep, bulging, all-engrossing". At daybreak they emerged onto the next icefield. Then there was a rocky section, smothered in powder snow. Colton took a sixty foot fall, but was unhurt and continued into a blue ice runnel. Then there was another icefield, from where they slanted left towards the very top of the Walker Spur. The subsidiary gully they had hoped to follow was impossible at first, so they had to

follow rock on its right wall, carried up on a wave of euphoric determination.

"It was mean stuff: deceptive, awkward and inevitably loose. ... Nick solved the problem of getting back into the gully bed by falling off:

'What's happening?'

'Nowt – just fallen off.'

We charged on up but then there were these two little ledges just asking to be sat upon, so much more comfortable than he cold wet snow on the other side and so much more convenient. So we sat down, just five minutes short, to dine on cheese and ham butties, with coffee by the gallon. Rare moments: we were asleep before the night came."

On that deceptively casual note of pure contentment, deliciously exhausted after nearly twenty-four hours non-stop climbing, MacIntyre ends his account of the first ascent of one of the great modern classic alpine climbs.

HIMALAYAN RENAISSANCE

Left
The 1970 route up the South Face of Annapurna brought a new level of technical difficulty to high altitude climbing. Here Mick Burke traverses fixed ropes on the Ice Ridge.

Below
This was a full-scale Himalayan siege, and it required an army of porters to transport all the supplies to base camp.

BETWEEN 1950 AND 1964 ALL THE WORLD'S fourteen 8,000-meter peaks were climbed. As with the Alps, a hundred years earlier, climbers tended to go for the easiest available lines to these previously untouched summits. Other, lower summits were also climbed, but by the mid-Sixties, mountaineers had still barely scratched the surface of the Himalayan ranges.

Travel to Central Asia was still, relative to today, very expensive. Much of the area was in any case closed to foreigners. Chinese-occupied Tibet was a no-go area. The unresolved Indo-Pakistani war of 1965 closed off a huge area of the Himalaya and Karakoram; and Nepal was closed to expeditions from 1964. Then, in 1968 news came through that Nepal was allowing climbers in again. In Europe, America, and Japan a new generation of mountaineers welcomed this chance to start out afresh – to attempt some of the summits previously considered almost impossible. They were also thrilled at the prospect of attempting new routes up the 8,000 meter giants – of trying some of the biggest, previously unimaginable, mountain faces on earth.

1970
ANNAPURNA SOUTH FACE
HASTON & WHILLANS

Waiting at the front of the queue was a 34-year-old British ex-army-officer called Chris Bonington. He and his wife Wendy had just moved to Manchester and were staying with their friends Nick and Carolyn Estcourt. "We arrived intending to stay for a few days until we had found a furnished flat, and ended by staying for two months, sleeping on their living-room floor with our eighteen-month-old son. By some miracle we did not get on each others' nerves – certainly a fine test of compatibility for any expedition."

It was on the wall of this living-room that they projected a slide of the 3,000-meter-high South Face of Annapurna, "and gazed and gazed – excited, then frightened." Several years earlier Bonington had taken part in the first ascents of two seven-thousanders – Nuptse and Annapurna II; this was decidedly bigger, steeper, and higher, with all the potential difficulties of extreme altitude. It was irresistible!

The nucleus of the team was Bonington, Estcourt, and Martin Boysen – a genial, laconic Biology teacher famous for his occasional bursts of temper and his natural genius at rock climbing. Next, Bonington invited Dougal Haston, whom he had met two years earlier while photographing the Eiger Direct, and Mick Burke who had been with him to meet the summit party in the blizzard. He also asked Ian Clough, with whom he had climbed the original Eigerwand route himself; Mike Thompson, an old friend from Sandhurst, came as food organizer. As the project snowballed into a major expedition requiring serious funding, Tom Frost, the famous Yosemite pioneer, was invited to keep the American media sweet. For deputy leader, Bonington chose his old mentor and alpine partner, Don Whillans, a pugnacious plumber-turned-climbing-celebrity famous for his ability to sink vast quantities of beer whist delivering pithy one-liners; he was also an extremely shrewd and capable mountaineer.

Over 3,000 meters high and finishing on an 8,000-meter summit, the South Face of Annapurna was in 1970 one of the hardest climbs that had ever been attempted. Bonington's British-American team followed a continuously difficult line up the left hand buttress. The huge reddish rock band near the top was turned on the left, but still gave several hundred meters of very hard climbing.

TEAM OF ALL TALENTS

It was an impressive assembly of big personalities with big climbing talents; and Bonington ran it on the lines of John Hunt's 1953 Everest expedition, leading from the front, juggling alternating pairs of climbers in the lead. The difference was that the South Face of Annapurna was much harder and much steeper than anything on the "normal" route up Everest.

Most of the team were in their late twenties, new to the Himalaya. For them it must have been a fantastic adventure just to trek up the gorge of the Modi Khola into the huge basin of the Annapurna Sanctuary. Deputy Leader Whillans was waiting when they arrived at base camp and pronounced, "It's going to be difficult, but I think it'll go all right."

The book Bonington subsequently wrote about the expedition, complete with diary excerpts and radio transcripts, is an interesting psychological study. Right from the start there seems to have been a

Left and Below
Martin Boysen (below) learned his climbing on the sandstone outcrops of southern England. In 1970 it was he who led one of the most spectacular pitches on Annapurna's South Face (left) tackling overhanging ice near the top of the Ice Ridge. The immense Rockband looms above.

feeling that the wily old fox, Whillans, and his taciturn young accomplice, Dougal Haston, were hogging the limelight, earmarked for the summit. Yet it was Martin Boysen who led one of the key sections, climbing vertical and overhanging ice at about 6,500 meters; Mick Burke and Tom Frost who cracked the key pitches through the Rockband at 7,500 meters, pulling off what was probably harder climbing than had ever been achieved before at that altitude. Above all, what shines through the occasional bickering is the sense of a team working together to pull off a fantastic new climb up a beautiful natural line – a bit like the Walker Spur but three times as big.

TRAGEDY AT THE ELEVENTH HOUR

They climbed it by laying siege to the mountain, fixing a lifeline of ropes all the way to Camp VI above the Rockband. Everyone, assisted by Sherpas on the lower section, took turns at carrying loads up the ropes. The siege went on for weeks and towards the end, as Bonington put it, they "drove themselves beyond the point of exhaustion." Plagued by bad weather in the final stages, Haston and Whillans spent nearly two weeks sitting it out at Camp VI, surviving on minimal rations, before pushing on to make a seventh camp, from where they set off on their summit bid, ploughing through cloud and snow to complete the first ascent of the South Face.

The monsoon was approaching fast and warmer temperatures were making the mountain more dangerous by the day. On the way down, Whillans said to Bonington, "You want to get everyone off the mountain as quickly as possible. It's falling apart. The whole place feels hostile somehow." Prescient words. Two days later, as the last climbers were coming down, stripping the camps, a huge ice tower collapsed, killing Ian Clough instantly. He had been passing through a dangerous zone where people always hur-

ried – the sort of risk almost unavoidable on a big Himalayan climb. For several weeks they had got away with it and then, on the last day, Clough was unlucky. Not for the last time, a triumphant Bonington expedition was soured by the loss of an old friend.

MAKALU WEST PILLAR
SEIGNEUR AND MELLET

Chris Bonington wasn't the only mountain impresario making news in the Himalaya in 1970. In Pakistan, Dr Herrligkoffer returned to Nanga Parbat, the mountain whose first ascent he had organized in 1953. This time he chose the gigantic Rupal Face, not as technically difficult as Annapurna's South Face, but considerably bigger – probably the biggest mountain face on earth. This expedition also ended in tragedy, when the young Tyrolean Reinhold Messner climbed solo from the top camp only to find his brother, Günther, following him. They reached the summit late in the day and ended up bivouacking in the open at nearly 8,000 meters before making a desperate escape down the far side of the mountain, unable to reverse

their steps from the way up. Günther Messner died in an avalanche during the descent.

Like Hermann Buhl before him, Reinhold Messner found Herrligkoffer aloof, autocratic, and litigious. The precise details of his solo summit bid and unauthorized traverse of the mountain remain contentious and relations amongst the surviving team members are still fraught.

Not so the French national team which tackled the world's fifth highest mountain, Makalu, in 1971. It was French climbers who had made the first ascent from the northwest, sixteen years earlier. Now they turned to the West Pillar which forms such a striking silhouette when you look from Everest, twelve miles away.

The leader was Robert Paragot. In 1959 he had taken part in the first ascent of Jannu – a stunningly beautiful, difficult peak near Kangchenjunga. On Makalu it was the same story: crack team of top French alpinists, equipped with the finest gear, working very hard to pull off a huge, demanding climb. The difference, twelve years on, was that they were attempting something much harder.

Makalu is the fifth highest mountain in the world and the crux of the West Pillar was a huge rockband

Above
The world's fifth highest mountain, Makalu, seen from the south, with the West Pillar profiled on the left.

Above

In this view from the summit of Everest, the world's third highest mountain, Kangchenjunga, dominates the distant eastern horizon, while the fifth highest, Makalu, towers just 12 miles away. It was first climbed in 1955 by a French expedition, following the Northwest Ridge which faces the camera. Now, in 1971, French climbers turned to the much harder West Pillar, profiled on the right.

well above 7,000 meters, where the team had to contend with rock climbing at Grade V and A2 (the second artificial grade). To contend with this level of difficulty, all the eleven climbers used oxygen for sleeping at the high camps; they also relied on oxygen for the final summit push. Much of the hard climbing was led and fixed by Bernard Mellet and Yannick Seigneur, a tall, blond, supremely confident man who lived up to his surname (translating as "Lord"). They were obviously good climbers, but on a project like this, mere technical proficiency is not enough. You need staying power. You need to keep going, week after week, maintaining momentum. You have to avoid getting ill. And you have to have that ruthless, competitive spark, so that, when the big day comes, you are prepared to stick your neck out, beyond all possibility of help, cut loose from the safety line of fixed ropes, and go for the top.

Seigneur and Mellet did that on 22 May, climbing on oxygen. At 8,040 meters they reached the point where the West Pillar merges with the Southeast Ridge, which had been climbed recently by a Japanese team. An old fixed rope helped them over one particularly difficult cliff and, at 5 pm, they stood on the 8,463 meters summit of Makalu.

KARAKORAM WONDERLAND

Amongst all the vast, sprawling mountain ranges of Central Asia, the most spectacular must be the Karakoram – the jagged watershed between the Indus river, which flows south to the Arabian Sea, and the Shaksgam which is soaked up in the sands of the Takla Makhan desert to the north.

Under the British Raj this region was incorporated into the extended province of Kashmir. During Partition in 1947, all of northwest Kashmir, including most of the Karakoram range, opted to join Pakistan. So the great giants such as Broad Peak, Hidden Peak, and K2 came under the control of the Pakistan government in Islamabad. During the Sixties, virtually the whole region was banned to foreign mountaineers and it was only in the mid Seventies – after President Nixon had brokered an uneasy truce between Pakistan and India – that the Karakoram opened up again.

As in Nepal, foreigners flocked to attempt new routes up the great eight-thousanders, with K2 being the most prestigious – and elusive – prize. But for real explorers the most exciting prospect was the vast wealth of peaks on which no-one had ever set foot.

Far Left
Wanda Rutkiewicz – the most forceful female high altitude climber the world has seen. In 1992 her single-mindedness finally got the better of her when she insisted on bivouacking, alone, near the summit of Kangchenjunga. She was never seen again.

Left
Martin Boysen leading the Fissure Boysen on the Trango Tower. It was here, in 1975, that he suffered the nightmare of a jammed knee.

1975
GASHERBRUM III
WANDA RUTKIEWICZ

During the Seventies and Eighties, few mountaineering nations equalled the record of the Poles. Regarding their record enviously, we in western Europe used to joke that they did so well because even the most spartan, dangerous, mountain climb was preferable to their life under the communist regime in Warsaw. They were certainly phenomenally tough. And they were good team players – men and women. Amongst Polish women climbers, the best known and most glamorous was Wanda Rutkiewicz.

In 1975 she led an expedition to attempt Gasherbrum III. Although not quite 8,000 meters, it does top the 26,000-foot mark. Its summit pyramid rises from a snow plateau immediately to the west of the slightly higher Gasherbrum II, which was being attempted the same year by a Polish men's expedition. To cope with the astronomical cost of hiring porters for the 100-mile approach march, the two teams collaborated, sharing a common base camp, and – at least initially – following the same route up the lower spur of Gasherbrum II.

The plan was for an all-women team to complete the ascent of Gasherbrum III. In the event two men joined the summit bid – Krysztof Zdzitowiecki and

Janusz Onyskiewicz, a future Polish cabinet minister and husband of the British climber Alison Chadwick, who with Wanda Rutkiewicz made the summit team up to four. The final pyramid gave a typical high altitude fight, with cold dry powder snow plastered onto dubious rock – "like swimming up a mountain of sugar," as Alison Chadwick put it. After a ten-hour climb from the top camp, the four of them stood on top of Gasherbrum III. Since 1964 it had been the highest unclimbed summit in the world. It was also the highest to have had its first ascent made by women.

1979
THE TRANGO TOWER
ANTHOINE, BOYSEN, BROWN, HOWELLS, CURRAN, AND RILEY

Ever since Martin Conway led his 1892 expedition up the Baltoro Glacier, every visiting expedition, with its long column of Balti porters, had gazed up at the stupendous granite towers which throng the lower reaches of the glacier, like clusters of gothic pinnacles. When Joe Brown came this way in 1959 with Ian McNaught-Davis, to make the first ascent of the Mustagh Tower, the two men were particularly taken by a striking monolith called the Trango Tower and vowed to return one day to climb it.

Right
The team which returned to victory on the Trango Tower in 1976: left to right – Malcolm Howells, Martin Boysen, Joe Brown, and Mo Anthoine, photographed by Tony Riley.

Below
The view which entranced Joe Brown in 1959. Trango Tower appears behind Great Trango (right) which was first climbed in 1977 by the crack American team of Galen Rowell, Dennis Hennek, Jim Morrisey, Kim Schmitz, and John Roskelley.

Sixteen years later they did just that. The expedition was organized by Brown's friend Mo Anthoine and the team included his friend Bill Barker, plus one of the stars of the Annapurna South Face team, Martin Boysen. After endless frustrating delays with flights to the remote outpost of Skardu, followed by tedious strikes by the Balti porters, they eventually reached a base camp beneath the Trango Tower, with barely two weeks left to find a feasible route and attempt to climb it.

The route involved the inevitable long approach up purgatorial scree slopes, then a long snow and rock gully to a shoulder, from where the final 700 meters of the tower reared up vertically – a giant, high altitude version of Europe's famous Aiguille des Drus.

Now the climbing was fun – steep, technical, and absorbing, with a growing panorama over the greatest mountain range on earth. The team took turns to lead, fixing ropes as they went. By the fourth day, Martin Boysen was pushing up a horribly overhanging crack, hoping desperately that things would ease above and give them a chance at the summit. To protect the pitch all he had was a single six-and-half-inch "bong" – an ultra-wide steel piton.

The climbing was brutal, even for someone of Boysen's ability. "Americans would call it an off-width crack; I called it something else. I was conscious of the total lack of protection, yet I had to keep the bong until it was absolutely essential. At eighty feet it was." He hammered in the bong, then shouted down to Mo Anthoine to watch the rope carefully as he launched himself up a final overhanging bulge, above which the angle relented. "I eased my knee gently into the crack, flexed it and move up. But then, when I tried to repeat the move, I found that my knee was stuck."

He was trapped on an overhanging cliff, several feet above his one piece of protection and ninety feet above his belayer, Mo Anthoine. Frantic to get in some kind of anchor, he pulled up the bolt kit on the rope and tried drilling a hole in the blank granite beside the crack. Famously impractical, he shouted down, "What the hell do I do with all these bits and pieces." Anthoine shouted instructions, but Boysen ended up dropping the drill, then collapsing "limp and defeated."

Hanging from his jammed knee, he contemplated death. "I choked out a single sob, the distillation of my despair. I would never again see my daughter Katie, my wife Maggie; never smell the warmth of love and life. ... Three hours slipped by and, as the sun moved lower, I was certain of my coming death. ... But surely there had to be a way out." Then he suddenly remembered the knifeblade piton in his pocket. He tried to cut away the

breeches around his knee, but the blade wouldn't bite, so he pounded it with his hammer to create a serrated edge.

"With this I cut and gouged the thick material within the crack with my last strength. Blood began to ooze thickly from my thigh, my fingers and knuckles were skinned, but I continued cutting without regard. At last I felt the material give. ... I started easing at the knee, but it would not budge .... [but then] my knee slipped out, and I half fell, half slid, to the bong – which held. I shouted to Mo and with great effort worked out how to descend. Mo waited. When I reached him, bloody and wrecked, but alive, I burst into the sweetest tears."

1976

That narrow escape from death marked the end of the attempt. Time, money, and patience had run out. But a year later they were back, marshalled by the ever-enthusiastic Anthoine, who had driven 5,000 miles all the way from North Wales with a new set of climbing gear and supplies, determined to climb the Trango Tower.

This time Anthoine, Boysen, and Brown were joined by Malcolm Howells, with Jim Curran and Tony Riley filming the climb. After many days'

Above
Kim Schmitz at Camp 3 on Gaurisankar. His companion, John Roskelley, spent nearly a week working from this cramped hovel.

Left
The curved white summit of the holy mountain, Gaurisankar, is on the left. The American-Nepalese route climbed straight up the huge sunlit precipice of the West Face "harder than the North Face of the Eiger." In the autumn Peter Boardman's team climbed the knife edge ridge on the right, leading to the lower South Summit (see overleaf).

work, they reached the previous year's highpoint – the Fissure Boysen. There were no jammed knees, but higher up, in the final chimneys of their route they found even harder climbing – a hideous frozen crack where the only way of making progress was hammering pitons insecurely between ice and rock. Then yet another groove almost halted them in their cracks. Witnessing the final race to the summit, late in the afternoon, Tony Riley wrote:

"Suddenly there was a shout and a cloud of snow containing Martin came plummeting out into space. One of the pegs he had been moving on had come out of the loose rock, and he stripped a couple more before he stopped. He gave full vent to his frustration, and Mo and I cowered under his verbal onslaught, each of us pretending he was probably talking to the other. After he'd finished with us, he directed his attention to the mountain, and hanging free on his rope with his fists above his head, he directed a flow of invective at the Trango Tower. Trango was finally conquered as a result of being shouted at by Martin."

An hour or two later they were on the summit of the Trango Tower and the following day Joe Brown and Malcolm Howells repeated the final pitches to the top, to complete an outstanding first ascent.

Right
Dorje Sherpa arriving at the precarious eyrie of Camp 3, en route for the summit.

A year after Mo Anthoine's team climbed Trango Tower, the Americans climbed its bigger, more sprawling neighbour, Great Trango. One of them, John Roskelley, was so taken with the area that he returned in 1979 to climb another stunning spire across the glacier, called Uli Biaho Tower.

Roskelley was one of the most prolific, successful Himalayan climbers in the world and his record of first ascents has hardly been equalled. Born and bred in Spokane, in the American Northwest, he had a reputation – rather like Britain's Don Whillans – for outspoken abrasiveness. He certainly didn't suffer fools gladly and he couldn't abide dithering. And he was unquestionably ambitious. But, as with any really fine mountaineer, his boldness was tempered by wily caution: he was – and still is – a natural survivor.

He also has a very long-suffering wife. The 1979 Uli Biaho trip followed back-to-back from the previous expedition, that spring, to Nepal, where Roskelley led nearly every pitch up a route 3,000 meters high. The mountain was Gaurishankar. Its two summits, Gauri, a manifestation of Shiva, and Shankar, "the Golden Goddess," are sacred to the Hindus who live in the lower valleys of Nepal. For a long time, before Everest was identified and measured, British surveyors thought it might be the highest mountain in the world; in fact, its higher north summit is 7,134 meters above sea level.

When the leader, Al Read, got permission for a joint American-Nepalese expedition to Gaurishankar, he hoped that they might be able to sneak round the back. But the Chinese were adamant that no-one could trespass into Tibet. So the climbers had to make do with the dauntingly steep West Face. Given the comparative inexperience of some of the Nepalese Sherpa climbers, they had to fix ropes nearly the whole way. Camp III was a single tent lashed uncomfortably to the not-very-flat top of a half-meter square boulder. From this hovel, Roskelley and Kim Schmitz spent four days fixing ropes up increasingly difficult terrain above. Then on 8 May 1979, Roskelley and Dorje Sherpa left the final fixed rope. So far, Roskelley had already found the climbing harder than anything on the North Face of the Eiger. Now he had to contend with one final rock overhang, which he climbed with aid at A3 standard, dangling in stirrups over a 3,000-meter drop.

The improbable West Ridge of Gaurisankar. Here on the first ascent in 1979, Tim Leach is only halfway up the 4 kilometres ridge "sated by days of constant tension on ice towers and cornices," as Peter Boardman put it. The red tent of Fawlty Towers camp can just be seen perched far below him, to the left.

At 5 pm that night Roskelley radioed base from Camp III to report that he and Dorje had just returned safely from higher summit – Shankar, the Golden Goddess.

It was a bit of a blow for the British climber, Peter Boardman, who had already committed to attempting the mountain that autumn. Undeterred, the British-Nepalese expedition set off bravely that October along the 3 kilometers of wildly corniced, knife-edged snow ridge to the right of the face, which the Americans had given a very wide berth. At least it was a new route, and at least it led to another virgin summit, Gauri. But it was a massive undertaking for a small team, as John Barry confided to his diary:

"We hardly seem to make any progress, even after an exhausting day's work. ... Don't like to be defeatist, but I think it is perhaps more than four men can chew. Suspect Pete feels the same." But they slogged on, meter by meter, moving sections of fixed rope as they progressed slowly higher. On the final push, Peter Boardman and Tim Leach from Britain, with the Swiss climber Guy Neidhardt and Pemba Sherpa from Nepal, committed themselves to some very steep climbing and a final bivouac in the bitter cold of November, just below the summit. The following morning, as Boardman subsequently related in *Sacred Summits*, they were rewarded:

"We were sated by days of constant tension on ice towers and cornices, and the safety of this gentle summit was a relief. We could stand without fear. We arrived on the ridge a few feet below the top, smiling. We had agreed not to touch the highest snows a long time before. Pemba attached a small Nepalese flag to his ice axe. For want of many words, we shook hands, our defences down."

1976
TWO ON CHANGABANG WEST WALL
BOARDMAN AND TASKER

Today Peter Boardman's body sits frozen above 8,000 meters on the Northeast Ridge of Everest, where he died in 1982. His companion – whose body has never been found – was Joe Tasker. Together they formed an extraordinary partnership and their most extraordinary climb was the first one they did together – the West Wall of Changabang.

Changabang is a shark's tooth of pale granite piercing the rim of the Nanda Devi Sanctuary, in India. It is the quintessential summit of dreams and, like so many of those summits, it was first climbed by a

team led by Chris Bonington. But the story didn't end there, in 1974. On the contrary, the sumptuous photos of Bonington, Scott and the rest of the Indo-British team just sent other climbers into a frenzy of desire. Bonington's team had, sensibly, found the easiest way up the mountain, round the back. The real challenge – crying out for someone to tackle it – was the soaring precipice of the West Wall – 1,700 meters of vertiginous rock, smeared with plaques and runnels of ice.

Like those early explorers, Kellas, Shipton and Tilman, Joe Tasker liked the idea of tackling a Himalayan peak with a team of just two climbers. In 1975 he did that up a new route on Dunagiri, with Dick Renshaw. It was probably the hardest thing ever climbed at that altitude by a two-man team, but they intended it merely as a warm-up for the West Wall of Changabang, on the other side of the glacier. In the event, they barely got off Dunagiri alive, and Renshaw suffered frostbite on several fingertips. Tasker escaped injury and was soon planning to return the following autumn to try Changabang. With his old partner Renshaw out of action, he asked Peter Boardman to join him. The rest, as they say, is history.

As far as Tasker could tell, there wasn't a single ledge worth the name on the West Wall of Changabang, so he envisaged sleeping in hammocks. To prepare for this sub-zero torture, he and Boardman spent several nights with their hammocks slung in a cold meat store in Manchester. However, when the time came, on Changabang, hammocks proved too miserable even for the notoriously ascetic Tasker. In the end they managed to make a kind of advance base, half-way up the wall, out of a tiny tent hung on a

Below and Right
Changabang – one of the most entrancing summits in the whole Himalaya. Chris Bonington's Indo-British expedition made the first ascent in 1974, by a route round the back. Two years later curly-haired Joe Tasker and Peter Boardman (below) arrived as an unsupported two-man team to attempt the soaring West Wall, profiled on the left, taking Himalayan climbing into a new dimension.

minute ledge cut from the ice. They took turns to sleep on the outside, where the tent fabric bulged out over a drop of a thousand meters.

As they had expected, the climbing was continuously steep and difficult, utterly absorbing, and beautiful. This was like doing one of the hardest, most technical climbs in the Alps, but on a peak of nearly 7,000 meters, far from any outside help or possibility of rescue. To climb the wall "alpine-style" in a single push seemed impossible, so they worked away at it, day by day, week by week, using several hundred feet of fixed rope to travel up and down. When the ropes were all used up, they had to lift them and move them higher up the wall.

And then, as in any big siege, there came the point where they just had to go for it – climbing continuously for three days, bivouacking where they could, and reaching the summit of Changabang. It took another three days, abseiling ropelength by ropelength, fighting to maintain concentration and avoid making a careless mistake, before they were safely down.

There have been harder climbs done since, even on the same mountain, and in much faster time, without the use of any fixed ropes. But at the time, in the bitterly cold shadow of that west face late in the autumn of 1976, Boardman and Tasker really did redefine what was possible in Himalayan climbing. They pointed the way to the future.

1978
EVEREST REDEFINED
HABELER & MESSNER

Reinhold Messner was born in the Dolomites in 1944. From the age of seven or eight he climbed almost every day. By his early twenties he had climbed virtually all the hard routes in the Dolomites, many of them solo, others with his brother Günther, whom he was to lose on Nanga Parbat in 1970. He never completely got over the death of his brother, and seems to have sought solace by driving himself even harder in the mountains, particularly on the highest mountains of all. Not for him the thrill of finding ways up previously unclimbed peaks. No – for Messner "first ascent" was less about what you climbed than how you climbed. He did, of course, find new routes up several of the 8,000 meter peaks, including Nanga Parbat, Manaslu and Gasherbrum I. But what really excited him about Gasherbrum I was the fact that he climbed it, in 1975, with just one companion – Peter Habeler – in just three days up and down.

The Northwest Face of Gasherbrum I was no Changabang West Wall, but it was still quite steep terrain. And it led to one of the highest summits in the world. Nothing like this had been done before on an eight-thousander. Three years later the same Tyrolean pair broke another record when they reached the summit of Everest without

Below
Reinhold Messner (left) and Peter Habeler kitted it out by the *Star Trek* wardrobe department for their historic oxygenless ascent of Everest in 1978. Two years later Messner returned to Everest, this time climbing from the north side (below left) to make the first solo ascent of the mountain.

Everest in the Eighties was an exciting place to be, but of all the new feats perhaps the most dazzling was the ascent made by two Swiss climbers, Erhard Loretan and Jean Troillet in 1986. It wasn't strictly a "first" ascent. The initial couloir had been climbed by a Japanese team six years earlier; the upper couloir had been climbed by Tom Hornbein and Willi Unsoeld during their epic traverse of the mountain in 1963; but the way the Swiss men climbed this very direct line up Everest's North Face was completely innovative.

They did a commando raid, dashing up and down the mountain before it really had time to notice that they were there – and before their bodies had time to suffer too drastically the deleterious effects of oxygen deprivation. The principle was revolutionary but blindingly obvious. Tents and sleeping bags weigh a lot and and slow you down. So why not leave them behind, rest in the day when it is warm, and climb by night?

Which is precisely what they did, leaving advance base (5,870 m) at 10 pm on 28 August 1986. By 11 am the next morning they were lounging in the sun, brewing cups of tea, at 7,800 meters. At 9 pm, well rested, they set off again into the Hornbein Couloir. It was bitterly cold and at one hard section they had to stop and wait for four hours, huddled together, before continuing at first light, to reach the summit of Everest at 1 pm the next day. They spent ninety happy minutes lounging on top of the world, then set off down, using good snow conditions to slide most of the way down the 3,000 meters North Face in just five hours. Total time for the round trip – 40.5 hours!

SWISS EXPRESS

7 am 19 August 1979. My brother Philip and I were standing on a domed snow summit above the valley of Hunza. We had just made the first ascent of a very minor, unnamed peak and much bigger summits crowded the horizon in every direction. Eighty miles to the northwest we could just see the huge pyramid of K2. The triple turrets of the Ogre were fifty miles away. Closer, just two valleys away, I suddenly noticed a mountain called Spantik. What drew the eye was its immense north face. The following year I spotted it again, at sunrise, this time from another mountain. Again I wondered about that great pillar, glowing pink in the morning sunshine. Must be granite, I thought. What an amazing climb it would be.

Above
Swiss ace Erhard Loretan triumphant on the summit of Everest in 1986, photographed by Jean Troillet. The two men took just 40 hours to climb up and down the North Face, finishing up the Hornbein Couloir (dark vertical gash just right of summit in picture opposite). They took the vaso-dilatory drug Adalat to improve circulation. What would the committee say if this were an Olympic sport?

supplementary oxygen. For Habeler that was enough. For Messner it was simply a prelude to the next step – to return to Everest in 1980 and, now that China had changed its foreign policy and was allowing foreigners into Tibet, to climb Everest's North Face – without any oxygen and completely alone.

Encouraged by Messner's example, other climbers inevitably followed. It was rather like Roger Bannister running the four-minute mile for the first time: once one person has broken the barrier, others think, "well maybe I could do that too." Thus, in 1984 a small Australian team climbed a new route up Everest's North Face, also without oxygen. In 1988 I achieved something similar on the East Face, with a four man American-Canadian-British team, parallel to another route which a previous American team had climbed the previous year, in 1983.

That unclimbed face of Spantik remained one of many hypothetical objectives – a remote possibility that might be realized if I could ever find the time and money and courage. Then, one day in 1987, the man in whose Islington house I rented a room, Victor Saunders, said, "Do you want to come to Spantik? I've got a permit for this summer." Suddenly that hypothetical pillar became a very exciting reality; but then, a few days later, Victor announced firmly, "Sorry, I've changed my mind: Fowler's coming."

Mick Fowler, a tax inspector by trade, was probably the finest young mountaineer in Britain. With Saunders he had pioneered some of the hardest mixed rock and ice climbs in Scotland. He had also climbed one of the hardest routes ever attempted in the Andes. He was in a completely different league. After a brief sulk, I had to admit, reluctantly, that a Fowler-Saunders rope stood a far better chance of success than a Venables-Saunders rope, on what looked as though it would be one of the hardest things ever attempted in the Karakoram.

It was. They spent July getting to base camp and acclimatizing by exploring the lower part of the spur – a huge gully followed by a long snow arête, leading to a final snow shelf beneath the pillar proper. As always in the Karakoram, the blazing sun was the big enemy, as Saunders explained in his book *Elusive Summits*:

"'The sun rose, having no alternative, into the nothing new.'"

"Whasat?" said Mick.

"Beckett. It's from *Murphy*," I said. "The next sentence is, 'Murphy sat out of it.' Which seems like a good idea. Let's get the tent up. What d'you think."

So they sheltered in their tiny nylon dome, whiling away the hot hours. Then reconnoitred a little further before descending to base camp to rest amongst the flower meadows beside the glacier. Then came back up again, only to be pinned down by snowfall for several days, before descending again, empty-handed, to base. It is a frustrating game, familiar to anyone who has been on a Himalayan expedition, which requires infinite patience and self-deluding optimism. But sit it out, and in the end, at the eleventh hour, you might just get lucky. They had almost given up hope when the weather brightened on 5 August. So they headed back up the glacier and the next morning set off in the dark to climb back up to their camp on the hanging glacier. On 7 August the climbing started in earnest.

LET THE CLIMBING BEGIN!

For 100 meters they climbed back up ropes they had left fixed earlier. Then they headed into a vertical sea of almost featureless rock slabs. What they had taken for runnels of firm ice turned out to be shifting rivulets of powder snow. As for that amenable golden granite, on close inspection it proved not to be granite at all, but smooth, compact metamorphosed limestone – marble.

Up this unhelpful tilted desert of marble they teetered and shovelled their way, grateful for the few cracks that took nuts or pitons for protection. That night they found a projecting rock flake where they could sit side by side. The next day, Fowler was delighted to find a dyke of dark shale, reminiscent of the rotten sea cliffs of Devon where he had pioneered so many new climbs. Saunders was less delighted:

"I removed the runners by pulling out the flakes they hung around. The next pitch was the continuation of the shale dyke. it formed a vertical black stripe, a shallow chimney of loose flakes, frozen in a glaze of

Left
Victor Saunders on the snow arête, approaching the real meat of the climb – the huge marble Golden Pillar of Spantik.

Right
Five days and several burnt bridges later, Fowler leads the final corner past a huge "ice ear" which hung right over the top of the route. "The snow-filled cracks offered no security. When Mick finished it looked as if the corner had been hoovered, and when I followed I knew I had been watching a virtuoso display."

clear ice. ... Very precariously I tiptoed upwards on the points of my crampons. After half-an-hour's work, I was looking down ninety feet of free-hanging rope."

On the third day on the pillar Saunders found himself leading another chimney. "It was just wide enough to squeeze an arm and leg into, and it was very, very steep." At the top he tried hammering a peg into a shallow crack, but one tweak of his hand and it fell out. So he simply anchored himself by bracing his body across the chimney. As Fowler led on up the next pitch, Saunders realized, "that this was an irreversible section. No safe pegs equals no abseil. In bad weather we could not climb down. We might not be able to even in good weather."

It was the ultimate climber's nightmare – the final burnt bridge. And it was now getting dark. Thirty meters above Saunders, Fowler at last found a belay – a single nut in crack. From that one piece of aluminium they suspended themselves for the night, Fowler hanging in his harness, Saunders standing in his rucksack, the bivouac tent draped over their heads.

"By the time the morning had taken the razor's edge off the cold, we had succeeded in reaching the final line of ramps. The situation was superb."

After all the trials and delays and doubts and anxious moments, the top of the Golden Pillar was in sight. The route finished with a vertical open-book corner. "The snow-filled cracks offered no security. ... When Mick finished it looked as if the corner had been hoovered ... and when I followed I knew I had been watching a virtuoso display." After that, they just had to climb out past a giant "Ice Ear" hanging out over the corner and pitch their tiny tent on top of the Ear. For the first time in five days they were on flat ground.

The next morning, 10 August, they set off at sunrise to wade through powder snow to the actual summit of Spantik, 7,027 meters above sea level. Only on the 11th did they start the descent, spending another night on the plateau before lowering themselves down onto a parallel spur to the Golden Pillar which would take them back to the base of the north face where they had started. To safeguard Fowler over the overhanging cornice onto the top of the spur, Saunders had to dig a huge hole in the plateau, brace himself in the hole as he paid out the rope. Fowler then belayed him from below, and at the end of one final long day they were safely back in base camp.

UNTOUCHED SUMMITS OF THE NEW WORLD

Left and Below

Fred Beckey (left) in heroic pose above the Garibaldi Meadows, British Columbia. Now still going strong in his eighties, he has probably made more mountain first ascents than anyone else in the world. His greatest early successes were in Alaska, where he made first ascents of Devil's Thumb and, with the famous Eiger veteran Heinrich Harrer, Mt Deborah and Mt Hunter (below right).

IN NOVEMBER 1996 I WAS SPEAKING AT THE annual gathering of the American Alpine Club in New York. At midday I escaped the conference room to find some food, and found myself in a Manhattan sandwich bar chatting with another speaker at the conference – a grizzled, wiry, septuagenarian with a stubbly face as deeply furrowed as the canyons of the wild west. Dreaming aloud in a gravely croak, he reeled off names of all the Himalayan mountains and valleys he still hoped to visit. Then, pulling out a wad of grubby greenbacks, he paid for my lunch and beer.

It was only afterwards that it dawned on me just how privileged I had been. This was the man who never had any money – the original climbing bum, the mountain tramp who had spent fifty years on the road, scrounging and making do, living out of the back of cars, stashing odds and ends of possessions at friends' houses all over the USA. This was also the man who had made more first ascents than anyone

else in America. In fact he had probably made more first ascents, than anyone, anywhere in the world. And he had bought me lunch!

Fred Beckey was born in Düsseldorf in 1923. When he was three his parents emigrated to America and settled in Seattle. From an early age Fred and his younger brother Helmey were drawn to the wild mountains of the Northwest – particularly their local North Cascades. At their parents' request, they joined the Boy Scouts and later the august local climbing club, The Mountaineers, but they quickly outgrew their tutors, forging home-made gear out of scrap metal to pioneer new climbs.

One of their earliest first ascents, in 1940, was of the appropriately named Forbidden Peak. No one knows how many first ascents Fred Beckey has subsequently made in the North Cascades of Oregon; they run into hundreds, and now, in his eighties, he is still exploring new ground. However, Beckey is known best for what he achieved in the bigger, wilder mountains north of Oregon. Ambitious from the start, in 1942 he and Helmey made the second ascent of Mount Waddington. This difficult, complex peak in the remote Coastal Ranges of British Columbia had been one of the great mountaineering prizes, first climbed in 1936 by Bill House and Fritz Wiessner. Wiessner was one of the best climbers in the world and almost reached the top of K2 in 1938. Now a couple of unknown young lads from Seattle had repeated his greatest climb.

Perhaps it was the common German origin, but Wiessner and Beckey hit it off, and Wiessner suggested that the brothers head further north to the BC/Alaska border to try a spectacular ice-smeared tower called the Devil's Thumb. In 1946, they did it, making the first ascent of the hardest peak yet to be climbed in Alaska.

By now Fred Beckey had graduated from the University of Washington, but had opted for part time work as a truck driver, leaving plenty of free time for climbing and starting work on the first of several historical guidebooks to the mountains of Oregon and Washington. In 1954 he returned to Alaska to pull off an extraordinary hat trick. First, with the German climber Henry Meybohm and a team from the University of Alaska, he climbed a new route up the North Peak of Denali. Not content with that, Beckey and Meybohm then went on to the untrodden Mount Deborah. On the way, in Fairbanks, they bumped into Heinrich Harrer, the Austrian veteran of the first ascent of the Eigerwand, so they invited him along too.

DEBORAH & HUNTER
BECKEY, HARRER, & MEYBOHM

Deborah, with its summit of 3,822 meters, had none of the giant scale and altitude of Denali; but it was still a big, wild, heavily glaciated mountain, with similar problems of cold and bad weather. The final half-mile section along the South Ridge gave the party the most sensational ice climbing they had ever done, climbing up and down of a series of cornices – overhanging turrets of snow and ice – with no possibility of evasion on the steep slopes below. The German-American threesome then travelled back to the Denali region to make the first ascent of the immense Mount Hunter.

With that kind of record, Fred Beckey would have seemed an obvious choice for the American Everest expedition of 1963, but he was turned down and, instead of achieving glory in Nepal followed by a hero's welcome at the White House, he consoled himself by making 26 first ascents in Oregon. He just wasn't the kind of biddable team player they were looking for. Now, still climbing in his eighties, he remains an awkward, cussed original with a legacy of exploration probably unequalled in the history of mountaineering.

BATKIN, SARTHOUS, & TERRAY ET AL

Heinrich Harrer wasn't the only foreigner to come sniffing around the unclimbed peaks of Alaska. Ten years after Harrer's ascent of Deborah, the great French climber who made the second ascent of the Eigerwand – Lionel Terray – flew in with a team of crack climbers. The plan was to attempt the Himalayan-scale South Face of Denali; but first Terray wanted a virgin summit.

Inspiration came from the self-appointed authority on Alaska's mountains, Bradford Washburn. Not only had Washburn made several first ascents himself – one whilst on honeymoon with his wife Barbara – but he also kept, at his Museum of Science in Washington, an unrivalled collection of large format aerial photographs of Alaska. He was one of the great landscape photographers of the twentieth century and his stunning black-and-white studies have nurtured the

imaginations of generations of aspiring pioneers. In 1964 he tempted Terray with his photo of Mount Huntingdon. It was dwarfed by Denali, but still a proud, independent mountain – a supremely elegant pyramid with a gorgeous ribbon of snow up its Northwest Ridge that Terray found irresistible.

Things had changed in Alaska since the pioneering days of Cook and Stuck. Now you just flew in by light ski-plane, bypassing all the mosquito-ridden tundra, to land directly on the pristine glacier beneath your mountain. But the actual climb up Huntingdon was no pushover. Even in May, the temperature rarely rose above –20° c. Operating from a snow cave at its base, Terray's team fixed ropes nearly all the way up the Northwest Ridge. Then on the ninth day, climbing the third big step on the ridge, traversing over the huge precipice of the West Face, Terray slipped and shot down a slope of bare ice, out of sight of his belayer, Jacques Soubis. Feeling a tug on the rope, Soubis assumed it was time for him to come up, but a moment later the rope was whipped from him and he felt himself tugged towards the abyss. By sheer chance, Sylvain Sarthou and Jacques Batkin had just tied the end of Terray's thin trail rope to a snow picket. This 5.5 mm line saved the lives of Soubis and Terray; but Terray fractured his elbow in the fall.

Convalescing back at base, Terray mused impatiently, "I must be an idiot. Why did I choose a mountain like this to climb at forty-three. At least in the Himalaya at base camp we could walk with our feet in grass." But the veteran of the Eiger, Annapurna and Makalu wasn't to be held back for long. Six days after the accident he announced that he would go back, pulling himself one-handed up 2,300 meters of fixed rope, to join the rest of the team pushing for the summit. Two days later, on 25 May, the advance team of Sarthou and Batkin reached the summit. Terray and the others followed a day later. Their warm-up for Denali had proved one of the hardest climbs of their lives and they contented themselves with this magnificent summit of Huntingdon, leaving the South Face of Denali for another great European alpinist – Riccardo Cassin.

TERRAY ET AL

The year after he climbed Huntingdon, Lionel Terray died in a rock climbing accident in the Massif de Vercors, near Grenoble. It seemed almost unbelievable that such a vibrant, apparently indestructible, life should end so abruptly. Between the Annapurna expedition of 1950 and his death in 1965, Terray led a

The photo by Bradford Washburn which fired up Lionel Terray to visit Alaska in 1964. The great ice steps of Mt Huntingdon's Northwest Ridge seem to float above the dark abyss on the left. The huge West Face on the right has provided stunning challenges for subsequent generations of climbers.

TAULLIRAJU ALPINE STYLE

When Terray's team made the first ascent of Taulliraju, it was assumed that a full-scale siege, with fixed ropes, was the only way to tackle such a hard six-thousander. By the Seventies, helped by more sophisticated gear, climbers were treating the Andean faces and ridges as super-alpine climbs, often getting up and down the mountain in two or three days, sometimes a single day. In 1982, on their first ever climb outside Europe, Mick Fowler and Chris Watts (pictured below) climbed a stupendous new route up the Southwest Face of Taulliraju, taking just their two 50 meters climbing ropes, a few pegs, nuts and ice screws, sleeping bags and enough food for a few days. At that stage it was probably the hardest climb that had ever been done in Peru.

Left
"Never, perhaps, in the whole history of mountaineering had the ascent of a peak been such sheer hard work." Lionel Terray's assessment of the first ascent of Taulliraju in 1964.

Below Left
This recent picture by Marko Prezelj shows the American climber Steve House dwarfed by Taulliraju's typically Peruvian ice structures.

Below Right
Chris Watts climbing up under an immense ice stalactite on the first ascent of the Southwest Buttress in 1982.

hectic life, roaming the globe, leading expeditions back-to-back, as well as regular guiding work in the Alps and filming. He had a huge appetite for new experience and was particularly enchanted by Peru.

Virtually all the big Andean peaks were still unclimbed in the Fifties. Unlike the great Himalayan peaks, the Andes could usually be reached within a few days of the road and in the easy-going atmosphere of Latin America, visiting mountaineers were also spared the excruciating bureaucratic hurdles and financial obstacles which Asian officials love to erect along the Himalayan path. The Andes were also considerably lower than the biggest Himalayan peaks. But they were no pushover. Close to the Equator, the snow here seems to stick to unbelievably steep faces. On the ridges, it forms surreal towers, cupolas, minarets and gargoyles – fantastic protuberances which seem to

defy gravity. These snow formations, dazzling above the dry tawny grass of the altiplano and brilliant turquoise glacial lakes, are a fantastic challenge.

Terray led several expeditions to Peru, where his most spectacular climbs were in the Cordillera Blanca, near Huaraz. Here he made first ascents of both summits of Chacaraju. The other outstanding first ascent was Taulliraju, climbed just a few days after Chacaraju Oeste, in 1956. First the team fixed three hundred meters of rope to attain the crest of the North Ridge. They rested at base camp, then returned on 17 August, reaching their former highpoint at 9:00 am. In his autobiography, *Conquistadors of the Useless*, Terray describes what happened next.

"The floury powder lay at an angle of over 60 degrees. Once a section gave way, but fortunately I was held on the rope by Sennelier after a fall of thirty feet. Each rope's length took over an hour, and it was not until three o'clock that we emerged from an ice overhang back onto the crest of the ridge, at the foot of a superb slab of granite fully a hundred feet high." Sennelier led this pitch and fixed a rope on it for the following day.

They bivouacked, then climbed on the next day, with the whole team – Maurice Davaille, Claude Gaudin, Raymond Jenny, Robert Sennelier, Pierre Souriac and Lionel Terray – reaching the summit at 2:00 pm. "More than fourteen hours climbing had been necessary to surmount 200 meters. Never, perhaps, in the whole history of mountaineering, had the ascent of a peak been such sheer hard work."

1974
CERRO TORRE – STORM-TOSSED TOWER OF PATAGONIA
FERRARI

Cerro Torre is the epitome of inaccessibility, the ultimate fantasy mountain – a soaring spire of smooth vertical granite, towering above the Patagonian ice cap, blasted by the malevolent westerlies which come screaming out of the Pacific Ocean. When they are cold, those winds plaster the tower with monstrous encrustations of white rime, stuck like icing to the rock. The actual summit is encased in a gigantic bulbous rime mushroom, which changes shape from day to day. And when the temperature rises, huge chunks of the mushroom collapse, crashing down on the walls below.

Over the last sixty years many, many climbers have frittered away days, weeks and months. waiting fruitlessly at the foot of the tower. They have come from all over the world, but the long saga of Cerro Torre's disputed first ascent is almost entirely an Italian story. It is a tragic-comic story, rich in human failing, with real heroes and villains.

The man at the heart of the story, Cesare Maestri, was in his youth a very fine rock climber, famous for his audacious solo ascents of some of the hardest climbs in the Dolomites. Then, in 1959, he returned triumphant from Argentina with the news that he had climbed the seemingly impossible Cerro Torre. Fellow mountaineers hailed his brilliant achievement; Lionel Terray called it "the greatest climbing feat of all time".

However, there was one mountaineer, Carlo Mauri, who voiced doubts. Mauri was a fine climber. He had accompanied the great Bonatti to the summit of Gasherbrum IV in 1957 and in 1958 he had attempted Cerro Torre himself, defeated by a combination of extreme technical difficulty and atrocious conditions. His team had tried the mountain from the great ice cap to the west, via a saddle which they called the Col of Hope. Maestri, by contrast, claimed to have climbed the mountain from the north, by what he called, less humbly, the Col of Conquest.

Maestri's problem was that he claimed to have climbed the upper face from the Col of Conquest in phenomenally fast time, whilst giving only the most vague details about how he had actually climbed it. His reports were inconsistent, with bivouac sites being marked in varying places on different photos. Over the years – nearly fifty now – since the claimed ascent,

his accounts have become steadily more vague and contradictory. Apologists like to put that down to the extreme stress he suffered on the climb. As for the improbability of his pulling off something so extremely hard, in such fast time, in 1959 – they attribute that to one of those rare surges of the human spirit, where a genius pulls out all the stops to achieve something almost superhuman.

But that isn't good enough. If you claim a landmark historic achievement, you make damned sure that you give a detailed coherent account of it. In fact, every detail is so clearly burned into your memory that you can't help giving a clear account. Maestri tried to fob people off with waffle. He also played the sympathy card, milking tragedy: his one companion on the climb, Toni Egger, was killed – according to Maestri, on the descent from the summit. The only other potential witness, an Argentine called Cesarino Fava, was down at base camp during the purported ascent.

In recent years, using equipment far superior to Maestri's, other teams have climbed to the Col of Conquest and beyond. In 2006 the an Argentine climber, Rolando Gabirotti, succeeded in climbing all the way up the Northwest Face to the summit, with Ermanno Salvaterra and Alessandro Beltrami. Like many others before them, they did not find a trace of Maestri's 1959 attempt – not a scrap of rope or a piton or a bolt – beyond a gear cache well short of the Col of Conquest.

Right
Scenes from Cerro Torre, clockwise from top left: Stefan Siegrist climbing past the Helmet during a rare repeat of the Ferrari Route; Maestri's infamous petrol-powered compressor still bolted to the granite near the top of the Southeast Face after 38 years; a rare sight of the Torre – Maestri's "Compressor Route" faces the camera, his earlier purported North Face route silhouetted on the right; the legendry gaucho, Don Guerra, brings climbers' supplies to base camp.

Left

Cerro Torre's elusive ice-cake summit is on the extreme right, with Maestri's purported North Face route dropping steeply left to the Col of Conquest. Dominating the background is the summit of Fitzroy, first climbed by Lionel Terray's team in 1952.

It now seems to be proved fairly conclusively that Cesare Maestri, like Cook on Denali, was a fibber. In fact, he seemed to confirm his own guilt by returning to Cerro Torre in 1970 to climb a different route, up the Southeast Face. This time, climbing almost entirely on rock, he took a diesel-powered compressor to power an electric drill. On some sections he created entire ladders of bolts beside perfectly good natural cracks. This time he did definitely get to within a whisker of the summit – the proof is there – but he did it by desecrating a beautiful mountain.

Carlo Mauri was also back on Cerro Torre in 1970, again trying from the Col of Hope. His team got quite close to the top but were defeated by the usual atrocious Patagonian conditions. One member of the team, Casimiro Ferrari, vowed to go back.

The chance came in 1974. It was the hundredth anniversary of the founding of the Lecco section of the Club Alpino Italiano and Ferrari wanted his group, the Lecco Spiders, to do something fitting to celebrate the anniversary. What better than to make the first undisputed ascent of a mountain etched deep in the Italian consciousness – Cerro Torre.

It took a whole month for the team of twelve to travel to Patagonia, reach the roadhead and then ferry supplies up to their windswept base on the Ice-cap. Then, in the southern midsummer, on Christmas Eve, they started work in earnest, carrying supplies up to the Col of Hope on the West Ridge. Above the Col the ridge rose in a series of snow mushrooms, leading eventually to a huge overhanging cornice called the Helmet, where they dug the tents in for Camp 5 on 26 December. Ferrari was thrilled:

"We were only 450 meters below the summit of Cerro Torre. In those three days the members of the team had pulled together in conditions which were quite unlike any they had ever known in the European Alps."

"A last pitch up flaky ice gullies and we emerged on the flat summit of Cerro Torre." Here Stefan Siegrist repeats that final crux of the Ferrari Route on a day of rare Patagonian sunshine, with Fitzroy looking in the background.

But then, all that excited hope was knocked out of them: "As the wind began to pound us again, we soon came to realize that merely to resist for any length of time would require new moral fibre and reserves of strength ... In the end we were stationary for three weeks ... and all the time anxiety and nervous tension grew in inverse proportion to the limited stocks of food. ... The temptation to abandoned the camp on the Helmet and retreat to the relative luxury of the lower camps was immense, but we knew well enough that only by sitting it out until the next fine spell would we have the remotest chance of success."

In the end, supplies got so low that seven of the men volunteered nobly to go down, to conserve food for a reduced summit team. On 6 January the weather cleared for a few hours, allowing them to climb onto the summit wall, before another storm drove them back to the tents for five more days.

On 13 January the weather improved again, but "it was far from perfect. The final cone of Cerro Torre stood out starkly clear at one moment, and at the next vanished from sight, obliterated by clouds chased round it by a violent wind. Our bemused eyes

had just time to pick out a route when the whole mountain slid out of sight and left us groping and bewildered." But they knew roughly where they were going, and continued groping through a ghostly vertical landscape of weird ice towers. They reached a huge rock corner – "an appalling icy cenotaph, many hundred of feet high, Luckily a more amenable line appeared –a bulging ice chimney." The chimney disappeared into monstrous cornices and, standing in stirrups, they had to edge out rightwards to a hidden ledge, from where they climbed up to a shoulder, then another icy chimney to the Foresummit.

"We were now a mere 30 meters form the top of Cerro Torre. A brief clearance in the mist revealed it, riding the seething clouds like a battleship on a stormy sea. Once glance at the final overhangs was enough to shatter any hope of a direct assault, but there was another possibility. ... In the end we had to traverse for three full pitches, with a ten meter descent on the way, before we rounded the last rib and saw the way open. A last steep pitch up flaky ice gullies and we emerged on to the flat summit of Cerro Torre. it was 5.45 pm on January 13 1974."

Right
Nowadays tour operators run popular climbing trips to Vinson Massif. The first ascent in 1966 was a very different affair, requiring complex logistical support from the U.S. Navy.

Far Left
Stefan Siegrist using modern ice
gear to climb the Helmet, on Cerro
Torre's Ferrari Route, first climbed
in 1974.

Left
The rarely seen west side of Cerro
Torre. The summit is in the top right
corner of the picture, with the Ferrari
route ascending from the right, and
the deep gash of Maestri's Col of
Conquest on the left.

At last, after sixteen years of false attempts and controversy, this most elusive summit had been reached through extraordinary teamwork and perseverance. Today, the first ascent of Cerro Torre is attributed, not to Cesare Maestri, but to Mario Conti, Daniele Chiappa, Giuseppe Negri and their expedition leader, Casimiro Ferrari.

NICK CLENCH ET AL

Not far south from Cerro Torre the South American continent breaks up into the archipelago of Tierra del Fuego, culminating in the bleak wave-lashed promontory of Cape Horn. There the Andes forms a big submarine loop, resurfacing sporadically in islands like South Georgia, before forming the curved finger of the Antarctic Peninsula.

Antarctica is a mountaineer's paradise. We have barely touched the potential. Thousands upon thousands of summits remain untouched, for the simple reason that they are extremely remote and very expensive to get to. The highest summit on the continent was only first identified in 1957, by the pilot of a US naval plane, and was named Vinson, after Carl Vinson, a Georgia congressman who was keen supporter of funding Antarctic research and exploration. The range which Vinson dominates was actually discovered much earlier, in 1934, when Lincoln Ellsworth and Herbert Hollick-Kenyon made the first aerial crossing of Antarctica. The mountains which they named Sentinel Range are also known as the Ellsworth Mountains, and they rise above the immense Ronne Iceshelf, 750 miles from the South Pole.

It required serious lobbying by the American Alpine Club to find the kind of money needed to get to these incredibly remote mountains, but after three years an expedition was organized, for the austral summer of 1966–7, co-sponsored by *National Geographic*, with the US Navy and National Science Foundation providing vital support in the field. Prominent amongst the climbers was Peter Schoening from Seattle, who in 1953 had saved six companions from plummeting to

Left
Antarctica's Ellsworth Mountains are some of the most vast and remote on Earth. The aeroplane in the lower picture gives some idea of the scale. It used to reach Vinson Massif in 1983, when Chris Bonington accompanied Dick Bass in his bid to become first person to climb all seven continental summits.

their deaths on the world's second highest peak, K2, with an extremely rapid, skilful ice axe belay. He had gone on to make the first ascent of one of Pakistan's other 8,000 meters peaks, Hidden Peak, in 1958, reaching the summit with Nicholas Clinch, who was a natural choice as leader of the American Antarctic Mountaineering Expedition.

The project took on a competitive edge with rumours that Woodrow Wilson Sayre was planning to beat the official expedition by flying to Antarctica in a private plane. This was the same man who had recently trespassed into Chinese-occupied Tibet to make an illegal attempt on Everest; on this occasion there were problems with the plane and he never reached the frozen continent.

Not so the official team, for whom all went smoothly, with naval transport from New Zealand to the American Antarctic base at McMurdo Sound, then a long flight over the continent in a Hercules fitted for ski landing. After placing three camps, Barry Corbet, John Evans, Bill Long and Pete Schoening reached the 4897 meters summit of Vinson on December 17. All the other climbers reach the summit on the following two days. The expedition also made first ascents of several other summits in the range, including the second highest in Antarctica, Mount Tyree.

SEVEN SUMMITS

Vinson was the last of the seven continental summits to be climbed. In order of height, they are:

ASIA – EVEREST 8,850 M
First ascent Edmund Hillary, Tenzing Norgay,
29 MAY 1953

SOUTH AMERICA – ACONCAGUA 6,960 M
First ascent: Matthias Zurbriggen,
14 JANUARY 1897

NORTH AMERICA – DENALI (MCKINLEY) 6,194 M
Harry Karstens, Walter Harper, Robert Tatum, Hudson Stuck,
7 APRIL 1913

AFRICA – KILIMANJARO 5,895 M
First ascent: Hans Meyer, Ludwig Purtscheller,
1889

EUROPE – ELBRUZ 5,642 M
F Crauford Grove, Frank Gardiner, Horace Walker, Peter Knubel,
28 JULY 1874

ANTARCTICA – VINSON 4,897 M
Barry Corbet, John Evans, Bill Long, Pete Schoening,
DECEMBER 17 1966

AUSTRALASIA – CARSTENSZ PYRAMID 4,884 M
Heinrich Harrer, Russel Kippax, Albert Huizenga, Phil Temple,
13 FEBRUARY 1962

The first person to climb all Seven Summits, in 1986, was the Canadian Pat Morrow (above) who chartered a special flight to Antarctica with the ace pilot Giles Kershaw, founding Adventure Network to fund this extremely expensive summer holiday. Adventure Network now runs regular summer flights between Chile and the ice runway at Patriot Hills, enabling hundred of people to climb Vinson. Morrow's claim to the Seven Summits depends on how you define the Australian continent: Carstensz, in Irian Jaya, is the highest summit in greater Australasia; Kosciuzko (2,228 m) is the highest in Australia proper and was, in the words of the Texan oil tycoon Dick Bass, "a walk in the park" when he climbed it to complete his alternative Seven Summits in 1985.

FREE ROCK

Left
Stephanie Bodet leading pitch 4 of Surveiller et Punir – one of the classic modern routes in the Verdon Gorge, Provence. Devoid of natural protection, the rock has been equipped with drilled bolts.

Below
The great rock climbing master from a different era – Joe Brown, probably Britain's finest ever pioneer of new climbs, photographed here in his heyday on the sea cliffs of Anglesey.

IN 1953 THE WORLD APPLAUDED AS A BRITISH/ Commonwealth expedition finally achieved what others had been trying for over thirty years – the first ascent of the highest mountain on the planet. Edmund Hillary and Tenzing Norgay became global household names. But there were lots of British climbers who weren't remotely interested in Everest, even though they would soon prove to be some of the finest mountaineers the world has ever seen. Many of them hadn't even been abroad; yet at home, on the small cliffs of this small island, they were starting a revolution in rock climbing, pushing at barriers, exploring where no-one had dared to go before. They were a bold, talented bunch, but there was one acknowledged master – a brave visionary with an eye for a good line – who seemed to be in a class of his own. He was called Joe Brown.

JOE BROWN

Joe Brown was born in Manchester in 1930, the youngest of seven children. His father – a jobbing builder struggling to find work during the Depression – had to take jobs at sea and died from an accident on board ship when Joe was only eight months old. As soon as Joe was old enough to be looked after by his brothers and sisters, his mother went out to work as a cleaner. During the Blitz, when Joe was ten, the house was badly damaged by bombs. It was a tough upbringing and by the age of fourteen he had left school to work for a builder. He earned ten shillings a week, and most of it went to his mother. But his boss did give him £3 10 shillings towards his first pair of boots, so that he could spend free Sundays out in the Peak District

That high ridge of moorland between the grimy industrial conurbations of Manchester and Sheffield was the great escape. From a very young age Brown loved roaming in the open country and soon discovered the gritstone edges. These escarpments rarely exceed 12 meters in height but the millstone grit – a hard, rough sandstone rippled and weathered into the most beautiful sculptural forms – is some of the finest climbing rock in the world. It's a tough training ground and in the Forties protection in its famous cracks was virtually non-existent.

The predominantly working-class climbers of the era enjoyed a special camaraderie, getting up at dawn to catch buses out to the edges, often sleeping rough, bivouacking in caves; and climbing with panache, dressed in baggy old clothes and plimsolls. Ropes were rudimentary and Brown famously made do with a length of old sash cord that his mother thought was no longer strong enough for a washing line.

The washing line is just part of the legend that has built up around Joe Brown, along with motor bike rides to the Lake District and North Wales, the first meeting with his only undisputed equal, Don Whillans, the founding of the elite Rock and Ice Club ... It was a very different world from today's scene, with its indoor climbing walls, sophisticated equipment and safety inspectors lurking round every corner. Brown and his friends had no formal training, few guidebooks, virtually no equipment. They learned

Right
Rhodesian climber Rustie Baillie making a 1965 repeat of Cenotaph Corner for John Cleare's and Tony Smythe's evocative book Rock Climbers in Action in Snowdonia.

Far Right
Another famous Cleare photo – this one of Pete Crew re-staging his most famous Cloggy climb: "Everyone knew it as the Master's Wall, and if Joe had climbed it that would have been the perfect name. But it seemed presumptuous, so we opted for the Great Wall."

STEEL AND ALLOY – THE PROTECTION RACKET

When Joe Brown succeeded on his second attempt in climbing Cenotaph Corner, he managed with just two pitons. Thereafter, he always tried to limit himself to a minimum of two pitons per pitch on any new route, ideally none. British climbers, limited to comparatively small, precious cliffs, have an ingrained antipathy to hammering steel into cracks, whether it is for direct artificial aid, or just to clip the rope in for protection.

The British ethic was never as rigorous – nor the technical standards as high – as on the famous Elbesandstein towers of Germany; but the outlook has always been similar. In the Fifties, pioneers like Brown and Whillans made do with the occasional piton. Other than that, they draped slings over rock spikes or threaded them round natural chockstones, often carrying a pocket-full of pebbles specifically for that purpose.

Then in the Sixties climbers began making artificial chockstones out of machine nuts, with the sharp threads drilled out to avoid cutting the rope slings threaded through them. Eventually someone had the bright idea of manufacturing "nuts" specifically for climbing, using new light alloys, instead of heavy steel. By the Seventies, when I started climbing, alloy nuts had become standard equipment, allowing even quite cowardly leaders to attempt hard routes with reasonable impunity. Nowadays there is a fantastic range of sophisticated nuts, as well as camming devices that can even hold in upside-down cracks.

as they went along, and within two years Brown was leading the hardest climbs around. At the age of seventeen he led his first new route, at a gritstone cliff called the Roaches. At the end of the following year, 1948, he top-roped Suicide Wall, the hardest climb in North Wales.

CENOTAPH CORNER
JOE BROWN

Like Cecil Slingsby and Frank Botterill in an earlier generation, Brown demonstrated what could be achieved by translating the skills learned on the small gritstone outcrops to the biggest mountain cliffs. In 1949 he made his first visit to Snowdonia's most hallowed cliff, Cloggy. Soon he had climbed all the existing routes and was putting up his own. In the summer of 1952, alone, he climbed six new routes on Cloggy. But his most famous, accessible, creations that summer were on a cliff called Dinas Cromlech, a short walk up the hillside from the Llanberis Pass road.

The first big success here, with Don Whillans, was Cemetery Gates. The theme fitted with an earlier route on the same cliff called Ivy Sepulchre and the route still waiting to be done – the 35-meter-high, plum vertical, uncompromising book corner which an earlier explorer, Menlove Edwards, had already named Cenotaph Corner.

Of all Brown's Welsh creations, this is the one every aspiring climber wants to lead. Nowadays, with bombproof alloy nuts and camming devices slotted into perfect clean rock every few feet, it is a very safe proposition. When Brown first attempted it, in December 1948, just after his Suicide Wall coup, he had to borrow five pitons, which he hammered in for protection, and to rest on while he scraped sodden clods of grass from the crack. Thirty meters up, struggling to place his last piton at the crux of the climb, he dropped his hammer. His second, Wilf White was hit a glancing blow on the head (helmets didn't appear until the Sixties), but once Brown had descended to collect the hammer, a groggy White encouraged him back up again. However, once he had placed all five pegs, Brown could go no further.

In 1952 he settled the score. Undaunted by cold wet weather, he wore socks over his plimsolls for extra friction on the greasy rock. As usual, he was extremely tenacious. Years of hard labouring had given him steel muscles. And his short frame was wonderfully lithe. One of his party pieces was to fold his feet behind his head then walk around on his hands. On the crag, this suppleness allowed him to keep his feet high, conserving energy and allowing him to reach for improbably distant holds. This time on Cenotaph Corner, worming his way out of the niche, he ended up splayed horizontal, parallel to the ground, until he could reach up and complete the most famous rock climb in Snowdonia.

1962
GREAT WALL
PETE CREW

By 1960 there was young pretender snapping at the heels of Joe Brown. He was called Pete Crew and he was making a name for himself on the blankest walls of North Wales. The great outstanding challenge was a particularly steep smooth section of the East Buttress of Cloggy. Brown had managed to get forty feet up it, leaving a piton hammered into a crack, its eye winking provocatively at anyone who dared to try and go higher. Crew tried in 1960, but failed. Two years later, working on a new guidebook to Cloggy, he thought he would try again, as it would be such a coup to get this new route into the book.

High on the wall he could see a thin crack which might offer protection; but he was determined to emulate Brown's rule of two pitons maximum. So he abseiled down from above, cleaning mud and grass from the crack, and pre-inserting five tiny pebble chockstones. Even with the chocks in place, when the big day came, and he was teetering on the sharp end of the rope, fifty feet above his last protection, he found himself running out of strength and facing a potential hundred-foot fall.

"By now I was getting desperate as I could not take much weight off my arms ... Just above the split chock the crack almost closed, so I spent the next ten minutes working a sling into this constriction using a peg. By this time I was absolutely shattered: I was half standing on the sling on the split chock and using a layback hold with one hand. [Then at last I could] sit in the sling and have a smoke ..." Nicotine and a good rest did the trick, and soon he had completed the route.

Crew concluded, "Everyone knew it as the Master's Wall, and if Joe had climbed it that would have been the perfect name. But it seemed presumptuous, so we opted for the Great Wall." As one of his contemporaries put it, "Only Crew had the determination and faith in his own ability to challenge the mystique of Joe Brown that was embodied in that wall." Now Great Wall has had hundreds of ascents. With modern precision climbing shoes and vastly improved protection, it is a reasonable undertaking for a competent leader at E4 grade, with a good nerve; and it goes completely free, with no rest points. But anyone with even a glimmer of imagination can see what a great first ascent it was in 1962.

SEASIDE ADVENTURES

Much of Britain's best climbing is on sea cliffs. The Himalayan explorer Tom Longstaff made one of the first coast climbs in North Devon, Scrattling Crack, in the late nineteenth century; Mummery climbed at Dover, and Aleister Crowley climbed the chalk cliffs of Beachy Head. In more recent times, in the 1960s, the North Wales set, hungry for new challenges, began to explore the hitherto untouched sea cliffs of Anglesey. But the most exciting sea cliffs were in the far north of Scotland and it was a doctor from Ullapool, Tom Patey, who delighted in exploring them.

Right
Sea cliff climbing remains a very British speciality. Here, in 1996, after several days effort, George Smith, belayed by Adam Wainwright, finally succeeds in climbing the top pitch of their new route, The Mad Brown, on the Anglesey sea cliffs. The "mosaic of loose rock," the difficulty of retreat, the awesome strenuosity make it a typical George Smith creation. Here he is seen in his favourite position – hanging upside down from uniquely inventive handholds.

Left
Tom Patey following Rustie Baillie, removing gear from the cussed overhanging chimney, during the first ascent of the Old Man of Hoy. Patey's death on another sea stack, four years later, was a tragic loss to mountaineering.

The Old Man of Hoy is actually quite young. Seventeenth-century maps show this point as a mere headland. By the early nineteenth century, paintings depicted a sea stack with two legs, hence the name, but one of the legs was subsequently washed away by a North Atlantic storm, leaving stack in its present form. The 1966 route follows more or less the line between sun and shade, facing the camera. Sandy Ogilvie is seen (right) approaching the crux chimney seen on page 148 and (far left) abseiling back down from the summit. Unseen in these pictures is his client on the climb, Ranulph Fiennes – training for the North Face of the Eiger.

1966
OLD MAN OF HOY
BAILLIE, BONINGTON, & PATEY

Patey's particular speciality was sea stacks – free-standing, wave-washed pillars with real unclimbed summits – Britain's answer to the desert towers of the American West. One stack in particular, caught his fancy. He phoned up Chris Bonington and assured him, "It's the finest rock pinnacle in the British Isles – three hundred feet high, as slender as Nelson's Column, sheer on every side and unclimbed."

"It" was the sandstone stack called the Old Man of Hoy, in the Orkney Islands and Bonington took the bait instantly, getting the sleeper train up to Inverness to meet the Doctor. In Orkney they joined the third member of the team, the Rhodesian climber Rustie Baillie. After a typical Patey night, filled with singing and malt whisky, they made a late start on the first day, climbing up the easier lower steps to a big ledge. Then Baillie traversed right, high above the sea, to battle laboriously up an overhanging chimney, bashing in pitons for aid, before abseiling back down as it got dark. The second day they got a little higher, but still had to return to base. Only on the third day did they reach the final corner, as Bonington recalled in his book *The Next Horizon*: "'It's my turn to lead,' I stated firmly and started up." And, true to form, after the desperate chimney below, Bonington bagged the best pitch of the whole climb – a soaring corner, plentifully endowed with good holds in the layered red sandstone, leading straight to a unique, previously untrodden, summit.

1973
AMERICA
DARBYSHIRE & LITTLEJOHN

In recent years, Scottish sea cliff climbing has taken off. Back in the Sixties and Seventies, Patey was almost a lone voice in the wilderness. However, down south, on the Devon-Cornwall peninsula, a climber who was probably the greatest pioneer of new routes since Joe Brown was discovering a treasure trove of untouched rock.

Like Joe Brown, Pat Littlejohn was more or less self-taught, operating initially out of the mainstream, unaware of just how good he was. Right from the start, as a teenager, living in Exeter, he was keen to explore new cliffs, find new routes. Climb-

Above
Pat Littlejohn started making first ascents as a teenager in the late Sixties and is still pioneering bold new routes all over the world.

Right
"Ahead the arête soars dramatically over an abyss filled with sea noise." Here, with advantage of modern protection gear, a climber repeats the final pitch of Littlejohn's America.

Left
Littlejohn leading one of is more recent sea cliff routes, Fay, on one of the spectacular rock fins at Lower Sharpnose Point.

ing with the slightly older Pete Biven and Frank Cannings, he quickly made his mark on the limestone cliffs at Berry Head, with routes such as Moonraker and Dreadnought, the latter working its way outrageously over the lip of a huge cave, with the waves crashing far below.

His greatest early partnership was with a young teacher-turned-thatcher called Keith Darbyshire. Together they explored mile after mile of the Devon and Cornwall coastline. It was a terrible loss when Darbyshire was killed (probably due to a breaking hold) in 1974. Before his untimely death he had accompanied Littlejohn on some stunning first ascents. Some of their boldest adventures were on the dark, north-facing cliff called Carn Gowla – a place every bit as forbidding, in its own way, as the North Face of the Eiger. In 1973, they climbed a route called Mausoleum – "a reverential ascent through massive features fashioned in cold hard stone." But what really drew Littlejohn's eye was the prow to its left – "a rib thrust out defiantly, crowned by a dome-shaped bastion of merciless verticality."

With its difficult approach, dodging the Atlantic waves, cut off from the land, it felt very committing. Recalling a phrase from a poem by Cliff Fishwick – "nothing but sea, America, and night" – Littlejohn decided that if he climbed this prow he would call it America.

Later that year he and Darbyshire were back, dodging the waves. "Beneath it, hyper tense and committed, we pull on damp trousers and damp PAs (rock shoes) after crossing the boulder in the nick of time". Half way up the second pitch the clouds began to drizzle, forcing Littlejohn to resort to aid: "I'm on a lichenous knife-edge trying to fathom a blank section. Raindrops clinch it and I stand on a peg and get moving. Ahead the arête soars dramatically over an abyss filled with sea-noise". At lease that overhanging arête was sheltered: "The rain hangs well away and is forgotten ... I proceed rapidly aloft, soon arriving at the bizarre focal point of this pitch – a prodigious raven's nest in which Keith later squats to rest. Above this, exposure and difficulty reach a climax, then a ledge is gained and solid protection cushions the impact of the steep final wall."

America is just one of scores of routes Littlejohn has pioneered around Britain's coastline. Not to mention all his first ascents in the Alps, and Russia, and the Grand Canyon, and Nepal, and Ethiopia and Kenya and ... the list is still being added to every year.

PETE LIVESEY

By tradition British climbers eschew competition. Or at least they are not overtly competitive: it's not quite the done thing. So they were a little shocked when a Yorkshireman who had tired of caving and athletics, turned his sportsman's drive to rock climbing. Whereas others had for years been quietly climbing harder new routes, endeavouring to eliminate "aid points" and climb totally free at the highest standards, the Yorkshire upstart, Pete Livesey, had no inhibitions about publishing his achievements. He was also amongst the first to train specifically for rock climbing, strengthening fingers, and cultivating endurance on the new indoor climbing wall at Leeds University.

And his achievements were phenomenal. Like Joe Brown, he inscribed his signature on Snowdonia's most public cliff, Dinas Cromlech, making the first ascent of the minutely-wrinkled right wall of Cenotaph Corner in 1974. That was soon eclipsed by an even harder route up the same wall, climbed by Livesey's protégé, an even more talented Yorkshireman called Ron Fawcett.

But enough of our little island. What was interesting was the way Livesey, Fawcett, and their friends

Left
Definitely *not* Pete Livesey: one of
the new breed of slickly dressed
continental free-climbers enjoying
Verdon's awesome verticality.
Christophe Bucher on Ecographie.

Above
Slightly closer to Livesey's Seventies
style: Chris Harris, reluctant to leave
the security of one of the very few
fixed pitons on The Fish, wonders
how on earth he is going to get
across the next section of seemingly
blank rock.

Jill Lawrence and John Sheard traveled to the eastern
Alps, to join locals like Nicho Mailänder making
first free ascents of some of the big limestone walls
which had previously relied on artificial aid. They
were also amongst the first outsiders to visit the
French domain of the Gorge du Verdon. As Livesey
put it, after his first visit to the gorge, 30 miles
north of St Tropez, "This place has primeval
grandeur, without a doubt, but everywhere drifts the
herbaceous fragrance of Provence."

GORGE DE VERDON

These sun bleached cliffs, 600 meters high, were a far
cry from the dank, mossy little crags of Wales. French
climbers only began to explore them in the Sixties.
Apart from a few well known training grounds, the
emphasis in France had always been on alpinism – on
the big mountains. There had also been little interest
in free climbing for its own sake: you just got up a
route as best you could, pulling on pitons or standing
in slings in the interest of speed and efficiency. Then
in the Seventies all that began to change. In Verdon,
climbers like Jean Claude Droyer discovered the most

beautiful, wildly improbable lines up immaculate grey
limestone. Where cracks petered out, even the
smoothest looking walls were beautifully wrinkled
and knobbled, with miraculous little solution pockets
– *gouttes d'eau* – where acidic water had etched holes
in the alkaline stone.

The great thing about Jean Claude Droyer and
the other pioneers of Verdon climbing is that they
protected their routes sensitively, generally hammering in pitons at main anchors, but relying on
removable nuts or threaded slings for intermediate
"runners." (The tragedy is that France, a country with
so much of the finest climbing in Europe, has subsequently led the way in wholesale drilling to fix bolts –
a pernicious trend which is spreading all round the
world). They were brilliant climbers and their route
names reflected their Gallic panache. Who could
resist the Voie Triomphe d'Eros or the soaring Eperon Sublime, where, as one crack line peters out, a line
of tiny finger pockets leads miraculously across an
apparently blank white sheet to another crack high
above the *maquis* scrub and the Verdon river in the
deep bed of the gorge.

The magnificent monolith Poi, in the
Ndoto Mountains of northern Kenya.
The East Face is the 650-meter-high
yellow wall on the right and
Wielochowski's route started up
its right hand edge. The rock is
compact and often crumbly, with
few sound cracks for protection. It
is also sprouts profuse vegetation.
In the photo opposite Wielochowski
is above the Arboretum, leading the
plant-filled chimney which led to
the Gashole.

A FISH CALLED IGOR

At the far eastern end of the Alps, in the Dolomites, there were also new stirrings. People were dispensing with "étriers" (stirrups) and climbing completely free up classic routes such as the North Face of the Cima Grande. And they were discovering new routes, in particular on the vast acreage of limestone on the South Face of the Marmolada. Modern Times was one such new route. The other famous new climb was The Fish, discovered by the Slovak climber Igor Koller.

Unlike the classic Dolomite routes, The Fish didn't follow a really prominent crack line. It was a subtle, tenuous line, linking faint features, yet avoiding the temptation simply to drill lots of holes. The crucial pitches, above the fish-shaped niche that gives the route its name, required imaginative use of skyhooks to link passages of hard free climbing. There are sections where the protection is widely spaced, so that if the leader falls, he or she will go a long way. You have to be subtly skillful and bold. Such was the power of Koller's vision in establishing this route that it quickly attained iconic status.

1983
POI — EAST FACE
CORKHILL & WIELOCHOWSKI

Ask most people about climbing in East Africa, and they might think of Kilimanjaro, or Mount Kenya. In fact there is wealth of summits throughout the region. When the British climber Andrew Wielochowski took a teaching job in Kenya in 1978, he was immediately attracted to the mountains of the North Frontier District. He was particular excited by a monolith called Poi, on the edge of the Ndoto mountains. Although a way had been found to the summit, there were huge untouched walls waiting to be climbed.

The chance to "have a look" came when local climber, guide, builder and pilot Mark Savage was flying up to the area to build a school. Wielochowski had a ride in the plane and from the village of Korr they drove over to Poi, with locals helping them to carry three days' water up to the foot of the 650-meter-high East Face. On this first attempt they got part way up the face before being defeated by a rotten sandy crack which wouldn't take ordinary rock pitons.

Back in Nairobi Wielochowski found a shop selling some 12-inch ice pitons, which he thought might work in the rotten rock. Savage was less sure and declined the invitation to fly Wielochowski back to

the north. But eventually Wielochowski found another climber, Ron Corkhill, who was keen to have a go, and who owned a landcruiser suitable for the rough overland journey. They set off in 1983.

Once again, local tribesmen were hired to help carry water to the foot of Poi. Then Wielochowski and Corkhill climbed back up to the rotten crack, where the 12-inch ice pegs did the trick, providing a secure anchor to protect the next moves through overhangs. That evening they reached the Tree in the Niche before abseiling several ropelengths back to the base, returning the next day up the ropes.

Then things got serious. Throughout the climb protection had been sparse. Often Wielochowski only found an anchor after 50 meters, so had no intermediate running belays. Later that day, reaching a bushy ledge he called the Arboretum, he realized how committed they were. "Retreat from the Arboretum was hard to conceive – a direct abseil would have sent us spinning into space ... and have left us hanging out of contact with rock 300 meters above ground. The ramp we had crossed was Poi's version of the Eiger's 'Hinterstoisser Traverse.'"

Supremely understated, he then goes on: "We relaxed and had lunch, because not far ahead we had spotted a chimney that would take us to the next major feature, The Gas Hole." Even so, they had to traverse 45 meters without any protection to reach the chimney and continue with only minimal belays up a vertical garden of cliff-dwelling shrubs to the Gas Hole.

Wielochowski led off left, trying to evade overhanging blank walls. When the rope ran out and there was no anchor, he just untied and carried on leftwards until he realized that there was no way round. So back to the rope, to retie and reverse his moves. In the end he had to climb a very hard, steep wall directly above the Gas Hole, with virtually no protection. Then at last the difficulties eased, they rushed up four easier pitches, grabbing increasing amounts of vegetation and emerging onto the summit plateau in the late afternoon. Losing their way on the descent, they stopped to light a fire, but a thunderstorm put it out, so they had to carry on in the dark, exhausted, until they could find a dry hollow to light another fire and warm their cold shivering bodies. The following day they staggered thirstily and hungrily back to the bottom of Poi.

YOSEMITE – FILLING THE SPACES

Ever since the first ascents of the Nose and Salathé Wall in the early Sixties, the Yosemite valley has been a Mecca for rock climbers all over the world. What makes it special is the "big walls" on Half Dome and El Capitan. When the British mountaineer Doug Scott teamed up with the Tyrolean ace Peter Habeler to make an early ascent of Salathé Wall, he entitled the ensuing article, "On the Profundity Trail".

The Nose and Salathé Wall were just the first of many lines which now make the El Cap guidebook look like a very busy street map. Soon after making the second ascent of The Nose, Royal Robbins and friends tackled the overhanging expanse to its right,

North America Wall, named for the prominent black streak resembling a map of their continent. Other lines began to fill the spaces. Amongst the great 1970s pioneers, Charlie Porter created Zodiac, Mescalito and The Shield, while Jim Bridwell climbed the evocatively named Pacific Ocean Wall. These routes took aid-climbing into a new dimension, with the climber relying on rurps (minute knifeblade pitons) or "birdbeaks" tapped into hairline cracks, or swages of copper hammered into tiny hollows, or skyhooks gripping the tiniest nubbins. Day after day the climbers would entrust their weight to these tenuous attachments, inching their way up the vertical granite desert, desiccated by the Californian sun. It was a skilful game that required courage, tenacity and creative artistry.

The problem was that the rock could only take so much hooking and bashing. On the old classics such as the Nose and Salathé Wall, the continual hammering in and removing of pitons turned once-hairline cracks into gaping wounds. By the Seventies, the best climbers realized that they could now gently slot alloy wedges – nuts – into the widened cracks. When Ray Jardine invented "Friends" – adjustable camming devices, the scope for "clean" and "hammerless" protection became almost limitless. Widening cracks also increased the scope for fingers: where aid had once been the only option, it was now conceivable that people might climb completely free.

THE FREEING OF EL CAP

And so it was that, in 1988, Salathé Wall, was climbed completely free for the first time by two Wyoming cowboys, Paul Piana and Todd Skinner. They took

Right
Yosemite evolution. In 1972 the legendary wall climber, Charlie Porter, made the first ascent of Zodiac, as a predominantly "aid" climb. Thirty-one years later the Bavarian brothers, Alex and Thomas Huber, managed to climb the whole 16-pitch route free, with no artificial aid, in just 2 hours, 31 minutes. Not content with that, Alex is seen here during a repeat ascent in 2004; this time the brothers shaved 40 minutes off their record, to complete the route in 1 hour, 51 minutes, and 34 seconds.

Left
Lynn Hill was the first person to free climb The Nose, in 1993. She then went back a year later and did it again, this time in a single day. Here she is seen above the fearsome Great Roof, cruising with comparative ease up Pitch 23, the Pancake Flake. (Compare the traditional aided ascent of the same pitch on page 94).

belaying each pitch, and climbed the whole 900-meter route free in a single day.

Things had come a long way since Warren Harding spent a total of 45 days engineering his way up the route in 1957. And they just got faster and faster. In 2005, having first free climbed The Nose in four days with his wife Beth Rodden, Tommy Caldwell returned two weeks later and free-climbed it in a short day, then rushed back down to the base of El Capitan to free-climb a second route, Freerider. Total time for the two routes, 23 hours, 23 minutes!

BAVARIAN WUNDERKIND

Freerider was the creation of two German brothers who have made Yosemite their second home. Alex and Thomas Huber grew up near Munich, and from an early age they and their younger sister were taken climbing by their father. By the time they were in their teens they had climbed most of the 4,000-meter peaks in the Alps; by their twenties they were climbing in the Himalaya. In 1991 Alex decided to concentrate on pure "sport" climbing – short routes, usually no longer than 30 meters, protected by bolts, where the whole emphasis is on pure technical difficulty.

Within this totally safe medium, he developed the ability to climb at the various highest standards. Then, confident in his technical ability, he turned to the big walls of the Dolomites, the Karakoram, and Yosemite. He climbed mainly with his brother Thomas and, with their long hair and prodigiously-honed torsos, they made a photogenic pair. On Salathé Wall Alex insisted on leading every pitch himself, claiming that this was the first true free ascent (Piana and Skinner had alternated leads). It was while climbing this classic that he noticed the possibility of another free variant up the wall, which became Freerider.

In 1998 the Hubers took on North America Wall. When I met Alex a couple of years later, I asked him about how he free-climbed out of the Black Cave, 600 meters up the wall. His dark eyes gleamed with manic intensity as he enthused, "It was an amazing pitch. You can place a cam right in the back of the cave, then there is nothing apart from one angle peg that long." He held up the end joint of his index finger. "You clip the peg and after that you can't place any nuts because you have to keep climbing. It's a long way and it would be a horrible place to fall."

Horrible indeed. And yet, a few weeks later the Hubers' free version of the wall, which they called El Niño, was repeated by two English climbers. One of them, Leo Houlding, was only just eighteen.

turns to free individual pitches and spent a total of thirty days on the route. On the final overhanging headwall pitch, Piana fell repeatedly – flying into space over a drop of 900 meters – before perfecting the sequence of brutal finger jams to succeed.

The Nose followed in 1993, with the brilliant Lynn Hill managing to finger jam her way past the Great Roof, then work out an astonishing sequence of moves on the Changing Corners pitch higher up. The route took four days. The following year she returned, starting in the dark, with Steve Sutton

GAMES CLIMBERS PLAY

Left and Below
"Cracks here and there, the odd crack and lots of exposure." Conrad Anker edges out from a hanging bivouac on Rakekniven, belayed by Jon Krakauer, with the immense Antarctic ice sheet stretching to infinity.

IN 1988, WITH THE U.S. CLIMBERS ROBERT Anderson and Ed Webster, and the Canadian Paul Teare, I climbed a new route on Mount Everest. Over the last twenty years I have given hundreds of lectures about that climb. Afterwards someone nearly always asks, "What's left to do after you've climbed Everest?" The answer is that the scope is unlimited. In fact, Everest has almost become an irrelevance: its summit just happens to stand at a height where humans can barely survive. But look down and around at the myriad other mountains, escarpments, sea cliffs and canyons around the globe and there is adventure to satisfy generations of climbers. The developments in mountaineering over the last few years have been breathtaking and for those of us lucky enough to live in the rich, industrialized countries, the opportunities for comparatively cheap travel have been unprecedented.

ANKAR, KRAKAUER, & LOWE

One please that is still not cheap to get to is Antarctica. It required the full support of *National Geographic* for some of America's finest mountaineers to fly in by C-130 transport plane to land on one of the blue ice runways of Queen Maud Land, then take a smaller plane for the final 40 miles to the Fenriskjeften Peaks – a cluster of extraordinary granite pinnacles piercing the polar ice sheet.

Although all sovereign claims to Antarctica are frozen under the Antarctic Treaty, this particular slice of the frozen cake is claimed nominally by Norway. So it is appropriate that the first climbing expedition to the Fenriskjeften was a Norwegian one, which succeeded in climbing the spire of Ulvetanna. Inspired by their photos, the American team set their sights on Rakekniven – the Razor. Alex Lowe was arguably the best all-round mountaineer in the world, famous for

Fantasy spires worthy of St Exupery's
Petit Prince pierce the Antarctic ice
sheet in Queen Maud Land.

his unflagging energy and enthusiasm. With him was his friend and regular climbing partner Conrad Anker from California. Rick Ridgeway had made the third ascent of K2 a few years earlier and was here to film with Mike Graber. Gordon Wiltsie was in charge of stills and Jon Krakauer, veteran of some epic Alaskan climbs in the mid Seventies, was the wordsmith.

So – a very talented team all round. They flew in at the end of 1996, then used skis to complete the approach. They tackled the plub-vertical front face of Rakekniven. In Anker's modest words, "the climbing was standard big wall stuff – cracks here and there, the odd flake and lots of exposure. The rock varied in quality – from crumbly rock affected by the freeze thaw process to solid Yosemite quality cracks".

Climbing crumbly, flaky rock in big boots, in sub-zero temperature is actually quite hard and time-consuming. After fixing the first four pitches, they abseiled off; then returned up the ropes, sleeping on portaledges – hanging tent platforms – thereafter, to complete the fifteen pitches over four days. In a sense, they were just repeating what they had done in many other parts of the world, but what a venue this was, with the immense expanse of the ice sheet stretching all around them. Conscious of his place in the world, Anker had this to say about the summit: "We thought we had the first ascent, yet the snow petrels (a wonderful coastal bird that nests on the cliffs to avoid the predatory skua) had landed and walked all over the snowy summit. Yes, the first human ascent but not the first sentient ascent".

EXOTIC BIG WALLS, BAFFIN ISLAND

Baffin, in Arctic Canada, is the world's fifth largest island. In 1995 an American photographer called Eugene Fisher published aerial photos of the island's east coast, describing "26 fjords, some 18 to 70 miles in length, that contain some of the tallest rock walls on earth, walls that exceed even the fabled faces of Mt Thor and Asgard [Baffin's most famous peaks] ... Yosemite would count as a minor side fjord if it were located along this vertiginous coast."

These were the ultimate sea cliffs! In fact, in 1992 Conrad Anker and Jon Turk had sea-kayaked into one of the fjords to do a climb, but now that Fisher's photos were in the public domain, others quickly followed. Rather than kayak in, most teams came in the early spring, paying the local Inuit to take them in by sledge when the fjords were still frozen.

The walls rising out of the frozen fjords were colossal. One of the biggest, Polar Sun Spire, was first climbed in 1995. Nearly as big was Great Sail Peak –

ALEX LOWE

They used to say that bringing Alex Lowe on a climb was cheating, he was that good. From the vertical ice falls near his home in Montana to the biggest Himalayan faces, he was good at everything. But what really made him stand out was that he loved what was doing and had a huge appetite for life. He certainly wasn't expecting to die when he set off in the autumn of 1999 with a team planning to make the first ski descent of the South Face of Shishapangma, in Tibet, and was simply doing a recce, walking up the lower dry glacier in trainers when a huge avalanche broke loose 2,000 meters above. Lowe, Conrad Anker, and Bridges were hit with a blast of compressed air. Anker was picked up and swept behind a boulder which protected him from the full force of thousands of tons of snow traveling at 70 miles an hour. The other two were less lucky. Anker is now married to Lowe's widow Jennifer and has become father to his friend's three sons. Here Alex is seen (far left) a year before his death, using skyhooks to aid up a granite flake on the stupendous 1,500-meter wall of Great Sail Peak, Baffin Island, working from the finest hi-tec overnight accommodation (near left).

1,150 meters of vertical and overhanging granite with only the most incipient crack systems, giving many days extreme aid climbing for Alex Lowe, Jared Ogden, Gordon Wiltsie, John Catto and Greg Child in 1998. Child, who comes from Australia, is one of the best all-round mountaineers in the world and one of the best writers on the subject; he is bright and sharp and eschews fine romantic notions. He called this exercise in subzero vertical suffering Rum, Sodomy and the Lash.

Even more masochistic was the climb done the following year by Utah-based Mike Libecki – the 600 meters high Ship's Prow hanging 600 meters over the frozen ocean. The climb was audacious, but half the adventure was getting there, traveling by dog sled with local guides Jaycko Ashevak, his nine-year-old grandson Benji and Imosy Sivugat. "At feeding time, we watched the 51-strong pack devour ten seals in just minutes. The dogs consumed everything except the blubber, which is too tough for them to chew. They even crunched down the bones. Blood and guts flew everywhere while we drank tea and watched the ten-hour sunset roll across the horizon. The next afternoon, after a week or so in the sleds, we reached our destination. While I set up base camp, my Inuit friends left to go back to Clyde River. As I watched them disappear around the corner of the Ship's Prow, I was instantly slapped in the face with utter solitude and total silence."

That silence was only broken over the next few weeks by the storms, when he had to hole up in his tent. The rest of the time he was travelling up and down his ropes, pushing the route up almost continu-ously overhanging rock. He eventually reached the summit in a storm. A few days later, determined to enjoy the miraculous summit view, he jumared back up his ropes to get his reward, before stripping the ropes and heading for home.

Some people might think Libecki was a little unhinged to contemplate spending five weeks alone on an overhanging monolith in the Arctic. But often it is these extremes of experience that enhance appreciation of life. Above all, it is the wondrous con-trast that makes life all the sweeter, as Libecki acknowledges when he concludes his account in the *American Alpine Journal*:

"Within just a few days I found myself at home in a garden with ripe tomatoes and basil. I knew I had to indulge in the fresh pesto, because in just a month I would be climbing huge granite domes on the other side of the world in Madagascar's warm sunshine. Why ration passion?"

MADAGASCAR

Madagascar was another of the big wall locations which suddenly sprang in to fashion in the 1990s. Unlike the pale bald walls of the Baffin fjords, the granite of the Tsaranoro massif was weathered gold, red and burnt umber, with pockets and wrinkles and firm edges on which the smooth malleable rubber soles of modern rock shoes could smear a tenuous grip. There were possibilities here for magnificent free climbing, but because of the paucity of continu-ous cracks, the climbs relied considerably on drilled bolts for protection.

PAKISTAN

The Karakoram mountains of northern Pakistan continued to lure ambitious rock climbers hungry for huge untouched walls. After the pioneering first ascent of the Trango Tower by Mo Anthoine's British team in 1976, others soon followed, finding other lines up the tower. Further east, above a village called

Hushe, visitors were entranced by another whole wonderland of towers and spires. As always, the inter-est is not so much in what people climb, but how they climb. Let's just look at two extreme contrasts.

In 1998 the American climber Conrad Anker arrived with the Canadian Peter Croft who was renowned for his ability to sprint up hard rock climbs (for instance, in 1990 he had climbed both of the two 900 meters high El Capitan classics – The Nose and Salathé Wall – in a single 30 ½ hour day). He excelled at moving very fast over steep rock, and Anker was no slouch either. Both of them were also highly experienced mountaineers, at home amongst the glaciated mountains at high altitude. They decided on the first ascent of a 2,500 ft high rock ridge on a peak called Spanser Brakk. Traditionally, one might expect to spend a few days on a hard climb like this, at altitude, carrying bivouac gear. But Anker and Croft pared everything down to a single rope, minimal rack of rock climbing gear, one water bottle each and a few "power bars" to maintain calorie levels. Then they started running. Uphill. Climbers will understand when I write that the difficulties included pitches graded 5.11a on the American system. Laymen will just have to accept that that is very hard climbing when you are operat-ing above 5,000 meters.

Above and Right
The granite walls of Madagascar's Tsaranoro massif are one of the most exciting recent "discoveries" for western climbers. Tony Lamprecht (right) is puzzling out the sketchy moves on the 8th pitch of a 600-meter route called Manara-Potsiny.

In complete contrast, the following year, a Catalan team of three set their sights on the 1,500 meters high West Face of Amin Brakk. This was almost as big as the Eiger, but much, much steeper – more like one of the hardest artificial wall climbs Sílvia Vidal had done on El Capitan, except that most of the hard climbing here was above 5,000 meters where, each morning, before the sun swung onto the face, temperatures would be sub-zero. Not to mention the regular snowstorms which tend to sweep through the Karakoram range every few days.

Unlike Anker and Croft on their free-climbing sprint, the Catalans were in for the long haul, literally. Altogether, Pep Masip, Miquel Puigdomènech and Sílvia Vidal hauled about 500 kg of supplies (much of it water) up the face. They expected to spend 28 days on the wall and actually spent 32. Commenting on this vertical existence, Vidal wrote in the *American Alpine Journal.* "Because we're talking about a lot of days with only two partners and above all living in a very reduced communal space, good relations with your partners are very important. We only had one book, which we re-read many times, and some games that we used to pass the time in bad weather."

As for the climbing, there were several pitches of A5. That's the hardest grade of artificial climbing, where you are trusting your weight to pieces of gear so tenuous that, should a piece rip, you will probably unzip all the others below, as you fly through the air. In other words, if a piece rips at 50 meters, you face a potential fall of 100 meters. One pitch led by Vidal relied almost entirely on copperheads – blobs of soft copper on the end of wire loops, hammered into the faintest depressions in a crackless corner. There was one blank traverse, where the Catalans had to resort to drilling 27 bolts. Other than those, and the abseil anchors they used to get back down, they left nothing on the wall.

MYRIAD VIRGIN SUMMITS OF THE HIMALAYA AND BEYOND

There are still hundreds of unclimbed peaks in the main Himalayan range stretching from Kashmir in the west to Tibet and Bhutan in the east. If you add the vast tangle of farther ranges which extend east through Southeast Tibet to Sichuan and Yunnan, the number runs to thousands. Strangely, most mountaineers are creatures of predictable habit who like to stick to the well-trodden path, generally choosing to climb well-known iconic peaks, leaving the unclimbed summits alone. But there are a few adventurous types who cannot resist the lure of the unknown. One in particular, has shown a voracious appetite for seeking out new challenges. Like Pat Littlejohn, he started his climbing life on the sea cliffs of Britain's southwest peninsula. He has also made first ascents of some striking sea stacks in the far north of Scotland. And his Himalayan record has been enviable. His name is Mick Fowler.

In India, Fowler teamed up with the American climber Steve Sustad to make the first ascent of a striking peak near the Tibetan border called Arwa Tower. He then turned his attention to the almost untapped ranges of southeast Tibet, making first ascents, in pretty lousy weather, of two striking pyramids in the Nyenchentangla Range, called Kajaqiao and Manamcho. But his most striking ascent was on a mountain in Sichuan which had already been climbed – the beautiful slender pyramid of Siguniang.

Left
Sílvia Vidal on the West face of Amin Brakk. Immediately below her is the faint corner climbed with tiny copperheads. Further below is the limited comfort of her team's hanging camp.

Right
Swiss climber Stefan Siegrist preparing an abseil after completing a new route up India's stunning Arwa Tower, close to the Tibet border. It was the prolific British explorer of new routes Mick Fowler who made the first ascent of the tower. In the portrait (below) he is seen closer to home, well powdered with chalk, during a first ascent on the White Cliffs of Dover.

2002
SIGUNIANG — NORTH FACE
FOWLER & RAMSDEN

The American climber Jack Tackle had been here in 1981, attempting unsuccessfully to climb the mountain from the north (a Japanese team made the first ascent from the other side, the following year). In 2000 Tackle met Fowler, who had developed an interest in the mountain, and they got talking about Siguniang. Tackle then, unwisely, showed Fowler his photos of the north face. "They were much more detailed than anything we had seen before and showed a series of smooth, ice-streaked granite walls cleft by a huge vertical fault line which was choked with something white. Whether or not this was ice or powder snow would make a big difference. Jack hadn't been close enough to look but the look in his eyes gave away what he thought."

A couple of years later, in May 2002, Mick Fowler arrived in the Siguniang national park to get close enough to see for sure. What he and Paul Ramsden, a safety inspector by trade, found was indeed ice – a miraculous vertical streak, a super giant, steeper, harder, wilder version of the Dru Couloir or the Super Couloir, hidden away on the flank of this exotic Chinese mountain.

On the first day they had to contend with 80° ice, sometimes worryingly thin. By nightfall it was snowing and they were crammed into a hideously uncomfortable bivouac inside their roughly suspended tent. In Fowler's words, "the night was excruciatingly uncomfortable, the ground ahead looked distinctly uncompromising and the regular roaring sound of spindrift avalanches was a constant reminder that our nice ice line was not a good place to be in bad weather. I was desperate for a drink but it was impossible to light the stove and melt snow in the confines of the flapping fabric. ... At some point I became aware that

it was getting light outside and Paul was lifting the zip section to peer out of the bottom. The steady swish of spindrift on fabric gave me a good idea of what it was like. He made no comment."

Nevertheless they carried on and were rewarded with improving weather, as the ice steepened to 95°. They spent another night in the "ice dyke" and in the morning Ramsden, the blunt Yorkshireman, pronounced, "That was a crap bivouac, Fowler. More steep ice today!" It was indeed steep and another snowstorm intensified the struggle, as Fowler described, following one of the steepest pitches, weighed down, unlike the leader, by a very heavy rucksack: "And so when I reached the overhang it was little surprise to find myself gasping uncontrollably and gulping in huge lungfulls of spindrift. With strength failing, I clipped into a less than perfect placement. Twice the ice failed and twice dangled free, marvelling that my heart could beat so fast."

But above the overhang the angle finally eased off and for the first time they managed to build a platform where they could pitch their tent in a position approximating to the horizontal, as Fowler explained with delight. "The temperature inside my sleeping bag was just right, there were no bits of rock sticking uncomfortably into me and for the first time on the climb I was bivouacking without half hanging from my harness. I contrasted the situation with the four star hotels I sometimes end up staying in during tax office work – overheated rooms, noisy guests, windows that don't open properly and not even a decent view. I concluded that this accommodation was not at all bad."

The following day, their fifth on the mountain, the climbing got easier, and although they did have to endure a final hideous "bum ledge" bivouac, by that stage they were virtually on the summit of Siguniang and all the discomfort seemed worth it, for pulling off such a stunning first ascent.

Above
Paul Ramsden traversing frighteningly steep ice (left), to join Fowler at a belay on Siguniang's awesome North Face (above, right). The route followed the blindingly obvious vertical streak of ice.

Right
Rob Owen "drytooling" through an overhang to gain the precarious icicle, on the first ascent of Haunted by Waters, near Banff, Canada.

CANADIAN MIXED

Mick Fowler was reared on the winter ice and mixed climbing of Scotland, but perhaps the world's finest ice climbing is in Canada, where standards are always being pushed higher and higher on the icefalls and huge mountain faces of the Rockies. Near the resort of Banff, huge sweeps of frozen water such as Sea of Vapours have long been testpieces for aspiring ice stars. Then, in the 1990s, local climbers began using their ice tools on vertical and overhanging limestone, "drytooling" to link sections of bare rock with free hanging icicles, at about the same time that the well known American, Jeff Lowe, was doing similar things in Colorado.

Canadian pioneers included Dave Thompson and Kefira Allen, one of the few women doing mixed climbing at the highest standard. The master Canadian was probably Will Gadd. On the new "mixed" grading system, he led the world's first M9, "Amphibian" with Helgi Christiansen. He then went on to lead the first M10 and the first M11 (in Iceland). Also very active in the Canadian Rockies are Scott Semple and Raphael Slawinski. A typical product of their art was a new route climbed in 2006, with the unlikely name The Doctor, The Tourist, His Crampon and Their Banana.

It is a meaty climb, 700 meters high, up the side of Mt Andromeda. And whereas earlier classic winter climbs would rely on continuous ribbons of solid ice, this uses subtler ephemeral smears and runnels, often hidden from below, lodged deep in cracks and corners, or plastered thinly across delicate traverses. In between you have to hook with ice axes and crampon tips on what tiny holds you can find on the dry limestone. It's detailed, precision work, greatly helped by the fine engineering of modern ice tools.

NORTH TWIN RE-INTERPRETED

It was this new dry-tooling expertise that enabled the brilliant Slovenian Marko Prezelj and American climber Steve House, to make a revolutionary ascent of one of the most forbidding, atmospheric north faces in the world – the North Face of North Twin. It is Canada's answer to the Eigerwand; but it is much harder than the Eigerwand and, until 2004, the original route climbed in 1972 by Chris Jones and George Lowe had never been repeated.

Jones and Lowe took six days on their ascent. It was one of the hardest alpine climbs that had ever been climbed, anywhere, and on the steep upper wall of compact limestone they relied heavily on aid climbing, hammering pegs into cracks. They did it in

summer; to repeat that kind of fiddly work in winter, at minus 30°c, would be desperately hard and extremely slow. But late winter – April 2004 – was when Prezelj and House chose to climb the face, gaining speed by hooking with ice picks where the pioneers had laboriously hammered and removed pitons. Nevertheless it was hard, as House admitted: "we didn't know if each pitch would go until we reached the end of the rack and/or rope and built an anchor. This kept the adventure high, a feeling we both consider important to a successful outing – more important than whether we complete a route."

The second bivouac, bang in the middle of the vertical upper wall, was on the biggest ledge they had seen all day – about the size of a boot. And it was a plastic boot that then added to their challenge, by being dropped into the void while House was changing into dry socks for the night. With studied understatement, he later commented, "It was an aus-

The concave triangle of North Twin's North Face is like a harder, steeper, scarier version of Europe's North Face of the Eiger. It was first climbed by Chris Jones and George Lowe in 1972. Here (below left) Marko Prezelj uses ice axes and crampons to make the first repeat of the route. In winter.

Right
Ivan Calderon follows a pitch of
tenuous free climbing, high on
Rainbow Jambaia. The free hanging
rope gives an idea of the angle.

tere pair that finished their dinner of soup and dehy-
drated mashed potatoes and rigged their tarp
overhead before squeezing on the ledge." Morning
brought the almost inevitable bad weather and spindrift avalanches, but they decided that advance was
easier than retreat, so House spent the day climbing
with one foot in just an inner boot, wrapped up in
plastic and sticky tape. Three days later, after a long
hike through a whiteout, over the Columbia icefield,
they were safely down.

2005
RAINBOW JAMBAIA
JOHN ARRAN ET AL

Anne Arran is one of the best women rock climbers
in Britain. Her husband John is one of the best anywhere, period. They love pioneering big new free
climbs on some of the world's most remote exotic
peaks and they have made a speciality of the tepuis –
ancient sandstone monoliths – of Venezuala. The
summit of one of these *tepuis* is the source of the
world's tallest waterfall, the Angel Falls. It has become
a popular site for base jumpers tempted by the
prospect of free-falling 1,000 meters into the jungle.

Even more outrageous is the prospect of climbing
up the huge overhanging wall behind the waterfall.
A Spanish team made the first ascent of this 1,000
meters high wall, which overhangs 60 meters in all, in
1990. The route was graded A4 – the second highest
grade of artificial climbing – and because some of
the rock was so loose, they called one section the
Derribos Arias – the "Demolition Zone." Undeterred
by the awesome overhanging nature of the cliff and
the dubious rock, the Arrans attempted a free ascent
in 2002 with the Venezuelan climber Ivan Calderón;
but travelling up and down the wall on lightweight
ropes, they discovered that the ropes were quickly
getting trashed: to continue with ropes in that state
would be suicidal.

They returned three years later, better equipped
with thick, substantial fixing ropes, prepared for a
long siege. This was a full scale expedition, requiring
careful planning for the charter flight from Bolivar to
the Kamarata valley, then a river journey by dugout
canoe, and finally a short walk, hauling all the gear to
the foot of what they hoped would be the biggest
overhanging free climb in the world. The 2002 team
was joined by Alfredo Rangel from Venezuala, Alex
Klenov from Russia, and Miles Gibson and Ben Heason from Britain.

Alfredo Rangel celebrating on the last rope length to the summit of Rainbow Jambaia, on the first free-climbed ascent of Angel Falls amphitheatre face – 31 pitches, 19 days, 1,000 meters high, 50 meters overhanging. The "Rainbow" appeared every day as the sun hit the world's highest waterfall. "Jambaia" is derived from the seven climbers' first name initials.

With a team of seven very strong climbers, the work could be shared out, alternating the mental strain of leading at the highest standard, with carrying up supplies to keep the hanging camps stocked. To give some idea of the logistics involved, they started off with 300 litres of water! The route was even harder than they expected, but it was possible to freeclimb it – just. At least it was for people accustomed to leading at British E7 grade. That's the seventh of eleven "extreme" grades denoting both technical difficulty and seriousness. It's the sort of climbing where you need very strong fingers to pinch narrow ribs in the stone, or pull sideways against slight edges, or crimp fingernail deep horizontal ledges. And you need the skill to slot micro wedges and mini-cams into faint cracks, all the time judging the solidity – or otherwise – of the surrounding rock. And you need lots of nerve to contemplate the possibility of falling over the yawning abyss, trusting to those micro-anchors to hold your fall. And when the odd tiny wire snaps, you still have to have the bottle to go up for another try.

As John Arran wrote in a subsequent article, after seventeen days of this, they were all feeling quite tired. To add to the general nervous strain, even their thick ropes had become worn by the constant pulling over edges. In several places, where the sheath was worn, they had had to cut and re-knot the ropes, adding to the difficulties of ascending and abseiling. And, for whoever was at the sharp end, out in front, the difficulty never seemed to let up. That day Arran was in front: "I just wanted the pitch to be over. Surely I'd done enough, running it out on 6b moves [hard!] from poor gear onto a nearly holdless and gearless face. And it had worked: somehow I'd reached an easing. Now I craved a belay to rest my aching limbs and congratulate myself on anyone of the hardest on sight leads I'd done in years." The next day, after leading the 31st pitch on the route, Miles Gibson let out a shriek of delight announcing that he had reached the top of the Angel Falls, and the day after that everyone followed, to celebrate amongst the unique, bizarre lost world plants on the summit of Ayauntepui. All they had to do know was abseil 1,000 meters back down the wall, stripping their ropes as they went.

MINIATURE PERFECTION

It's easy to get excited about the biggest overhanging free climb in the world; less easy, perhaps, to be impressed by climbs so small that you don't even need a rope. But climbers have always loved to play

on boulders. Oscar Eckenstein, who took part in the first climbing expedition to the Karakoram in 1892, took his bouldering very seriously. The Parisian mountaineer Pierre Allain perfected his technique on the sandstone boulders in the Fontainebleau forest and gave his initials to the smooth-soled rubber climbing shoe he invented – the PA – forerunner of all modern rock shoes. But it took an American to elevate a casual pastime into high art, complete with its own grading system.

John Gill, born in 1937, was a maths professor at the University of Southern Colorado until he retired in 2000. He was also a serious gymnast who could, for instance, climb a 6 meter rope in just 3.4 seconds, from a sitting start. Arms only! And do several one finger/one arm pull-ups in succession. He was seriously strong and he applied that strength with scientific precision to rock climbing, in particular to the boulder problem. The boulder is the climber's version of the haiku – minimalist perfection, with everything condensed into one short sequence of exquisitely hard moves, which may rise no more than a couple meters off the ground.

When I was a child I loved bouldering. It was just something I did for fun, without realizing that it had an actual name, unaware that in California at the time there was a man called John Gill perfecting sequences of moves harder than anyone had ever done before. Much, much later, in the Nineties, when I was a middle-aged and fairly experienced climber, I went along one evening to a rather fine, sculptural cluster of boulders in Wales I had always fancied, and was startled to find groups of people with chalk bags, special brushes for cleaning holds, special pads to cushion falls, and even a special book with names and grades for all the problems. My casual childhood game had become a sport in its own right, with every available lump of rock labelled, described, quantified and graded. And, of course, the equipment manufacturers had cashed in with a whole new range of products.

Above
Bouldering on the exquisitely eroded ancient sandstone rocks in South Africa's Cedarberg mountains.

Right
One of Mike Robertson's deep-water-solo friends in flight off his beloved Dorset sea cliffs.

However, the great joy of bouldering is that you don't actually need a huge amount of gear. In fact, all you really need is a pair of rock shoes. However, good boulderers are tackling such outrageously big problems – with the potential of falling 10 meters or more – that sophisticated crash pads can actually guard against some very nasty injuries. The other bit of equipment – introduced back in the Sixties by John Gill – is gymnast's chalk, to improve grip on fingerholds. To my mind, the introduction of chalk has been one of the great tragedies of modern climbing: the telltale white slashes point up holds, removing much of the mystique of finding the hold for yourself; they also disfigure the natural colour, texture and sculptural beauty of the rock itself, which is one of the main reasons for going climbing in the first place.

Be that as it may, bouldering has become hugely popular, because it is enormous fun and is comparatively safe. And the scope, worldwide, is limitless. Serious boulderers now travel the world to repeat celebrated problems by modern stars such as the Swiss climber Fred Nicole. In South Africa, a country with some of the biggest and best mountain crags anywhere in the world, visitors are now arriving exclusively to climb on the boulders of Rocklands in the Cedarberg, north of Cape Town, drawn not by size, but by the exquisite colour and texture of these fantastically weathered natural quartzite sculptures.

Bouldering can be taken to huge heights if you know you can fall off with impunity. Assuming you can swim, that all becomes possible over deep sea water: provided you avoid belly flops, falls of 30 meters or more are contemplatable. The great joy is that you climb without all the encumbrance or ropes, harness and runners. In recent years "deep water soloing" has become hugely popular, particularly on Britain's Dorset coast, near the home of photographer Mike Robertson, who spends several weeks every year touring the world to find new seaside climbs.

Dave MacLeod dancing his way up a beautifully ripped sheet of gneiss on the Hebridean island of Lewis, to make the first ascent of Flock Talk. An outstanding young Scottish climber, MacLeod excels at traditional climbing relying on natural protection. And buckets of courage. His route Rhapsody, at Dumbarton Rock, was the world's first E11 rock climb.

1968
THE TOTEM POLE
EWBANK & KELLAR

Australia has beautiful rock climbing and some of the best is in Tasmania, particularly on the island's sea cliffs. The most famous feature is the Totem Pole which John Ewbank described nicely: "Take a matchstick. Change it into Dolerite. Multiply it 1600 times. Stand it upright in a heavy swell, then swim away before it topples over." Ewbank made the first ascent with Alan Kellar in 1968. Their route used artificial aid at A4 standard. Repeating it many years later, in 1996 Steve Monks and Simon Mentz spotted what looked like a line of tiny holds up the opposite edge. Their hunch proved correct and the following day they made the first free ascent of this stunning sea stack.

2001
LHOTSE MIDDLE
VINOGRADSKY, TIMOFEEV, BOLOTOV, & KUZNETOV

The last of the main eight thousand-meter peaks, Shishapangma, was climbed in 1964. However, there remained subsidiary summits to these giants. Kangchenjunga, for instance, has four summits over 8,000 meters. By the end of the twentieth century there was just one of these summits left – the middle summit of Lhotse.

The main summit of Lhotse, fourth highest peak in the world, was first climbed by the Swiss mountaineers Ernst Reiss and Fritz Luchsinger in 1956, as part of the same expedition which made the second ascent of Everest. The eastern peak, Lhotse Shar was climbed in 1979. In 1990 Lhotse's gigantic South Face (almost as big as, but harder than, Nanga Parbat's Rupal Face) was climbed for the first time by a large Russian team. And in 2001 it was the Russians again who applied their extraordinary perseverance and teamwork to reaching the highest unclimbed point on the surface of the earth – 8,414 meters Lhotse Middle.

The problem with Lhotse Middle, was that it was a fearsomely steep pinnacle or dubious rock, crowned with giant meringue-blobs of snow, connected to the main summit by the most fiendishly knife-edge ridge. Tackling that kind of ground at sea level would be

Left
"Take a matchstick. Change it into Dolerite. Multiply it 1,600 times. Stand it upright in a heavy swell, then swim away before it topples over." John Ewbank's description of Tasmania's Totem Pole. He made the first ascent, using artificial aid, in 1968. Here Steve Monks and Simon Mentz make the first free ascent, by a new route.

Above
8,414 meters above the base of the Totem Pole, the Middle Summit of Lhotse was the world's ultimate unclimbed summit, until a brilliant Russian expedition made the first ascent in 2001. Yuri Koshelenko took these pictures a day after the first party reached the top.

tricky; starting the hard climbing at over 8,400 meters, it was an almost impossible challenge.

The Russians got round the problem by doing a canny traverse, from the famous South Col, across a huge snow shelf on the northeast face of Lhotse, in Tibet, avoiding the crazy ridge and getting to a point almost directly beneath the tantalizing Middle Summit. They spent most of April climbing the traditional Everest approach to the South Col, stocking camps with food and oxygen. Then in the first week of May, alternating teams took the task of pushing on across the Northeast Face of Lhotse.

On 22 May Evgueni Vinogradsky, Sergei Timofeev and Alexei Bolotov, all from Ekaterinburg, together with Petr Kuznetov, occupied Camp 5 at 8,250 meters, almost directly beneath Lhotse Middle. The next morning, aided by oxygen, they left for the summit, fixing ropes as they climbed a spectacularly steep corner to reach the elusive ridge, where they had to

descend slightly to a gap beneath the final pinnacle. They continued, breathing bottled oxygen, ploughing through immense snow mushrooms and by 3.00 pm all four climbers had pulled through the final cornice to perch on the summit.

That night of 23 May all four men were safely back at Camp 5. Then other team members had their turns. On 24 May Gleb Solokov, Yuri Koshelenko and Nikolai Jiline climbed all the way from the South Col to the summit and back in a single day; on 27 May Viktor Volodin and Vladimir Yanochkin did the same. It seems remarkable that so many members of the team were still fit enough for such a demanding summit day on what must be some of the steepest terrain ever attempted at that altitude. What a triumph to get eight members to the top and how encouraging that the "Master of Sport" and four times "Snow Leopard" winner, Evgueni Vinogradsky, did so in his fifty-fifth year!

Gleb Solokov, plugged into supplementary oxygen, perches on the fragile crest of Lhotse Middle, 8,414 meters above sea level, as clouds swallow up famous 6,000-meter peaks of Sola Khumbu, far below.

ANDERSON & HOUSE

From sunny seaside bouldering to the biggest mountain face on earth, the barriers keep being pushed back. In the summer of 2004 Steve House and Marko Prezelj, emboldened by their recent success on the North Face of North Twin, headed for Pakistan with American friends Steve Swenson and Bruce Miller. In the Karakoram they pulled off a dazzling string of first ascents, including two extremely hard routes to the 6,974 summit of K7. Steve House climbed his K7 route completely alone. As if that were not enough, he then enrolled Bruce Miller for his next project, on the other side of the Indus river – the gigantic, 4,000 meters high Rupal Face of Nanga Parbat.

Nanga Parbat has always inspired extremes of effort. It was here that Mummery made his futuristic attempt on the Diamir Face in 1895. The same mountain saw a string of heroic, often tragic, German attempts through the Thirties. Hermann Buhl's eventual solo ascent in 1953 is one of the great legends of mountaineering. Reinhold Messner completed the first ascent of the Rupal Face in 1970, only to lose his brother during an epic escape down the Diamir Face. Haunted by the loss of his brother, he returned several times, eventually, as if in expiation, making a completely solo ascent of the face, reaching the summit for the second time, in 1978.

Young Steve House climbs with similar messianic fervour, always trying to go steeper, harder, faster. Determined that alpinism should progress, he wanted to climb the Rupal Face by a new direct route, much harder than the original 1970 route, and to do it in pure alpine style – just two climbers, carrying what they could on their backs, continuing as far as they could, with no radios, no porters, no support team, no fixed ropes. And, that summer of 2004 they almost pulled it off. However, after five days, as they headed for the summit, Miller realized that House's chest infection was becoming serious:

"I waited for an hour watching Steve draped over his axe. He was barely moving. Ghosts of past partners were talking to me. I climbed down to Steve and said, 'You're going too slow. You're sick. You're not going to get any better here at 7,500 meters.' Steve admitted that, yes, he was hurting, but the thought he could recover – we could bivouac just below. That was the moment I realized I hadn't really known him. ... It was beyond his understanding that he was subject to some of the same limitations as less fanatical climbers. He was making decisions based mainly on the risk of not reaching the summit. The risk of dying was a secondary concern. I listed my priorities in the

reverse order. That made our partnership perhaps essentially balanced for the Rupal Face, somewhere between bold and crazy." So Bruce Miller, the family man of 41, persuaded his younger companion to descend. And even that – over 3,000 meters down the still difficult "Messner Route" was no pushover.

A year later the driven younger man was back at the foot of the Rupal Face, this time with a new partner, Vince Anderson, to share the fraught leads up immense rockband, separated by icefields, climbing mainly at night to avoid the threat of stonefall and avalanches. As Anderson put it, "the frequency and scope of the avalanches made me realize that climbing this face alpine-style was the safest way to go. The risks were acceptable once, but not for numerous excursions along fixed ropes."

On the third day, half way up the wall, where House had previously headed left towards the Messner Route, this time they continued direct, tackling more very hard mixed climbing. Their fourth bivouac was on a knife edge of snow excavated to make a ledge less than a meter wide, with the tent draped over the edges. The following night it took them hours to excavate a ledge, then melt snow for vital brews to rehydrate. When the alarm went at

Below
Climbing unroped onone of the "easier" sections, Vince Anderson approaches one of the huge rock bands on the Rupal Face direct route. It took him and House six days to reach the summit, and another two days to descend the original "Messner Route."

Right

The Rupal Face of Nanga Parbat, 4,600 meters high, is probably the biggest mountain face in the world. The original 1970 "Messner" route took the shadowy ice slopes curving up from the left. Anderson and House tackled the face head-on, taking insome very steep rock bands in a direct line to the summit.

1:30 am the next day, Anderson hadn't slept at all. It took the whole day to reach the summit and by the time they regained their tent they had been on the go for 24 hours. Two days later, after the interminable descent of the Messner Route, they were safely down. Anderson concluded, "We were transformed by our experience on the Rupal Face. Steve realized a lifelong dream and vanquished the pain of last year's rebuff. I discovered my physical, intellectual, and emotional limits, and pushed them much farther than I had imagined possible. Having annihilated our outer sins, perhaps we glimpsed, if only for a moment, our true selves. Neither of us will ever be the same."

Indeed. How could anyone ever be quite the same person after pushing themselves so far beyond the normal parameters of human existence? Some people might think that Anderson and House were simply crazy. In fact, for all the risk, their success depended on years of experience, meticulous planning and bold imagination. It was a triumph of the human spirit and proof that the scope for vertical exploration is almost unlimited.

INDEX

Page numbers in *italic* type refer to pictures or their captions

A

Aas, Monrad 60
Abruzzi, Luigi Amedeo, Duke of 42, *42*, 46
accidents
 Eiger 73–4, 104
 Everest 65, 124
 Matterhorn disaster *26*, 31–2
 Nanga Parbat 61, *82, 83*
 Shishapangma 165
Aconcagua 143
Agassiz, Louis 23
Agissizjoch 23
Aiguille, Mont 13, *13*
Aiguille d'Argentière 26
Aiguille de Trélatête 26
Aiguille du Plan 69
Aiguille Grépon 67, *67*
Aiguille Verte 26
Alaska *34*, 35–9, 42, 131–2
Allain, Pierre 176
Allen, Kefira 171
Alphubel 33
Alpine Club 23, *23*, 26, 42, 67, 100
alpine style ascents 68
Alps 11, 13–33, 67–75, 99–109
 Dauphiné 27
 Eastern 69, 72
 "Golden Age" of Alpine climbing 23–33
altiplano 42
Amin Brakk 168, *168*
Ampato, Mount 12
Ampferer, Otto 33
Anderegg, Jacob 33
Anderegg, Melchior 31, *31*, 33
Anderson, Peter 37
Anderson, Robert 161
Anderson, Vince 184–5
Andes 12, 32, 42–3, 135, 136–41
Andromeda, Mount 171
Anglesey *145*, 148, *149*
Anker, Conrad *7, 160, 161*, 164, 165, 166
Annapurna *76*, 77–9, 85
Annapurna II 111
Annapurna
 North Face *76*, 78
 South Face *110*, 111–16, *112–13, 114*
Antarctica 141–3, 161–4
Anthoine, Mo 106, 118–21, *119*
Aoraki 44–5, *44, 45*
 Zurbriggen Ridge 45
Arctic 164–6
Argentina 136–41
Arizona 96
Arnold, H. 55
Arran, Anne 173, 175
Arran, John 173, 175
artificial climbing 70
Arwa Tower 168, *169*
Aschenbrenner, Peter 82
Asgard, Mount 164
Atkinson, John 49

B

Aufdenblatten, Alfred 68
Austrian Alpine Club 75
avalanches 61, 68, 78, *82*, 165
Ayauntepui 173–5

Baffin Island 164–6, *164–5*
Baillie, Rustie *146, 148,* 152
Ball, John 23, 26
Balmat, Jacques 17–18
Baltoro Glacier 118
Band, George 85
Barker, Bill 106, 119
Barrill, Big Ed 35–6, *36*
Barry, John 124
Bass, Dick 143, *143*
Batian 47, *47*
Batkin, Jacques 132
Bauer, Paul 57, 61
Baxter-Jones, Roger *104*
Beachy Head 148
Beckley, Fred *130,* 131–2
Beckley, Helmey 131
belaying 30, *50*
Bell, Jim 54–5
Beltrami, Alessandro 136
Ben Nevis 53–5, *54*
 Green Gully 54–5
 Tower Ridge 54
Bennen, Johann-Joseph 32–3
Berger, Karl 33
Berner Oberland 23, *24–5*, 32–3
Berry Head 153
Bhutan 168
Bietschorn 32, 33
big wall climbing 89
Biven, Peter 153
Black Canyon 96
Blümlisalphorn 33
Boardman, Peter 124, *124,* 126
Bodet, Stephanie *144*
Boivin, Jean Marc 106
Bolivia 42–3
Bolotov, Alexei 181
Bonatti, Walter 99–101, *100*
Bonington, Chris 101, 102, 108, 111–16, *115,* 124, *143,* 152
boots *see* equipment
Bortis, Josef 23
Boss, Emil 45
Botterill, Fred 50
Bouchard, John 106
bouldering 175–7, *176, 177*
Bourdillon, Tom 80
Boysen, Martin 111, *114,* 115, 118–21, *118, 119*
Brenta Alta 70
Bridwell, Jim 158
British climbers 42
 Alpine Club 23, *23,* 26, 42
 "Golden Age" of Alpine climbing 23–33
British Columbia *130,* 131
Broad Peak 83–5, *84, 85, 86–7,* 117
Broad Stand 49
Brocherel, Joseph 46–7
Brooks, Alfred 35
Brown, Joe 8–9, 85, 118–21, *119,* 145–8, *145*
Browne, Belmore 35–6, 37
Bruce, Geoffrey 64, *64*

C

Bryn, A.B. 60
Bucher, Christophe *154*
Buhl, Hermann 81–5, *83, 84, 85,* 184
Burgener, Alexander *30,* 67
Burke, Mick *110,* 111, 115
Burma 57
Butler, Samuel 44

Calderón, Ivan 173, *173*
Caldwell, Tommy 159
Campanile Basso 33
Canada 171
Cannings, Frank 153
capacocha 12
Carn Gowla 153–4
Carrel, Jean-Antoine 27–8, 30, *30*
Carstensz Pyramid 143
Cascade Mountains 131
Cassin, Rattim 70
Cassin, Riccardo *71,* 75, 132
Catto, John 165
Caucasus 68
Cecchinel, Walter 105
Cedarberg Mountains *176,* 177
Cerro Torre 136–41, *136, 137, 138–9, 140*
Chacaraju 135
Chacaraju Oeste 135
Chadwick, Alison 118
Chamonix valley 13, 17, 19
Changabang 124–6, *124*
Charles VII, King of France 13, *13*
Chen San 85
Chiappa, Daniele 141
Child, Greg 165
Chimbarazo 32
Cho Oyu 85
Chogolisa 85, *86–7*
Chomiomo 58
Chouinard, Yvon 90, *90, 93*
Christiansen, Helgi 171
Cima di Ball 33
Cima di Fradusta 33
Cima Grande 70, *70–1,* 72, 157
Civetta 70
Clark, Jack 45
Cleare, John *146, 147*
Clinch, Nicholas 85
Clogwyn Du'r Arddu (Cloggy) *see* Snowdon
Clough, Ian 101, 111, 115–16
Coastal Ranges 131
Coleridge, Samuel Taylor 49
Collie, Norman 54, *54*
Colorado 95–6
Colton, Nick 108–9
Comici, Emilio 70–2, *70*
Compagnoni, Achille 85, 99
Conti, Mario 141
continental Seven Summits 143
Conway, Martin 42–3, *42,* 118
Cook, Frederick 35–9
Cook, Mount *see* Aoraki
Cook, Thomas 26
Corbet, Barry 143
Cordillera Blanca 135
Cordillera Real 42–3
Corkhill, Ron 157–8
Couzy, Jean 85

Crew, Pete *147*, 148
Croft, Peter 166
Crowley, Aleister 57, 148
Croz, Jean-Baptiste *28*
Croz, Michel 26, *26*, 28, 31–2
Curran, Jim 120

D

Darbyshire, Keith 153–4
Davaille, Maurice 135
Davidson, E.C. 37
Deborah, Mount 132
deep water soloing 177, *177*
Denali 35–9, *36*, *37*, *40–1*, 143
   North Summit *34–5*, 37, 132
   South Summit *34–5*, 37–9
   West Buttress *38*
Dent Blanche *28*
Destivelle, Catherine 101
Detassis 70
Devil's Bridge *23*
Devil's Thumb 131
Devil's Tower 70
Devon-Cornwall peninsula 148, 152–4
Dhaulagiri 85
Diamond 96
Diemberger, Kurt 83–5, *84*
Diener, Peter 85
Dinas Cromlech 147–8, 154
   Cemetery Gates 147
   Cenotaph Corner 9, 146, 147–8, 154
   Ivy Sepulchre 147
Disgrazia, Monte 33
Dixon, Marmaduke 45, *45*
Djuglosz 101
Doje 85
Dolent, Col 26
Dolomites 26, 33, 70–2, 157
Don Guerra *137*
Donyo Sabuk 47
Dorje Sherpa 121, *121*, 124
Dorset 177, *177*
Douglas, Lord Francis *26*, 28–32
Dover 148, *169*
Droyer, Jean Claude 155
drugs *see* stimulants
drytooling 171, *171*
du Faur, Freda 44, *44*
Dülfer, Hans 70
Dumbarton Rock *179*
Dunagiri 124
Dych Tau 68

E

Eckenstein, Oscar 176
Ecographie *154*
Ecrins, Pointe des 26
Ecuador 42
Edwards, Menlove 147
Egger, Toni 136
Eiger 23, *24–5*
   Death Bivouac 73, 74, *103*, 104
   Eiger Direct 102–4, *102*
   Eigerwand 72–5, *74*, 102–4
   Götterquergang 75
   Hinterstoisser Traverse 73, 74
   North Face *22*, 72–3, *73*, 102–4
   Stollenjoch 73

eight thousand meter summits 77–85, 111
El Capitan *88*, 89, *89*, 92–5, 158–9
   Freerider 159
   Mescalito 158
   El Niño 159, 166
   North America Wall 158, 159
   The Nose *89*, 92–5, *93*, *94*, 158–9, *158*
   Salathé Wall *92*, 95, *95*, *96*, 158–9, 166
   The Shield 158
   Zodiac 158, *159*
Elbesandstein 55, *55*
Elbruz 143
Eldorado Canyon 96
Ellsworth, Lincoln 141
Ellsworth Mountains 141, 143
Eperon Sublime 155
equipment 30, *49*, *90*, 135, *165*
   alpenstock 17–18
   birdbeaks 158
   boings 119–20
   bolts 95, 155, 168
   boots 30, 45, *49*, 52, 54, 74, 78
   camming devices 146, 158
   chalk 177
   chockstones 52, 146, 148
   "cleaning" a pitch *91*
   copperheads 168
   crampons 104
   electric drill 137
   fixed 155
   friends 158
   hammocks 124
   helmets 147
   ice axes 104
   ice screws 55, 104
   jumars 104
   karabiners 70, 73–4
   knot-jamming 55
   nuts 90, 146, 158
   oxygen sets 64, 65, *65*, 79, 80–1, *80*, 117
   PA climbing shoes 176
   pitons 33, 52, 55, 70, 89, 90, 95
   ropes 32, 49, 55
   rurps 90, 158
   skyhooks 89, 158
   stirrups 70
Esais *39*
Esposita 75
Estcourt, Nick 111
Evans, Charles 80, *80*
Evans, John 143
Everest 8, 51, 52, 54, 78, 79–81, 85, *117*, 143, 161
   early expeditions 58, 64–5, *64*, 77
   first parapente jump 106
   forty hour ascent 127
   Hillary Step *81*
   Hornbein Couloir 127
   oxygenless ascent 126–7, *126*
   solo ascent 127
Explorers Club 35

F

Fa Hian 11
fascism 70, 75
Fava, Cesarino 136
Fawcett, Ron 154–5
Fenriskjeften Peaks 161
Ferrari, Casimiro 137–41

Fiennes, Ranulph *151*
Finch, George 64, *64*, 65
Finsteraarhorn 23
Fish, The *155*, 157
Fisher, Eugene 164
Fitchen, Joe 95
Fitzgerald, Edward 45
Fitzroy *136*, *137*
Flatirons 96
Fleischbank 70
Flock Talk *178–9*
Foraker, Mount 37, *40–1*
Forbes, James 23
Forbidden Peak 131
Forrer, Ernst 85
Fowler, Mick 128–9, 135, 168–70, *169*
fraudulent climbing claims 35–8, *36*, 136–7
Fred, Johnny *39*
free climbing 55, 145–59
Frost, Tom 90, *92*, *93*, 95, 111, 115
frostbite 78, 83, 124
Fuji, Mount 12
Fyfe, Tom 44–5

G

Gabarrou, Patrick 106
Gabriotti, Rolando 136
Gadd, Will 171
Gallwas, Jerry 90
gangrene 78
Gardiner, Frank 143
Gasherbrum peaks 85, *86–7*, 118, 126
Gate of the Mists 47
Gaudin, Claude 135
Gaurishankar *120–1*, 121–2, *122–3*
Gersdorf, Baron von 18
Gesner, Konrad 13
Gibson, Miles 173, 175
Gill, John 176–7
Gillman, Peter 104
Giordano, Felice 28
glaciers 13, 23
global warming 101
Götner, A. 61
Gotthard Pass 23
Graber, Mike 164
grading systems 50, 55, 171, 176
Graham, Alex 44
Graham Brown, Thomas *52*, 68–9
Graham, George 44–5
Graham, Peter *44*
Grandes Jorasses 26, 33
   Central Couloir 106–9, *108*, *109*
   North Face 72, *72*
   Pointe Walker 31
   Walker Spur 75, *75*
Graven, Alexander 68
Great Gable 49
Great Sail Peak 164–5, *164–5*
Green, William 45
greenhouse gases 26
Gréloz, Robert 69
gritstone 145, 147
Grove, F. Crauford 143
Guglia de Brenta 33
guidebooks 50
Guillen, Señor 43
Gunnison 96

Gyalzen Norbu Sherpa 85

H

Habeler, Peter 65, 68, *96*, 126, *126*, 158
Hadow, Douglas *26*, 30–1
Half Dome 89–90, 95, 158
Haller, Albrecht von 13
hallucinations 69, 83
Hannibal 11, *12*
Harder, Gilbert *63*
Harding, Warren 89, 90, *90*, 92–5, 159
Hargreaves, A.B. *52*
Harlin, John 101–4, *103*
Harlin, John III *106*, 107
Harper, Walter 38–9, *39*, 143
Harrer, Heinrich 74–5, *74*, *130*, 132, 143
Harris, Chris 155
Hartmann, Hans *57*
Harvard Mountaineering Club 61
Haskett-Smith, Walter Parry *48*, 49–50, *54*
Haston, Dougal 102–4, 108, *108*, 111, 114–15
Haunted by Waters *171*
Hauptdrilling 55
Hauptwiesenstein Rostkante 55
Heason, Ben 173
Heckmair, Anderl 74–5, *74*
Henneck, Dennis *119*
Hepp, E. 61
Herford, Siegfried 50–1, *50*
Herrligkoffer, Karl 81–2, 116
Herzog, Maurice 77–9, *77*, 85
Hesleden, Dave *109*
Hidden Peak 117, 143
Hillary, Edmund 80–1, *80*, 143
Hill, Lynn *158*, 159
Himalaya 8, 57–65, 77–83, 111–29, 168–70
Hindu Kush 57
Hinterstoisser, Andreas *72*, 73
Hirondelles, Col des 33
Hitler, Adolf 75
Holland, Charles 50
Hollick-Kenyon, Herbert 141
holy mountains 12
Hooker, Joseph 57
Hornbein, Tom 127
Houlding, Leo 159
House, Bill 131
House, Steve *135*, 171, 172–3, 184–5
Houston, Charles 61–2
Houston, Oscar 79
Howell, Ian *51*
Howells, Malcolm 118–21, *119*
Huber, Alex 159, *159*
Huber, Thomas *158*, 159
Hudson, Charles *26*, 28, 30–2
Hughes, Luke *72*
Hugi, Professor 23
Huizenga, Albert 143
Hunt, John 79, 81
Hunter, Mount *130*, 132
Huntingdon, Mount 132, *132–3*
Hupfauer, Sigi 104
hypothermia *83*

I

Ichac 77
Illimani 42–3, *43*
Imanishi, Toshio 85

India 61
Ingalls, Huntley 96
Irvine, Sandy *64*, 65

J

Jager, Claude 105
Jannu 116
Jardine, Ray 158
Jenny, Raymond 135
Jiline, Nikolai 181
Jöchler, Sepp 85
Jones, Chris 89, 171
Jones, Eric 101, *101*
Jungfrau 23, *24–5*, 73

K

K2 *42*, 61, 70, 85, *86–7*, 99, 117, 143
K7 184
Kabru 60
Kailas, Mount 12
Kaisergebirge 70
Kajaqiao 168
Kala Gandaki 77
Kangchenjunga 8, 57, *58–9*, 61, 85, *117*, 118, 180
Karakoram *42*, 57, 83–5, 111, 117, 128, 166, 168, 184–5
Karakoram Pass 11
Karpinski, Mount *63*
Karstens, Billy 38–9, *39*, 143
Kashmir 57, 117, 168
Kasparek, Fritz 74–5, *74*
Kaufmann, Ulrich 45
Kellar, Alan 180
Kellas, Alexander 58, 65
Kempter, Otto 82
Kennedy, Edward 23, *28*
Kenya 46–7, 157
Kenya, Mount 46–7, *46*, *47*
Kershaw, Giles 143
Khumbu Icefall *78*, 79
Kilimanjaro 46, *46*, 47, 143
King, Terry 108
Kippax, Russel 143
Kishtwar Shivling 7–8, *7*
Klenov, Alex 173
Klondike gold rush 35
Knubel, Joseph 68
Knubel, Peter 143
Koller, Igor 157
Komito, Steve 96, *97*
Kor, Layton 96, *96*, *97*, 102–4, *102*
Kosciuzko 143
Koshelenko, Yuri 181, *181*
Krakauer, Jon *7*, *160*, 164
Kronig, Johann *28*
Kurtz, Toni 73–4
Kuznetov, Petr 181

L

La Paz 42, *43*
Lacedelli, Lino 99
Lachenal, Louis 77–8, *77*, 85
Lagarde 69
Lake District, (English) 49–51
Lambert, Raymond 79
Lamprecht, Tony *167*
Larch, Josef 85
Lauwo, Yohanas Kinyala 46

Lawrence, Jill 155
Leach, Tim *122–3*, 124
Lear, Edward *58–9*
Lehne, Jörg 104
Lemur Wall 9
Les Drus *98*, 99–101, *99*
Lhotse *78*, 85, 180–1, *181*, *182–3*
Libecki, Mike 165–6
Little Switzerland 55
Littlejohn, Pat 152–4, *152*, *153*
Livesey, Pete 154–5
Lloyd, Thomas 37, 39
Long, Bill 143
Longland, Jack 51–3, *52*
Longs Peak 96
Longstaff, Tom 148
Loretan, Erhard 127, *127*
Lost Arrow 89
Lowe, Alex 161, 164, *164–5*, 165
Lowe, George 171
Lowe, Jeff 171
Lower Sharpnose Point *152*
Luchsinger, Fritz 85, 180
Lyskamm West 33

M

McGonagall, Charley 37
MacIntyre, Alex 104, *104*, 108–9
MacKinder, Sir Halford 46–7
McKinley, Mount *see* Denali
MacLeod, Dave *178–9*
McNaught-Davis, Ian 118
Mad Brown *149*
Madagascar 166
Maestri, Cesare 136–7, 141
Mahdi 99
Maiden *see* Jungfrau
Mailänder, Nico 155
Makalu *78*, 85, *116*
    West Pillar 116–17, *116*
Mallet, Mont 33
Mallory, George 51, 54, *61*, 65, *78*
Manamcho 168
Manaslu 85, 126
Mannering, George 45
maps 23
Maquiagnaz, Antoine 42, 43
Maquignaz, Joseph *22*
Marmolada 70, 157
Masip, Pep 168
Matterhorn 26–31, *28*, *29*, 66
    Fürggen 67
    Hörnli ridge *28*, *29*, 30, 66
    Italian Ridge *30*
    North Face *66*, 72, 100
    Pic Tyndall *30*
    South Ridge *66*
    The Teeth 67
    West Face *66*, 67
    Zmutt Ridge *30*, *66*, 67, 68
Matthews, William 23
Mauri, Carlo 99, 136–7
Mehringer, Karl 73
Meier, Martin *73*
Mellet, Bernard 117
Mentz, Simon 180
Mer de Glace 13
Merkl, Willi 81

Merry, Wayne 95
Messner, Günther 116, 126, 184
Messner, Reinhold 65, 68, 116, 126, *126*, 184
Meybohm, Henry 131–2
Meyer, Gottlieb 23
Meyer, Hans 46, 143
Meyer, Hieronymus 23
Meyer, Johann-Rudolf 23
Micheluzzi 70
Miller, Bruce 184
Mima Zaxi 85
Modi Khola 114
Mönch 23, *24–5*
Monk *see* Mönch
Monks, Steve 180
Mont Blanc 13, *16–17*, 17–19
    Aiguille du Goûter 17
    Brenva Face 19, *31*, 68, *69*
    Central Pillar of Frêney 101
    Dôme du Goûter 17
    Monte Bianco 19
    North Face 17–19
    South Face 19
Mont Blanc du Tacul *105*, 106, *106–7*
Moorcroft, William 57
Moore, A.W. *31*
Moravec, Fritz 85
Morrisey, Jim *119*
Moses 11–12, *11*
Motenvers 13
Mummery, Albert Frederick *30*, 67–8, *67*, 148, 184
Murith, Abbé Laurent-Joseph 13
Mussolini, Benito 70
Mustagh Tower 118

N

Nanda Devi 61–4, *61, 62, 63*
Nanga Parbat 57, 61, 75, 81–3, *82, 83*, 85, 116, 126
    Diamir Face 68, 184
    Rupal Face 116, 184–5, *184–5*
Napes Needle *48*, 49–50
Napoleon Bonaparte 11, 77
Nawang Dorje Sherpa 85
Ndoto Mountains 157–8
Negri, Giuseppe 141
Neidhardt, Guy 124
Nelion 47, *47*
Nepal 57, 77, 79, 111
New Zealand 44–5
Nicole, Fred 177
Nima Dorje Sherpa 85
North Twin 171–3, *172*
Norton, Edward 65, *65*, 77
Norway 60
Nuptse 111
Nyenchentangla Range 168

O

Oberaarhorn 33
Odell, Noel 61–4
Ogden, Jared 165
Ogilvie, Sandy *150–1*
Ogre *see* Eiger
Old Man of Hoy *148*, *150–1*, 152
Ollie, César 46–7
Omei Shan 12
Onyskiewicz, Janusz 118
Oregon 131

Oudot, Dr 77–8
Owen, Rob *171*
oxygen, use of 64, 65, *65*, 79, 80–1, *80*, 117

P

Paccard, Michel-Gabriel 17, 18–19
Pakistan 117, 166, 168
Paradis, Marie 19
Paragot, Robert 116
parikrama 12
Parker, Herschel 35–6, 37
Pasang Dawa Lama 77, 85
Pat, Morrow 143, *143*
Patey, Tom 101, 148, *148*, 152
Pauer, Paul *58*
Pauhunri 58
Pause, Walter 33
Peak District 53, 145
Peary, Robert 36
Pellissier, Louis 42
Pelmo, Mount 26
Pelvoux, Mont 27
Pemba Sherpa 124
Penhall, William *66*, 67
Peru 12, 135
Peters, Rudolf *73*
Petherick, Mary 67
Petit Dru 101
    Bonatti Pillar *98*, 99–101, *101*
    Drus Couloir 105
Petrach 11
Phildius, Eberhard 54
Piana, Paul 158–9
Pigott, Fred 51, 52–3
pilgrimage, places of 12
Pillar Rock 49
Piz Linard 23
Poi *156–7*, 157–8
Polar Sun Spire 164
Pooli, Nino 33
Porter, Charlie 158, *158*
Porter, John 106
Pratt, Chuck *93*, 95
Preuss, Paul 33
Prezelj, Marko 171, 172–3, *172*, 184
prussiking 95
Puigdomènech, Miquel 168
pundits 57
Purtscheller, Ludwig 46, 143

Q

Queen Maud Land 161, *162–3*

R

Raeburn, Harold 54
Rainbow Falls 173–5, *174–5*
Rakekniven *6–7, 160*, 161, *161*, 164
Ramsden, Paul 169–70, *170*
Rangel, Alfredo 173, *174–5*
Read, Al 121
Rébuffat, Gaston 78
Reinhard, Johann 12
Reiss, Ernst 85, 180
Renshaw, Dick *7–8, 7*, 124
Ridgeway, Rick 164
Riley, Tony 120–1
Rimpfischorn 33
Rishi Gorge *61, 62*

Roaches 147
Robbins, Royal 89–90, *92, 93*, 95, 101, 158
Robertson, Mike 177, *177*
Roch, André 69
Rock and Ice Club 145
Rocky Mountains 96, 171
Rodden, Beth 159
Roskelley, John *119, 120*, 121, 124
Rossi, Roland 70
Rost, Hans 55
Rowell, Galen *119*
Rübenson, C.W. 60
Rucksack Club 51, 52
Ruinette 26
Ruskin, John 23, 26
Rutkiewicz, Wanda 118, *118*
Rwenzori 46

S

sacrifice, human 12
St Bernard Pass 11
St Elias, Mount 42
Salathé, John 89
Salvaterra, Ermanno 136
Samson, George 50–1, *50*
Sarthou, Sylvain 132
Saunders, Victor 128–9, *128, 129*
Saussure, Horace Benedict de *16–17*, 17, 19
Savage, Mark 157
Saxony 55
Sayre, Woodrow Wilson 143
Scafell Crag 50
Scafell Pike 49, *50*
    Central Buttress 50–1
    Great Flake 50–1, *51*
Schelbert, Albin 85
Schjelderup 60
Schlaginweit, Adolf 57
Schmid brothers 72
Schmitz, Kim *119, 120–1*
Schmuck, Marcus 83–5, *84*
Schoening, Peter 85, 141, 143
Schrammtorwächter 55
Schreckhorn 32, 33
Scotland 53–4, 148, 152
Scott, Doug *94*, 95, 158
Scrattling Crack 148
sea cliffs *145*, 148–54, *148, 149, 150–1*, 177, *177*, 180
sea stacks *150–1*, 152, 180
Sea of Vapours 171
Sedlmayer, Max 73
Segogne 69
Seigneur, Yannick 117
Sella, Alessandro *22*
Sella, Gaudenzia *22*
Sella, Vittoria *22, 56*
Semple, Scott 171
Sennelier, Robert 135
Sentinel Range *see* Ellsworth Mountains
Sentinel Rock 89
séracs 17
Seven Summits 143
Sheard, John 155
Sherpas 58, 77–8, 79, *115, 121*
Sherrick, Mike 90
Ship's Prow 165–6
Shipton, Eric 47, 61, 64, 79
Shishapangma 85, 165

Shivling 8
Sichuan 168
Siegrist, Stefan *137, 138–9, 140, 169*
Siguniang 168–70, *170*
Sikkim 57, 58
Silvretta mountains 23
Sinai, Mount *10*, 11–12, *11*, *13*
Siniolchu *56*, 57, *58*, 61
Skilbrum 85
Skinner, Todd 158–9
Slawinski, Raphael 171
Slingsby, Cecil *54*, 60
Smith, George *149*
Smith, Gordon 106, 108
Smythe, Frank 52, *52*, 65, 68, 69
snowblindness 78
Snowdon
    Clogwyn Du'r Arddu (Cloggy) 51–3, *53*, 147, *147*, 148
    East Buttress 51, *53*, 148
    Longland's Climb 53
    Pigott's Climb 51
    Pinnacle *53*
    West Buttress 52–3, *53*
Sodnam Doje 85
Sola Khumbu 79, *182–3*
Solokov, Gleb 181, *182–3*
Somervell, Howard 64–5, *65*
Sorenson, Tobin 104
Soubis, Jacques 132
Souriac, Pierre 135
South Africa 177
Southern Alps 44–5
Spanser Brakk 166
Spantik 127–9, *128, 129*
Spider Rock 96
Standing Rock 96, *97*
Steck, Al 89
Stephen, Leslie *23*, 32–3
Stetind 60
stimulants
    coca tea 83
    Maxiton 78
    Pervitin 82
stonefalls 108
Strobel, Gunther 104
Strubich, Emanuel 55
Stuck, Hudson 37–9, 143
Suicide Wall 147
Surveiller et Punir *144*
Sustad, Steve 168
Sutton, Steve 159
Swenson, Steve 184

T
Tackle, Jack 169
Tasker, Joe 124, *124*, 126
Tasman, Mount 45
Tasmania 180
Tatum, Robert 38–9, *39*, 143
Taugwalder, Peter *23*, 28, 30–1
Taulliraju *134*, 135, *135*
Teare, Paul 161
Temple, Phil 143
Tenzing Norgay 79, 80–1, *80*, 143
tepuis 173–5
Terray, Lionel 77–8, 85, 132, 135, 136
Tête de Valpelline 26

Thedule Pass 28
Thompson, Dave 171
Thompson, Mike 111
Thor, Mount 164
Tibet 12, 57, 79, 111, 168
Tichy, Herbert 85
Tilman, Bill 47, 61–4, 79
Timofeev, Sergei 181
Titicaca, Lake 42
Titlis 13
Tizzoni 75
Totem Pole 96, 180, *180*
tourism 26, 45
Trango Tower 118–21, *118–19*
Tre Cime de Lavaredo 70–2, *70–1*
Triolet 69
Troillet, Jean 127
Tsarahoro *9*
Tsaranoro massif 166, *166, 167*
Tsung Ling 11
Turk, Jon 164
Turner, J.M.W. *12*, 23, *23*
Tyndall, John 26, 27–8, *29*, *30*, 32–3, *32*
Tyree, Mount 143

U
Uli Biaho Tower 121
Ulvetanna 161
Unsoeld, Willi 127
Utah 96

V
Velan, Mont 13
Venables, Stephen 7–8, *7*
Venetz, Benedikt 67
Venezuela 173–5
Ventoux, Mount 11
Verdon Gorge *144*, *154*, 155
Vidal, Sílvia 168, *168*
Vigne, Geoffrey 57
Ville, Antoine de 13
Vinatzer 70
Vinogradsky, Evgueni 181
Vinson Massif 141, *141, 142*, 143
Voie Triomphe d'Eros 155
Volker, Alois 23
Volodin, Viktor 181
Vörg, Wiggerl 74–5, *74*
Votteler, Roland 104

W
Waddington, Mount 70, 131
Wager, Lawrence 65
Wagner, Benno *9*
Wainwright, Adam *149*
Wales 51–3, 147–8
Walker, Horace 31, 143
Walker, Lucy 31, *31*
Wang Fuzhou 85
Ward, Michael 79, *80*
Washburn, Bradford *30*, 72, 132, *132–3*
Wastwater 49
Watts, Chris 135, *135*
Watzmann 82
Webster, Ed 161
Weisshorn 27, *29*, 32–3
Wenger 32
Western Cwn *78*, 79, *79*

Wetterhorn *22*
Whillans, Don 101, 104, 111, 114–15, 145, 146, 147
White, Wilf 147
Whymper, Edward 26–31, *26*
    Scrambles in the Alps 27, 32
Whymper, Pointe 26
Wielochowski, Andrew *156*, 157–8, *157*
Wien, Karl 61
Wiessner, Fritz 70, 77, 131
Wigram, C. 28
Wilder Kopf-Westkante 55
Willenpart, Hans 85
Wills, Sir Alfred 26
Wiltsie, Gordon 164, 165
Windham, William 13
Wintersteller, Fritz 83–5, *84*
Wolf, Kaspar 13
women climbers 67, 118
    Aoraki 44
    Matterhorn 31
    Mont Blanc 19
Wu Zongyue 85
Wugk, H. 55
Wyn-Harris, Percy 47, 65

X
Xu Jing 85

Y
Yanochkin, Vladimir 181
Yosemite Valley 89–95, 158–9
Young, Geoffrey Winthrop 52, 68
Yungden 85
Yunnan 168

Z
Zdzitowiecki, Krysztof 118
Zermatt 27, *28*, 32
Zhang Junyan 85
Zinalrothorn 32–3
Zurbriggen, Matthias 45, 143
Zurfluh, Heinrich 68

ACKNOWLEDGEMENTS

Producing a book like this is a big team effort. I would like to thank my editor Jenny Doubt, designer Ashley Western, production manager Geoff Fennell and tireless picture researcher Emma O'Neil. Also the many friends and colleagues around the world who have helped source pictures and information. Particular thanks are due to Anna Lawford, Honorary Keeper of the Alpine Club Photo Library. Also (with apologies for any unintentional omissions): Conrad Anker, Stefano Ardito, Steve Bartlett, Fred Beckey, Christian Beckwith, Margaret Body, Simon Carter, Ken Crocket, Cubby Cuthbertson, Jo Cuthbertson, Frances Daltrey, Kurt Diemberger, Thorbjørn Evenold, Mick Fowler, Horst Höfler, Huntley Ingalls, Chris Jones, Steve Komito, Lindsay Griffin, Chris Jones, John Harlin, Steve Komito, Anna Lawford, Pat Littlejohn, Bernard Newman, Dick Renshaw, Simon Richardson, Raphael Slawinski, Victor Saunders, Andrej Stremfelj, Ludwig Trojok, Ed Webster, Andrew Wielochowski, Ken Wilson and Ray Wood.

A comprehensive bibliography would take up a whole book this size, and I can only list a few of the most useful sources. I would like to thank John Harlin III for permission to quote from the invaluable *American Alpine Journal*, in particular for the concluding section on Nanga Parbat, and Steve Goodwin, Editor of the *Alpine Journal*. Another indispensable source was my treasured collection of old copies of Mountain Magazine. Pat Littlejohn's account of America came from Mountain no.34, Cerro Torre's first ascent from no.38, Louis Adoubert's Drus Couloir account from no.44, Alex MacIntyre's witty Grandes Jorasses story from no.53 and Pete Livesey's enthusing on Verdon from no.61.

Other sources:
Abode of Snow – Kenneth Mason (Diadem/The Mountaineers 1987) (indispensable history of early Himalayan climbing)

Alps – Stefano Ardito (Swan Hill 1996) (Mont Blanc first ascent)

Climbing in North America – Chris Jones (University of California Press 1976) (Mt McKinley, Deborah, Standing Tower and Yosemite)

Conquistadores of the Useless – Lionel Terray (Bâton Wicks 2001) (Huntingdon and Taulliraju)

Eiger Direct – Peter Gillman & Dougal Haston (Collins 1966)

Elusive Summits – Victor Saunders (Hodder & Stoughton 1990) (Spantik Golden Pillar)

Hermann Buhl – Climbing Without Compromise – Horst Höfler (Bâton Wicks/The Mountaineers 2000) (Nanga Parbat and Broad Peak)

Himalaya Alpine Style – Andy Fanshawe & Stephen Venables (Hodder & Stoughton 1996)

Mont Blanc – Discovery & Conquest of the Giant of the When The Alps Cast Their Spell – Trevor Braham (The In Pinn 2004) (Alpine Golden Age)

Mountain Men – Mick Conefrey & Tim Jordan (Boxtree 2001) (Matterhorn and Mt McKinley)

On Thin Ice – Mick Fowler (Bâton Wicks 2005) (Siguniang North Face)

On Top of the World – Climbing The World's 14 Highest Peaks – Richard Sale & John Cleare (HarperCollins 2000)

Summit – 150 Years of the Alpine Club – George Band (Collins 2006) (Alpine Golden Age)

The Ascent of Nanda Devi – W H Tilman (*H.W.Tilman – The Seven Mountain Travel Books* – Diadem/The Mountaineers 1983)

The Black Cliff – The History of Climbing on Clogwyn d'yr Arddu – Peter Crew, Jack Soper & Ken Wilson (London 1971) (early Welsh rock climbing)

The Bolivian Andes – Sir Martin Conway (1900)

The Eiger Obsession – John Harlin (Simon Schuster 2007)

The First Ascent of Mount Kenya – Sir Halford MacKinder (C.Hurst & Co 1991)

The Mountains of My Life – Walter Bonatti (2000) (Bonatti Pillar)

Summits & Secrets – Kurt Diemberger (Diemberger Omnibus, Diadem/The Mountaineers 1998)

Trango – The Nameless Tower – Jim Curran (Dark Peak 1978)

Welsh Rock – Trevor Jones & Geoff Milburn (1986) (early Welsh rock climbing)

PICTURE ACKNOWLEDGEMENTS

The publishers would like to thank the following individuals and organisations for supplying images for this book. Every effort has been made to contact the copyright holders. Please contact the publishers if any credits have inadvertently been omitted.

Abraham Brothers' Photographic Collection /Alpine Club Photo Library, London 48.
Alamy /Blickwinkel 70-71; /Roger Cracknell 11/North Africa 10; /FAN travelstock 166; /INTERFOTO Pressebildagentur 24-25; /Dirk V. Mallinckrodt 154; /Robert Preston 112-113; /Galen Rowell/Mountain Light 134.
Alexander Turnbull Library, Making New Zealand Collection, Wellington, New Zealand /Emmeline Freda Du Faur with Alec and Peter Graham/ F-1296-1/2-MNZ 44 bottom.
Alpine Club Photo Library, London 23 bottom, 31, 33 right, 42 top, 53 bottom, 54 left, 64, 67.
Archiv des Deutschen Alpenvereins 57 bottom, 58 left.
Anne & John Arran/www.thefreeclimber.com /Anne Arran 174-175; /John Arran 173.
Baton Wicks Archive /Walter Brunskill 50 top; /George Sansom 50 bottom; /Ken Wilson 114 bottom.
Fred Beckey 131.
George Bell 172 top.
Chris Bonington Picture Library /Chris Boningon 102, 103, 108, 110, 111, 115, 142 bottom, 148; /Ian Clough 114 top; /Peter Boardman 122-123; /Joe Tasker 124, 125.
Bridgeman Art Library /Abbot Hall Gallery, Kendal, Cumbria, UK 23 top; /Bibliothèque nationale, Paris, France, Archive Charmet 18; /Private Collection 11, 13 top; /Royal Geographical Society, London, UK 16-17; /The Stapleton Collection/Private Collection 27.
Willi P. Burkhardt, Buochs, Switzerland 19.
Canterbury Museum, WA Kennedy Collection /G E Mannering/1975.203.11586 45 top.
Simon Carter/Onsight Photography 8-9, 180, 144, 167.
Christie's Images 17.
ED COOPER PHOTO 88, 130.
Corbis UK Ltd /Theo Allofs 137 bottom right; /Robert van der Hilst 13 bottom; /Earl & Nazima Kowall 82 right; /Danny Lehman 36 bottom; /Craig Lovell 14-15; /Reuters/Antony Njuguna 47 right; /Galen Rowell 36-37, 89 bottom, 118-119 bottom; /Joseph Sohm/Visions of America 136; /Sandro Vannini 98; /Jim Zuckerman 43.
Dave Cuthbertson/Cubby Images 178-179.
Glen Denny 90 top & bottom.
Leo Dickinson/www.Adventure Archive.com 101.
Kurt Diemberger 84-85.
Epicscotland 54-55.
John Evans 141 right.
Roger Everett 155.
Mick Fowler 128, 135 right, 170 left & right.
Tom Frost, Aurora Photos, Inc 91, 92-93.
Getty Images /Aurora Photos/Mario Colonel 20-21; /Walter Daran 39; /Hulton Archive/Express Newspapers 26 bottom.
John Harlin III 106-107.
Hedgehog House /Jean-Paul Ferrero 46 left; /Nick Groves 45 centre & bottom; /Jim Harding 89 top; /Dean Johnston 44 top; /Colin Monteath 38; /Hugh van Noorden 117; /Dick and Pip Smith 78-79 bottom, 120 bottom; /Tom Till 28.
Steve House 184.

Huntley Ingalls 96 right, 97.
Photo by Harish Kapadia 61.
KEYSTONE - FRANCE, CAMERA PRESS LONDON 74 right.
Yuri Koshelenko 181 left & right, 182.
Keith Ladzinski 176, 177 top.
Alan Leary 53 top.
Bill Long 141 left.
Mark Lynden 169 bottom.
Mary Evans Picture Library /Illustrated London News 65 left.
Bobby Model / M-11 156-157.
Martin Moran 32 bottom.
www.mountaincamera.com/John Cleare 29, 51, 62, 66, 69, 75, 79 top, 105, 118 left, 145, 146, 147, 152, 153 top; /Henry Day 76; /Leo Dickinson 126 right; /Alan Hinkes 86; /Colin Monteath 142 top; /Doug Scott 185 right.
Baiba Morrow 143.
National Museum of Wales 58.
The Ohio State University Archives, Frederick A. Cook Society Collection 36 top.
Ian Parnell 153 bottom.
Marko Prezelj, mark@amebis.si 40, 135 left, 137 top right, 173 Bottom;
Andrew Querner 171.
Richard Renshaw 7 top.
Simon Richardson 109 left & right.
Frank Richter 55 left & right.
Tony Riley, Cumbria Picture Library 118 right, 119 top.
Eric Roberts, courtesy of Ann Roberts 63.
Mike Robertson 177 bottom.
John Roskelley 120 top, 121.
Royal Geographical Society /George Band 80 top; /Alfred Gregory 80 bottom left; /Edmund Hillary 1, 80 bottom right; /J.B. Noel 65 right.
Doug Scott 94-95, 96 left, 104, 116.
Victor Saunders 129.
Vittorio Sella, © Fondazione Sella, Biella 22, 42 bottom.
Copyright SMC Image Archive 49 top & bottom.
Fotograf Lars Thulin AB 60 top & bottom.
Jean Troillet 127.
© Tate, London 2008 12.
TopFoto 82 left, 83 left; /Alinari 70 left, /Vittorio Sella 56; /Topham Picturepoint 26 top, 100; /Ullsteinbild 3 left, 74 left, 83 right; /World History Archive 32 top.
Stephen Venables 46 right, 47 left, 68, 73 left & right, 81, 99, 126 left, 150-151.
Silvia Vidal 168.
Visual Impact GmbH /Dennis Burdet 169 top; /Thomas Ulrich 4-5, 137 top left & bottom left, 138-139, 140 left & right.
© Bradford Washburn, Courtesy Panopticon Gallery, Boston, MA 30, 34-35, 72, 132-133.
Andrew Wielochowski 157 right.
Gordon Wiltsie, AlpenImage, Ltd 2-3, 6-7, 160-161, 162-163, 164-165.
Ray Wood Photography 149.
Heinz Zak 158-159.